COCKTAIL ECONOMICS

FINANCIAL TIMES

In an increasingly competitive world, it is quality
of thinking that gives an edge—an idea that opens new
doors, a technique that solves a problem, or an insight
that simply helps make sense of it all.

We work with leading authors in the various arenas
of business and finance to bring cutting-edge thinking
and best-learning practices to a global market.

It is our goal to create world-class print publications
and electronic products that give readers
knowledge and understanding that can then be
applied, whether studying or at work.

To find out more about our business
products, you can visit us at www.ftpress.com.

COCKTAIL ECONOMICS

Discovering Investment Truths from Everyday Conversations

VICTOR A. CANTO

FT Press
FINANCIAL TIMES

Vice President, Editor-in-Chief: Tim Moore
Executive Editor: Jim Boyd
Editorial Assistant: Pamela Boland
Development Editor: Russ Hall
Associate Editor-in-Chief and Director of Marketing: Amy Neidlinger
Publicist: Amy Fandrei
Marketing Coordinator: Megan Colvin
Cover Designer: John Barnett
Managing Editor: Gina Kanouse
Senior Project Editor: Kristy Hart
Copy Editor: Krista Hansing
Indexer: Erika Millen
Senior Compositor: Gloria Schurick
Manufacturing Buyer: Dan Uhrig

FT Press
FINANCIAL TIMES

© 2007 by Pearson Education, Inc.
Publishing as FT Press
Upper Saddle River, New Jersey 07458

**FT Press offers excellent discounts on this book when ordered in
quantity for bulk purchases or special sales. For more information,
please contact U.S. Corporate and Government Sales, 1-800-382-3419,
corpsales@pearsontechgroup.com. For sales outside the U.S., please
contact International Sales at international@pearsoned.com.**

Company and product names mentioned herein are the trademarks or registered
trademarks of their respective owners.

Printed in the United States of America

First Printing May, 2007

ISBN 0-13-243273-0

Pearson Education LTD.
Pearson Education Australia PTY, Limited.
Pearson Education Singapore, Pte. Ltd.
Pearson Education North Asia, Ltd.
Pearson Education Canada, Ltd.
Pearson Educación de Mexico, S.A. de C.V.
Pearson Education—Japan
Pearson Education Malaysia, Pte. Ltd.

Canto, Victor A.
  Cocktail economics : discovering investment truths from everyday conversations /
Victor A. Canto.
     p. cm.
  ISBN 0-13-243273-0 (hardback : alk. paper) 1. Portfolio management.
2. Investment analysis. 3. Investments. I. Title.
  HG4529.5.C358 2007
  332.6—dc22
                          2006101589

To Ana Rosa

CONTENTS

ACKNOWLEDGMENTS

Thinking about the origins of this book takes me back to my days as an assistant professor at the University of Southern California Graduate School of Business where I tried to share with my students, initially with little success, much of what I had learned at the University of Chicago. Inadvertently my students sent me on a long journey to improve my skill of delivery and mastery of the content of my economic lectures. For that I will always be grateful to them.

In order to engage my students and to share my interest in policy issues—in particular the fiscal and regulatory legislation passed by elected officials at the federal and local levels—I developed the concept of cocktail economics. In my lectures, time and again using contemporary issues, I illustrated how top-down incentives and disincentives affect both economic behavior and the performance of the economy. In particular I tried to teach my students how to trace the impact of government policies through the economy. The final objective was to develop simple and elegant solutions to the public policy issues discussed in class.

In time my interest in the interconnection of policy and economic behavior evolved. After leaving USC in the mid-1980s I focused more and more on the impact and implication of government policies. But it was not until 1997, at which point I had started my own firm with the encouragement of my wife, Ana, and three daughters, Vianca, Victoria, and Veronica, that I decided to focus on what I really had become interested in: I had found that seldom does the analysis of government action apply to the strategies that are vital to business managers, financial analysts, and investors in general. With this in mind, I set forth to discover the investment implications of policy actions, information that would of course be useful to investors, portfolio managers, and financial analysts, but also to corporate strategists, government officials, and the policymakers themselves. This book represents the sum of the knowledge gained on this front in my professional career. For the reader I hope it represents a new path for investing—the extra step that demands to be taken.

Along the way, in developing my theories on investing, I have met many wonderful people, many of whom have become great friends. Sometimes, during difficult times, people find out who their true friends really are. In 1997, as I began my new firm, Harlan Cadinha, Herb Gullquist, Robert Doede, John Rutledge, David Walsh, Christian Carrillo, and Danielle Andrews were wonderfully supportive and proved to be exceptional friends. More recently I have gotten to know David Cleary, Dyke Benjamin, Christopher Komosa, John Reese, Chris Foster and Neil Rose, and in one way or another I have benefited from their friendships. Charlie Parker, Robert Webb, and Larry Kudlow have always been supportive and encouraging.

One person without whom this project would not have become reality is Chris McEvoy. His dedication, initiative, and many editorial suggestions greatly enhanced the manuscript. Andy Wiese and Erik Walters were outstanding research assistants.

ABOUT THE AUTHOR

Victor A. Canto is Founder and Chairman of La Jolla Economics, an economic consulting firm located in La Jolla, California. He was Director, Chief Investment Officer, and Portfolio Manager of Calport Asset Management.

Dr. Canto taught finance and business economics at the University of Southern California (USC) from 1977 to 1985 and has served as Visiting Professor at both the Universidad Central del Este in the Dominican Republic and the University of California at Los Angeles (UCLA). He was a consultant to the Financial Council of Puerto Rico; an advisor to the Finance Minister as well as Dominican Republic's Central Bank. Dominican Republic.

Victor Canto has authored, edited, or coedited a number of books, including *Investment Strategy and State and Local Economic Policy*, *The Determinants and Consequences of Trade Restrictions in the U.S. Economy*; and *Currency Substitution: Theory and Evidence from Latin America*, as well as *Understanding Asset Allocation*.

His work has appeared the *Wall Street Journal*, *Investor's Business Daily,* and *National Review on line,* and many leading economic journals, including *Economic Inquiry*, *Journal of Macroeconomics*, *The International Trade Journal*, *Journal of Business and Economic Statistics*, *The Southern Economic Journal*, *Applied Economics*, *The CATO Journal*, *Public Finance*, *The Journal of International Money and Finance*, *The Journal of Wealth Management*, *The Financial Analysts Journal*, and *The New Palgrave Dictionary of Money and Finance*.

FOREWORD

I have a great job. I travel the world, give speeches, advise corporations, nurture companies, write about investing, and talk about investing on television. It's the kind of job that has its share of perks, one of which is that I get to meet smart people who truly grasp the ins and outs of investing in stocks and bonds. A vast amount of investment advice is available today, and much of it is garbage. But among the smart advisors—the accurate ones—are those who understand that investments behave in certain ways for a certain set of economic reasons, and that there's a right and wrong way to invest during each and every economic moment. Right now is an economic moment. Is your money invested according to the distinct set of economic circumstances that define it? Is your money where it should be?

I count Victor Canto among today's best and smartest advisors—a select group, to be sure—and for very good reason. When it comes to economics and investing, and the permanent marriage of the two, Victor knows what he is talking about and has proven it over the decades. He has made money in both good times and bad, for many a satisfied client. This is an important detail: Victor never *wills* his investment advice. For Victor and today's sharpest financial advisors, things are what they are. Sometimes the stock market is trending up, other times down. Still other times it's as flat as a pancake. But the good ones know how to invest in each circumstance. Simply, they know where the money should be at all times if it is to have the best chance of turning into more money.

I am happy to say that Victor has now done all investors, including myself, an important service: He has written a widely accessible book about the marriage of economics and investing, and the crucial ties that bind the two. If I had to sum up Victor's book in a few words, I'd say it's the story of how big ideas make the investment world go 'round.

Big ideas matter. And they should matter *a lot* to investors who want to make meaningful money in the stock and bond markets.

For instance, technology is a big idea—and a personal favorite of mine. I've had my eyes on technology since my earliest days as an investor. You've probably noticed it, too. Technology has dramatically changed our lives in a historically short period of time. One day not so long ago, we thought the fax machine was the most amazing piece of office equipment ever conceived. Who faxes now? Hardly anyone: We e-mail important documents to whomever we want. Pay phones once were standard technology. But with the glacial advance of the cell phone, they're dropping like dinosaurs. This is how most of us think of technology—in terms of how it affects our everyday lives. This is micro stuff and important stuff. But how about looking at technology from a macro perspective, as a big idea?

The technology revolution has led to higher economic growth, more productivity, lower inflation, and, correspondingly, lower interest rates. The rationale goes like this: Because the Internet has made everything in the office go faster, it has reduced the amount of time it takes to do a dollar's worth of business. That has both enhanced productivity and resulted in faster growth, which shows up in higher gross domestic product. Because more is being produced with less effort, this process brings about lower prices and, hence, lower inflation. And when inflation is low, there's every reason why interest rates also can be low.

This progression deserves a "wow." One big idea—technology—has influenced so many other big ideas, each critically important to the direction of the economy and the stock and bond markets that reflect that economy.

Consider inflation. Higher inflation reduces the value of all income streams, whereas falling inflation does the opposite. Obviously, this is a powerful animal, one that is best contained in a manageable range. And that's where the Federal Reserve comes in, a big idea in its own right.

When the Fed perceives potentially higher inflation, it tightens, or extracts money from, the economy. It does so by raising interest rates. For a time, higher interest rates can partner with a vibrant economy. Traditionally, this is a stock moment rather than a bond moment. But what happens when the Fed keeps raising rates to crush inflationary pressures? Well, it just might put the brakes on the economy. And when those brakes slam too hard, the economy might well fall into recession, perhaps one marked by deflation. What then? Well, for one, the bond markets will cheer. Bond traders love bad news, particularly the recessions and deflations that make the bonds they sell more valuable.

Here, one big idea (the Fed) can turn a couple of other big ideas (inflation and interest rates) on their heads, the result being the collapse of a monstrously big idea (economic growth) and the wholesale transfer of investor money from one big idea (stocks) to another (bonds).

Whew.

Here's another big idea: taxes. The economy's potential to grow and the likelihood that stocks will climb disproportionately relative to bonds each are enhanced when tax rates are lowered, particularly taxes on capital and investment. Write that down, memorize it, and believe it. It's a favorite big idea that I share with investors who know how to make money.

Regulations matter, too. Do governments need to set the rules for the businesses that operate within their economic boundaries? Well, if societies are to have order, they must. But it's all a matter of degree. High regulations—lots of rules—depress the ability of businesses to be profitable. Low regulations, on the other hand, unleash the profit-making prowess of businesses. Write those down, too.

Capital is a big idea, big and beefy. *Capital* is another word for *money* or *wealth,* and it moves to where it is most welcome. And where it ends up is often an excellent place for *you* to put *your* money. What makes capital most welcome? Two familiar big ideas: low taxes and low regulations. Just look at Ireland. For decades, this island was pretty low on the list of capital-friendly international locales. But a lot changed toward the end of the twentieth century. First, it got a lot quieter in the north: The desire for peace and prosperity at last trumped the decades-long spiral of guns, conflict, and killing. Foreign businesses and investors began to take notice. But what really attracted the world's capital was the island's shift to lower taxes and regulations. The guns silenced and the government-induced barriers to investment lowered. As a result, Ireland today is blanketed in green, and I don't mean the kind the cows eat.

Do the small things matter? Sure. I have written that the more time company managers spend thinking about customers and products, and the less about financial indicators—many of which relate to those big ideas I'm talking about—the better our companies will perform. Same for stock pickers. If stock picking is to be done with good results, it should be left to those who can properly scrutinize the products, management, customers, and profitability of our public companies. Thinking small, or in a very precise and targeted way, can lead to big corporate profits and, likewise, big investor gains.

But a word to the wise: Most investors don't have the time or skill to be successful stock pickers, to play investing small ball day after day. All investors, however, can play investing big ball with excellent results, while saving themselves a lot of sweat and heartache.

When I say "big ball" here, I'm talking about asset allocation, the big idea that goes like this: Basically, no single investment is a loner in an asset-allocation world. It is a security that falls into one of a few asset categories. Let's call these categories A, B, C, and D. Each moves above and below the water line of average returns at different times and to differing degrees. Sometimes it is an A and B moment; other times, allocating to C and D might make you the most money. So how to pick the winners? Well, *critically and fundamentally,* changes in government policies related to taxation, regulation, the value of currencies, interest rates, and inflation go a long way toward determining these movements. In other words, asset allocation is the big idea of big ideas in the investing world; it is the crossroad where economics and investing meet.

Naturally, when you arrive at any crossroad, you are faced with the same question: Which way to turn? Just as naturally, you answer that question based on the information you're carrying around.

Information will forever be a huge big idea, both the good *and* the bad kind. Good information produces winners with regularity, whereas bad information usually corresponds with the losers. Of course, if you keep acting on bad information, the poor results you produce are yours and yours alone. You've earned them. But I've long held that losing is an important big idea if it becomes an opportunity to learn. When you get on a horse, sometimes you'll get thrown. *Riding itself is chancy.* But you become a better rider by getting tossed, standing up again, and mounting once more. Indeed, if you take your lumps and *learn from them,* you'll pretty soon notice that you are riding farther, longer, and faster.

In this same vein, I have said before that bruises, not books, are life's best teachers. But here I stress that I'm an avid reader of books—good books, that is—who understands the value of the information they provide.

And now to the biggest idea at hand: Victor Canto has written a book that not only will lessen the incidence and magnitude of your investment bruises, but also will teach you about all the big ideas that have so very much to do with making *significant* gains in the stock and bond markets.

Listen to Victor, *think big,* invest appropriately for each economic moment, and prosper.

—John Rutledge, Chairman, Rutledge Capital, LLC

PREFACE

My first teaching experience was a disaster. The year was 1977, and the venue was the University of Southern California in Los Angeles. It was an important time for me. I had just left the University of Chicago with a doctorate in economics, along with a full head of ideas and plenty of energy. Economics wasn't only my vocation; it was my passion. I was about to jump into action at USC's graduate school of business. What could be better?

A root canal, perhaps.

My initial feeling was one of awkwardness. It turned out that most of my students were older than me. They also were a much different sort than my colleagues back in Chicago—people who could consume large portions of economic theory at a sitting. My students at USC worked during the day and went to school at night. They went to business school to learn how to make money, how to get a better job, how to succeed. They were practical people, and they wanted little more than the action points they could apply to their business lives. Theory? Theory didn't stand a chance with this crowd. At the time, the late 1970s, residential real estate prices were climbing about 1 to 2 percent a month in the Los Angeles area. This had my business students ravenous for knowledge about real estate finance—and finance in general—and turned off by even a whiff of macro- or microeconomics. My impression was that some of my students viewed economics as a minor inconvenience, at best, while most found it a major nuisance—a requirement that had to be satisfied before they could pursue their fortunes.

My youthful penchant toward showing off probably didn't help matters any. From the outset, I overemphasized the analytical aspects of economics, which I thought to be my forte, and quickly found that most of my students did not share my enthusiasm. The stark differences between teacher and student were reflected in the poor evaluations I received at the end of the semester. I was devastated at the time. Worse, analytics aside, I simply could not understand why my students were not as passionate as I was about economics in general. Doesn't everyone interested in success in life carry around a pair of economic viewing glasses through which they study their surroundings, calculate, and plan for the future? Many of my students commented in their evaluations that they failed to see how the textbook, or even the subject, would help their careers. After all, many of them already were working. And outside of perhaps the finer points of real estate and the letters *MBA* after their names, many figured they already possessed what they needed to get ahead.

I knew then, as now, that no one ever knows everything he or she needs to get ahead, that life and experience instruct and challenge us each and every day. But my students were *certain* that economics need not be part of their life programs. Teaching economics to MBA students seemed like a daunting task at the time. But I would recover.

The next semester, I told my students that even if they did not accept how economic theory could aid their careers, they could benefit from its study in at least one way: Economics, I revealed, was an excellent conversation piece. If grasped even to a nominal degree, it could elevate their status in all manner of social situations, from the cocktail party, to the business luncheon, to the client dinner. Wouldn't it be nice, I asked, if they could discuss with confidence the important political and economic issues of the day? (I note here and do throughout this book that political and economic issues forever are intertwined.) At the very least, they should know what the economic and political issues *are,* and if they wanted to show off a little, their opinions should be informed because the person with an informed opinion best articulates a position.

I suggested that we try this approach for a while, calling it *cocktail economics.* By definition, we would apply economic theory to the everyday events that might be discussed over, well, cocktails. For my part, I hoped the approach would spark a fire of interest in the subject. If it didn't, we could fall back on the course outline. The students agreed, and cocktail economics was a go.

Most of my MBA students subscribed to *The Wall Street Journal,* so I suggested at the outset that we go over the paper's editorial page each class. (In all honesty, I suspect that most of my students agreed to this as a way of reducing the time spent on the textbook. But one has to start somewhere.) A few rules were in play: First, if an editorial discussed some policy action in Washington, the students needed to figure out the breadth of the initial impact of that action. Would the policy affect the economy as a whole or just a region or an industry? To answer this, they needed to identify the nature of economic "shocks," those disruptions to the economic trajectory that are either natural or manmade. Would the shock in question affect the demand or supply side of the market? The succeeding step was to determine how the economy would return to a state of equilibrium in the wake of a shock. Would this occur through a change in price or a change in output? I argued that if consumers and/or suppliers exhibited a degree of flexibility, the bulk of the adjustment back toward equilibrium would occur in the form of quantity changes (or the shift in the amount of a product or good in the economic pipeline), with little or no change in price. On the other hand, if inflexible factors were at work—for instance if there was little give in a supplier's production capacity—prices would have to change to clear the market and restore equilibrium.

This last analysis, it turns out, was dear to the hearts of my students. Because they were businesspeople, I asked them simply to think of who would benefit and who would lose in the aftermath of each shock we studied. My students all wanted to be on the side of the "winners" in life, so at the very least, they were intrigued.

With cocktail economics set in motion, my classes initially became livelier—even entertaining. And to the extent that my students were able to correctly answer each question related to the editorials we surveyed, I reminded them that they could now carry these informed opinions to the office, bar, or restaurant—anywhere they met with clients, colleagues, or even friends. Their skills at arguing and debating would only improve across this process. Finally, I told them that, if nothing else, cocktail economics would teach them how to better tell a story and maybe even enhance their ability to identify good investments.

This scheme soon took on a life of its own, with frowns turning to smiles and nodding-off being replaced with straightened backs and wider eyes. Correspondingly, my ratings as a teacher improved, and I felt very satisfied: I had found a way to both motivate my students and engage them in economic thought.

It has been more than 25 years since I began using this method, but I still find it gratifying when my former students mention it. The chance meetings are few and far between, but nearly every time, the conversation starts the same way: "Professor Canto, I'll always remember cocktail economics." Sometimes they mention that they still use this approach, that they return to it every time they have a big decision to make.

In this book, I have applied the cocktail-economics approach to my theories on investing. I have attempted to be conversational and to employ guiding anecdotes to help reduce what can be complex economic theories to the common-sense basics. But these are powerful basics. Whereas some of my former students might apply cocktail economics to their big life decisions, you will be encouraged to apply it to your investment portfolio—a place where the right decisions can usher in true prosperity.

INTRODUCTION

The Above-Average Opportunity

The investment strategy I set forth in this book is not a stock-picker's method. Lots of people still think this is what investing is all about—finding those diamond stocks in the rough that will deliver wealth and all the trappings of Easy Street. There's nothing at all wrong with stock picking, which, when practiced with an eye to detail, has made many an investor rich. At the micro level, finding the best companies—based on profits, product lines, market shares, P/E ratios, stock multiples, etc.—within the best-performing sectors is a rigor taken on by many successful investors. But my investment plan specifically is concerned with the big picture, with the broad macro worldwide forces that act on all investments.

In essence, my method applies a set of "top-down" principles that enable you to accurately select the winning asset classes within each economic "cycle" or definable economic period (typically between a point of low performance to one of high performance). Intrinsic to this strategy is the belief that the separate asset classes—such as the stocks of large or small companies, or the shares of domestic or international corporations—each act in ways that are uniquely attached to the full range of economic variables.

Here's an example: In 1964, a tax cut was signed into law that lowered the top income-tax rate from 91 percent to 71 percent. If you think 91 percent was quite high—confiscatory, to say the least—you are correct. So lowering that rate assuredly would have made some taxpayers happy. Let's measure how happy:

A 91 percent tax rate leaves only 9 take-home cents per dollar of income. When that tax rate is reduced to 71 percent, the take-home increases to 29¢. Thus, the 1964 tax-rate cut *more than tripled* the take-home rate for high-end earners subject to this tax.

Because high-end earners back in 1964 suddenly had more capital available, they were able to put it into action by investing it, saving it, spending it, expanding their businesses, and perhaps hiring more workers. All these activities are positives for economies, and the economy of the mid-1960s was no exception.

The 1964 income-tax cut, coupled with the tax cuts of 1962 on investment and capital gains, helped activate one of the longer economic expansions in American history: Unemployment declined from 6.7 percent to 3.8 percent in 1963; capacity utilization (a measure of the output of factories and industries) increased more than 8 percentage points to 91.9 percent in 1966; the real gross national product (GNP) grew at a compound annual rate of 5.7 percent between 1963 and 1966, compared with just 4.1 percent during the previous three years; and while government spending expanded 5 percent more than GNP between 1960 and 1963, GNP grew slightly faster than government spending between 1963 and 1966.

I point out the rate of spending in relation to the rate of economic growth (or GNP growth) because it has been argued that the increase in economic activity during this period was a result of accelerated government spending. But with the ratio of spending to growth falling, it becomes clear that the tax cuts strongly contributed to the economic expansion.[1]

Two quick notes are in order. To present my investment strategy using the cocktail-economics approach, my methodology has necessarily become more specific. First, instead of merely jumping off random editorials in the *Wall Street Journal*, I use historic examples to illustrate and explain the key big-picture concepts of investing explored in each chapter. A second important distinction is that the macroeconomic analyses contained herein are not dependent on a person's political leanings. That tax cut of 1964, for instance, was not a Republican event, with the GOP being the party most often associated with the desire to lower tax rates. The 1964 rate cut was shepherded by Democratic President John F. Kennedy and signed into law by his Democratic successor, Lyndon B. Johnson.

Facts matter more than politics. And what matters most to a successful investment strategy is both the quality of the economic analysis and the insights derived from that analysis. This is a lot like cocktail economics—a correct filtering of information is essential. But what I provide in these pages is a framework of filters that have proven over many years to accurately identify which asset classes will perform best (or worst, or neutral) in each economic environment. Can asset-class swings be predicted? Yes. Furthermore, as investors, can we time our actions to those swings? Yes again.

This might sound like powerful stuff, and it is. In my experience, any investor who faithfully applies such a program has little option but to perform better than the great many investors who do not.

Much better.

A Predictable Course for Each Asset Class

Beyond random luck, foul play, or a highly tuned ability to pick stocks company by company, truly successful long-term investing cannot occur without a sound idea of how the many top-down macroeconomic forces—taxes, regulations, inflation, interest rates, war, peace, trade barriers, etc.—act on the investment vehicles themselves. And here I stress the idea of *truly* successful.

Too many financial planners and advisors have investors believing that average is good enough. To be sure, average is not bad. If you invest in a broad range of stocks and bonds and stick to your allocation decisions for a long enough time period, you are certain to come out ahead. And ahead, in this case, will likely be near the middle of the pack. But what if I told you there is a way to capture the upside of each economic cycle that will have you ahead of the pack for most of your investment life? You might hesitate, thinking you were being sold a get-rich-quick scheme—which, assuredly, is not my plan. Rather, this book sets forth an intuitive approach to investing that takes into account all the macroeconomic forces that act on the performance of every possible asset class. When these forces are understood, an economic cycle can be described in terms of how the different asset classes will perform in it. With this knowledge secure, all an investor needs to do is shift to the asset classes that are forecast to rise and step away from the ones that predictably will fall—or do nothing at all, if staying put is the best course of action.

If I told you that road accidents are likely to increase in foul weather, you might yawn in response. Everyone knows that. But if I said that small-capitalization stocks (shares of public companies that are relatively small in size) are likely to do better than larger company stocks in uncertain economic environments, such as when new regulations or higher taxes have been set into place or threaten to be signed into law, I might get your attention.

This is but one of several provable relationships between the macroeconomic environment and the separate asset classes that we discuss. These relationships are easy to learn and, if you invest, to apply. But I stress that it is important for the investor interested in true success to understand all the variables that make for the relationship between economic policy and asset-class movement. Simply, successful investors need to know *why* groups of stocks do what they do.

Why? Let's go back on the road.

Why are there more car accidents in inclement weather? Several factors might be at play: lower visibility, slick road surfaces, inadequate equipment, the random driver who makes hell for everyone else. You know all these, and successful drivers take each of these factors into account. Another yawn. But what if I were to ask, "*Why* do small-caps perform better than large-caps in uncertain economic environments?" The key factor here might be the capability of a smaller company to adjust to a new economic environment more quickly than a larger company—something akin to a sprinter being able to beat out a long-distance runner, if only at the start of a race. Someone who yawns at this relationship just might not be interested in making money.

I have written somewhat academically about these relationships in a book called *Understanding Asset Allocation*, a work I am very proud of that sets forth my strategy for cyclical asset allocation in an in-depth, analytical manner. By "cyclical," I mean cycles—the prices of investment assets move in certain directions during specific economic environments for a knowable set of reasons. By "analytical," I mean plenty of charts, historical data, theorems, formulas, and scrutiny. The subject in the pages ahead is the same. But hopefully I have presented it as if I were back talking to my business students at USC. In essence, where my previous book was an analytical study, this book is practical. Just as my students looked for practical ways to apply the economic theories forced upon them, I here set forth how truly successful investing is a product of a practical application of one's sound understanding of the various macroeconomic forces.

Simply, if the prices of stocks and bonds will move in predictable directions when certain economic conditions are in play, there's no reason for an investor not to act on that information.

In what follows, I offer snapshots of how this book attempts to bring you to this point of confidence.

The Investment Precedent

My initial task is to impress upon you the importance of investing in general. I know of no sounder activity for wealth accumulation, if properly performed, than investing in a mix of stocks and bonds over the long haul. And at no time in history have more Americans been involved in this activity. Still, not every American is convinced. It's common to run into folks who think of Wall Street as just another Las Vegas, people who believe that the risks of investing seems too great while the returns appear too random. I know this to be hogwash. But I'd still like to convince you, for certain, that investing in the markets is as sound and prudent an activity as you can be involved in—as sound as, say, owning a house.

Who doesn't want to own a house, doesn't see the value in it? Scant few. Hence, if you can understand why home ownership is vital to your wealth and security over the long run, I believe you'll have no difficulty comprehending how long-term investing in the stock and bond markets is crucial to your financial well-being.

The follow-up to this is that not all investing plans are alike. As I noted, too many investors have been lured into the belief that average gains are the best they can hope for. Sure, average is not bad at all. If you purchased a broad group of stocks 25 years ago and sold that allocation today, you might be looking at triple-digit capital gains (as measured by share-price appreciation), generally and historically speaking.

Just for fun, let's look at some of the big winners during this period. If you owned a share of Coleco Industries, the makers of the Cabbage Patch doll and Donkey Kong, for the last 25 years, you would have witnessed its price increase by more than 434 percent. If you bought and held Chrysler, you would have seen a 426 percent gain. Reading & Bates, the offshore drilling company? That stock climbed just over 181 percent in the last 25 years.

But now I'm sounding like a stock picker. Chances are, few people bought and held shares of just one of these stocks for the last two and a half decades. Chances are, most investors in this period purchased and held a variety of stocks and bonds. And in doing so, they acted just like homeowners: They bought, they held, and when the time was right, they sold, at a healthy profit.

But a lot went on while they were holding their investments. The prices of their shares went up and down or stayed flat, periodically and often violently—and not just company by company, but group by group. Their small-caps might have climbed while their large-caps wallowed; their value stocks might have gone on a tear while their growth stocks descended; their domestic stocks might have nudged tentatively upward while their international shares charged significantly higher.

If you involve yourself in a broad allocation and spread out your investments across the major classes of stocks and bonds in proportion to their market capitalization, over time you will do well. But in doing so, you will never capture (except by the whim of your original allocation) all the upside when one class of stocks breaks away from the pack. Meanwhile, you always will capture (again, by the whim of your original allocation) the downside movement of each class of stocks and bonds you hold. But all this will average out for you, if only because the average long-run upward performance of asset classes is for real. In other words, groups of assets that move away for a period from their long-run performance averages tend to return to their long-run performance averages. Wall Street types call this "mean reversion." So if you buy and hold your portfolio of stocks and bonds, just as you would buy and hold a house, but perhaps adding to your portfolio paycheck to paycheck (just as you might with a 401[k] plan), you will gain by the average long-run performance of your original allocation. Not bad at all. But not great. This book is interested in great.

An Eye on Elasticity

In an up-trending market, all investors like to own the stocks or groups of stocks that have the greatest *sensitivity* to the market—or the stocks that will climb the most when the market is rising. Pinpointing which group of stocks or asset class will do this and at what times is the essence of my program for investing. Because there is little or no chance that stocks will generate negative returns over the long run, by buying and holding the most sensitive stocks at the right times, you maximize your long-run returns. But how does one identify such sensitivity?

Let's return to cocktail economics. I asked my students at USC to initially determine which segment of the economy would be affected by a policy action coming out of Washington, D.C.—or, for that matter any shock, from new taxes to new technologies, to global political events—that can impact an economy. Next, they were to determine which side of the market, supply or demand, would be affected by the shock. The final step was to determine the price changes and/or output changes that would return the market to its equilibrium. (Just as with stocks, economies or markets tend to return to their long-run levels of performance.) This brought up the concept of sensitivity, a term I often use interchangeably with *flexibility* or *elasticity*. Just like rubber bands, certain aspects of economies—such as companies, industries, production capacities, and resources—are elastic in nature; they can adjust lower or higher to meet the requirements of demand or supply. Conversely, just like oak trees, certain aspects of economies are stubborn and immovable. It follows that an understanding of which variables will bend and which will not is central to figuring out which stocks will outperform or underperform when economic shocks occur.

In many cases the all-important study of elasticity applies to location: the physical location of a company, a resource, a policy action, a natural occurrence, etc. Within these parameters, an elastic or flexible company might be one that shifts its production away from a suddenly high-regulation area to another in which the regulatory burden is much lower. An inflexible company, on the other hand, might see half its production capacity destroyed by a tsunami, with no capability to locate that lost production elsewhere.

Taken to a broader level, the investor who can correctly identify the elasticities inherent in classes of stocks possesses an excellent tool for determining the winners and losers through each economic cycle.

Over the years, I have found that the energy sector provides a wealth of examples for this "location effect." Remember those rolling blackouts in California a few years back? In the simplest of terms, this shock occurred because the added demand for power in the state outpaced the capability of suppliers to deliver it. So put yourself back in my class at USC for a moment. Which companies would be best suited to survive this shock, and which would be most hurt by it? Thinking in terms of location, the California companies with inflexible or inelastic modes of production would clearly suffer the most: If Company A has two plants, one in Santa Barbara and the other in San Diego, there is simply no way it can escape an energy shock within California. In contrast, if Company B also has two plants, but located in San Francisco and *Santa Fe,* it has an immediate advantage over Company A if it can shift production to its New Mexico facility.

This is a very quick rendering of the location effect, and we examine it in greater detail later. But the idea should be clear to any investor: Always determine the impact of an economic shock in terms of both location and the elasticities of the companies in that location.

Traveling from the Source to the Tilt

Over the years, I often have turned to energy as a way of illuminating even the most basic principles of investing—in particular, the idea that no one should ever put all his eggs in one basket. Investors like one thing above all else: higher returns, regardless of the asset classes that provide it. Similarly, in the winter, people in cold climates (for the sake of argument) might like one thing above all else: warmth at a good price, regardless of the fuel source that provides it. In both cases, the source of the result pales in importance to the result itself.

In the most pragmatic sense, investors want to make money. They do so by investing in small-caps, large-caps, value stocks, growth stocks, international shares, domestic shares, Treasury bonds, T-bills, and various combinations of each. People in cold climates, meanwhile, want to stay warm in the winter without going bankrupt. They look for the best-priced fuel they can bring into their homes, alter their fuel usage, better insulate their homes, etc.—anything to keep their energy bills within budget while staying warm. This simple logic instructs that the various *sources* of the results we seek ought to be correctly chosen to provide us with the sought-after *results*.

One period in American history bears out this parallel in a most instructive way: the energy crisis of the 1970s. Investigating this decade from the point of view of fuel—the source that would deliver American consumers their desired result—most interestingly enables us to construct a "benchmark" portfolio that is properly allocated for the long term. But remember, we're interested in capturing all the upside the market has to offer. So by "benchmark," I mean "beginning"—a thoughtful distribution of your eggs (your money) into several baskets (the various asset classes). And from this allocation you *tilt* from time to time based on your ability to properly evaluate each macroeconomic shock that comes along.

Tilting properly, however, requires some talent, and you need to develop a certain skill set to mature from an average investor to an above-average performer. Sadly, insight regarding the interrelationship of investing and economics is too often lacking these days. For instance, it never ceases to amaze me when a business story in the newspaper makes an inference about the profitability of a company, the performance of the stock market, or a macroeconomic variable such as the rate of GDP growth by looking solely at price changes. What can an increase or decrease in the price of something tell us about the profits that thing is generating or the quantities of it that are being transacted? The answer is, not very much. And without knowledge of profit and quantity shifts, we cannot make informed decisions on how to respond to news of a price shift. The challenge, then, is to discover the supply-and-demand conditions underlying movements in price (in effect, pinpointing the true nature of each economic shock) to make that price movement a reliable indicator. In this way, we turn what I call price "smoke" into a price "signal," a valuable piece of information that enables you to act properly within your portfolio.

A Timing for Everything

When the nature of an economic shock and the elasticities of the different companies, industries, and asset classes with respect to that shock are determined, a simple investment strategy emerges: Buy the stocks of the companies or asset classes that will benefit from the shock and avoid those that will not. This strategy has paid enormous dividends for my clients over the years. But it also has asked my clients to look more sharply at macroeconomic forces than ever before and to understand, that for every economic action, there is a *predictable* market reaction. As a result, the better my clients have understood these relationships, the further in advance they have been able to make the proper adjustments to the portfolios they manage.

Timing is an essential element of a cyclical asset-allocation strategy, although you will still benefit if you correctly adjust your allocations after an economic cycle has established. That said, you want to activate your tilts early enough to capture as much of a cycle's upside as possible. This is not to say that investment forecasts based on a sound rendering of the macroeconomic environment will be correct every time; sometimes the forecasts will be off.

It's just like the weather, an analogy I incorporate to describe the fundamentals of forecasting and timing. Sometimes it rains when the weatherman predicted sun, and other times it is sunny when the forecast called for showers. But the farmer out in the field always has a hand up on the weatherman. When he sees black storm clouds on the horizon, he can make the safe assumption that bad weather is coming and pull his tractor into the barn. In doing so, he uses additional information to his advantage. Or, in the abstract, he has applied his educated rendering of the variables to his decision rules for when or when not to take action.

This information advantage applies to the investment strategy I'm setting forth. The better you get at it, the easier it will be for you to timely apply a macroeconomic analysis to your decision rules for when and how to adjust your investments. You want to stay as close to top-down information as possible, essentially becoming the farmer who watches the skies, not just the weatherman who looks at the radar. In fact, it's preferable that you wear both these hats.

Tax- and monetary-policy changes, natural disasters, shifts to the underlying inflation rate and the rate of GDP growth—these and many other events constitute shocks to the economic system and dictate periods when certain types of assets will outperform others. Here you want to wear the farmer's hat: If you can see the storm clouds as they relate to these events, you very well might be able to anticipate cyclical changes in the economy and the stock markets they will deliver. To improve this forecast, you want to put on your weatherman hat, collecting the forecasts of seasoned pros who can corroborate your opinions.

Indeed, don't get the feeling that you'll be left standing out in the field gazing into the sky, attempting to figure out the relationships between economic shocks and investing on your own. Throughout this book, I outline the precise conditions under which the exposure to the various classifications of stocks and/or bonds should be increased or decreased. Then, using historical data, I illustrate the potentially significant benefits of such a cycle-driven strategy.

A Strategy of Strategies

Shocks, cycles, elasticities, location effects—this investing story has many twists and also many levels of convergence. In the pages ahead, I also describe how the various macroeconomic forces might or might not move independently of one another and show that there is no way to rule out the fact that some conditions might occur simultaneously. This means that investors can employ *multiple investment strategies* either alone or simultaneously. What are these strategies?

Investors today might be most familiar with "passive" strategies that invest in shares of funds that mirror the performance of the various stock indexes. When the market goes up, the passive investor does well. When the market drops, the passive investor goes down with it. As the prices of stocks collectively move upward over time, this is a very safe strategy for long-term wealth accumulation. And although it is not, in my firm belief, the best method for attaining all the upside that markets have to offer, there are certainly times when an all or partial passive approach to investing makes the most sense. Similarly, sometimes going "active" is preferable—times when you want to select stocks in certain categories that will benefit most from the macroeconomic environment.

For instance, when the stocks of smaller companies (small-caps) project to outperform the stocks of larger companies (large-caps), my research bears out that an active, stock-picking approach to small-caps might be in order. Another approach concerns uncorrelated or nontraditional investments that are chosen on the belief that they will outperform the market for some reason. Hedge funds, which employ sophisticated investment strategies, fall into this category. The fees can be high for entry into these funds. But sometimes you want to stick your toe into these high-end active waters, just as sometimes a long swim in the lower-end passive pool makes the most sense.

You might notice that there is a "pair-wise" default to this investment program. Sometimes you want to lean large-cap, other times small-cap. Sometimes you want to go "active," other times "passive." So although there appear to be many moving parts to this plan, the implementation will not be too complicated as long as you keep in mind that there always will be one choice over another when it comes down to the nitty-gritty of adjusting your portfolio from time to time and from cycle to cycle.

Before we jump in, I'd like to leave you with a very cocktail-economics way of thinking about the application of this strategy. *Question:* How do you turn a martini into a Gibson? *Answer:* You put an onion in it. And if you'll allow the gin and vermouth in the glass to represent the sphere of economic forces, the onion in the glass can represent the range of investment decisions you can make based on your rendering of these forces. Onions have layers, just like this multilayered investment plan. The first layer consists of building a benchmark allocation to the various asset classes. The second layer consists of an application of a macroeconomic forecast to one of four different pair-wise asset choices: large-cap versus small-cap, domestic versus international, value versus growth, and stocks versus bonds. The third and final layer consists of deciding among the various active and passive strategies. The end result is a cyclical asset allocation that will have you best positioned to take the most advantage of the stock and bond markets through every economic cycle.

Glass, for now, dismissed.

Endnotes

1. Victor A. Canto, co-authored with Douglas H. Joines and Robert I. Webb, "The Revenue Effects of the Kennedy and Reagan Tax Cuts: Some Time Series Estimates," *Journal of Business and Economic Statistics* 4, no. 3 (July 1986): 281–288.

2. Since the 1964 tax cut became law in midyear, with about half of the reductions in tax rates retroactive to the beginning of that calendar year, the full reduction in tax rates became effective in calendar year 1965. By targeting the period between 1963 and 1966, we can capture the full effects of both the 1962 and 1964 tax cuts.

1 —————————————————

The Buy-and-Hold Connection: Investing Fundamentals, Courtesy of the American Homeowner The American Dream—or Reality?

This book has a good deal to do with the fundamentals of investing, and a good deal more to do with how to perform at a higher level than the great herd of investors who settle for average results. But before turning to above-average performance, my first duty is to convince you that even average investing is well worth your time. In this chapter, we investigate the very concept of average investing—and from what I believe to be a very distinctive and instructive point of view:

I believe that if you can truly understand the dynamics and payoffs related to buying and living in a home, you will stand on a rock-solid foundation from which to invest in the stock and bond markets. In other words, this foundation is the average on which we build an above-average strategy.

When stacked against each other, home-owning and stock market investing form a weighty parallel because each activity so completely instructs the other. You see, homeowners and stockowners are identical in many ways. They desire the returns that their investments will generate and, more important, believe that these returns will, in fact, materialize. They display levels of risk that, in relation to returns, are satisfied by their investments—basically, their fear of "getting burned" is low. The lingo attached to each of their activities is much the same as well. Let me throw a few terms at you, all of which we discuss in this chapter: *buy-and-hold, price appreciation, transaction costs, capital gains, imputed income, leverage,* and *total returns.* Taken together, these terms set the parameters of performance for investors of all stripes. And for homeowners in general, they set the parameters for *average* performance.

When it comes to buying and living in a home, average is the established and profitable American way. Think of it this way: If you invest in something and it appreciates in relation to a historical average that has proven to deliver substantial positive returns, then you win. You make money. *Average,* here, equates with *success*—and with homeownership: In general, the prices of all homes go up over time. So if you invest in a home, you stand to gain on that investment. This is why you "buy," and it is one of the two dominant forces that drive homeownership. The second force has to do with why you "hold" that investment. For now, I state plainly that you hold it until it becomes profitable to sell it.

Already you should sense a parallel between owning a home and owning a portfolio of stocks and bonds. Each you buy, and each you hold. Simple enough. But *simple* will empower you in the pages ahead as we transfer the fundamentals of home-owning into the foundational rules for investing in the stock and bond markets.

The American Dream: As Real as Ever

Millions of Americans understand the value of investing in residential real estate. They start small, and when the time is right, they sell, at a profit, and move to a bigger place. Some call this the American Dream, but it's not a dream at all. At this writing, homeownership in the U.S. stands near 69 percent—up from 63 percent in 1970, 55 percent in 1950, and 48 percent in 1930.[1] That's an impressive climb. At no time in history have more Americans owned homes—that's yet more evidence that this is not only the land of opportunity, but also the land of personal responsibility. After all, what's more responsible than taking advantage of an investment that's almost certain to make you better off? True, no investment is 100 percent guaranteed. But historically, homeownership comes pretty close.

Most Americans know this. They know that home prices usually go up over time, so much so that the fears attached to home-owning relative to other forms of investing are very low. They know that if they hold on to their properties long enough, they might very well enjoy a nice payday if they decide to sell. The data backs this up, and conversations at the kitchen table verify this reality every day: "You paid *how much* for your house 20 years ago? And now it's worth *how much*? Holy cow." Americans also know that owning and living in a home is a low-tax activity; in fact, for most Americans, it is a tax-free activity, a tremendous incentive to buy rather than rent.

These are the basics of the buy-and-hold strategy as it relates to residential real estate. But with participation rates in this strategy near 70 percent today, buy-and-hold becomes an authoritative force worthy of deeper investigation. Who are these buyers and holders, and what are the range of factors that both motivate and guide their actions?

In what follows I'll introduce you to two: Their names are Jennifer and Carlos, and their actions in relation to the buy-and-hold formula are like a textbook.

The Motivating Force of a Demand-Led Expansion

Jennifer and Carlos are a lot alike. After finishing college the same year, they each landed good jobs in the same U.S. city. They worked hard, saving and planning, and as luck would have it, they purchased homes in the same suburban development during the same month three years later. The units they liked went for $200,000 a piece, and they each figured they could live happily with one bedroom and one small bath until they decided to settle down and have families. After a few years of bumping into each other nearly all the time, the two began to date, and it wasn't all that long before Carlos proposed to Jennifer. At the five-year mark of homeownership and only six months before their wedding day, they put their units up for sale— but they had gauged the market accurately and knew that selling wouldn't be too difficult in a short period of time. And they were right. Their sales went quickly and profitably, and with cash in hand, they began their lives together deeper in the suburbs, where the homes come with in-ground pools, big lawns, and two-car garages.[2]

A nice story with a happy ending? Sure. But the forces of economics and fundamental investing behavior are swirling behind the scenes.

When Jennifer and Carlos shopped for their original homes, they each noticed two things: First, a lot of properties were available. Second, prices overall seemed pretty steep. But this latter fact didn't turn them off, if only because they believed that prices would continue to increase the longer they put off making a purchase. So they entered the house-hunting market with enthusiasm—in effect, joining the very powerful group that today drives America's *demand-led* housing expansion: Simply stated, steady economic growth in America over time has led to a steady increase in the demand for homes. As the population has become larger and more affluent, it has increasingly looked to own residential real estate, raising the demand for this particular good.

In economic terms, any such demand-led expansion can be satisfied through either price increases, increases in supply, or both. In the U.S. example, an upward shift in the demand for homes has produced a movement along the "supply curve" that has resulted in higher prices *and* higher output (or more homes).

Jennifer and Carlos might not have been able to state this like an economist, but they understood it well enough: Homeowners profit very simply because they buy and hold properties. Buying and holding allows people to take advantage of the secular uptrends in home prices, while riding out any short-term downward fluctuations in prices. This is an insurance policy on success. Buy something at $1, hold it while its value increases despite any bumps along the way, and sell it at $2—or more. That's the one-two punch for homeownership, just as it's the winning combination for investing in the stock market.

Buy and Hold, but for How Long?

There's one obvious follow-up question to all this: How *long* does one hold? Foresight is part of the answer—one holds a home until selling it is profitable, a time in the future that one can easily calculate by studying price movements in a neighborhood. But I'll argue that another, equally influential force goes a long way toward determining buy-and-hold behavior: It is the *transaction cost*—and, in fact, it's what kept Jennifer and Carlos in their homes long enough for the two to finally get together.

In the U.S., the average homeowner owns a house for between four-and-a-half and seven years. This holding period can be explained in good part by the transaction costs associated with the purchase and sale of a home combined with the expected increase in average home prices. Technically, a transaction cost is the difference between the price a purchaser pays and the net price a seller receives. In this regard, it is similar to a sales tax: It drives a wedge between the price the consumer pays and the price the seller pays. In tax terms, the dynamic is simple and often minimal. Seven cents on the dollar doesn't feel like all that much when you buy a $10 shirt. In the case of residential real estate, however, transaction costs can be substantial and often determine the point at which homeowners feel "free" to sell their properties.

Continuing with the story of Jennifer and Carlos, they were each able to sell their properties for $240,000. Five years earlier, the purchase price in both cases was $200,000, so it looks as if they each cleared $40,000—a 20 percent gain. But if the transaction costs each suffered $20,000, or 10 percent, they each realized only half that amount ($40,000 – $20,000 = $20,000), for a 10 percent gain net of transaction costs. Jennifer and Carlos both did well, but those transaction costs mattered.

Transaction Costs (Greatly) Influence Holding Periods

I've gone through the pain of moving several times during my marriage, so I can attest to the fact that transaction costs can be significant. Today, based on average realtor fees, we can set the initial transaction cost at around 6 percent. Any financing involved in the transaction adds some costs (bankers and lawyers need to get paid, too). And you can also throw in moving expenses as well as the psychological costs to the family members who are moving. (Psychological costs might be hard to calculate, but they do exist.) Putting all this together, we can make a reasoned estimate that the transaction costs involved in purchasing residential real estate could easily exceed 10 percent of a home price in general.

So if a family moves, how long will it take before the price appreciation of their new house makes up for the transaction costs incurred in selling their old one? Well, since 1960, the median house price has gained an average of 5.6 percent per year. This means that the transaction cost of an initial purchase and move, using the estimates we just made, is equivalent to at least one year's worth of home appreciation (5.6 percent) and probably two years or more. Viewed this way, one can safely argue that, unless forced to move by circumstances, any move a homeowner makes based purely on investment considerations requires a holding period long enough to attain returns that at least make up for the original transaction costs.[3]

Here it would seem that upward-trending home prices are the true friend of the homeowner; they will systematically, and in a relatively short period of time, compensate for transaction costs incurred. But what if home prices in an area are going down? Should homeowners in the neighborhood panic? The answer, based on the data and personal experience, is more than likely a big "No."

Riding Out the Dips: A California Story

Once again, no investment is 100 percent guaranteed. Sometimes pockets of the housing market are infected by price declines—such as Texas during the oil-price drop of the 1980s, California in the early 1990s, and Northern California after the Internet bubble popped in 2000. But these are fluctuations around the long-term trend. Although home-owning is not always a sure thing on a shorter-term basis, the longer you own a property, the greater your chances are of navigating through any disturbances in the market.

In my home state of California, real-estate prices declined by a third in the early 1990s. Worse, in many cases, home prices fell *below* the value of mortgages. In California, home loans are "nonrecourse," meaning that when homeowners walk away from mortgages, creditors must either chase them down or take possession of their vacated properties. In general, creditors have chosen the latter. So back in the early 1990s, the temptation to abandon a home in California and let the creditor worry about it was great. But did those who took this option act prudently (at least, in a cold, economic sense)?

This is a simple calculation. Using the average annual gain of the median home price, 5.6 percent, we can figure out how many years a sample California couple in the early 1990s needed to wait to recapture the full value of their property. (Central to this calculation is the belief that home prices can recover from situations such as the one that occurred in California. But the long-term trends for home prices in the U.S. are simply too positive and reliable not to be banked on.) Let's assume that our California couple held a home loan with an 80 percent loan-to-value ratio (meaning that the value of the loan was 80 percent of the home price) when the price shock occurred. So a 30 percent decline in the value of their home meant their loan was worth 10 percent *more than* the value of their home. That is, the California couple was suddenly 10 percent underwater. Time to flee? Well, we now know this 10 percent deficit to be in the neighborhood of two years' worth of home appreciation, on average, or 5.6 percent plus 5.6 percent. So if the California couple held on to their house for just two years more, they may very well have been made "whole" again.

On the other hand, had they jumped, they would have lost even more than their original investment. The loss the bank or lender would have realized if the house were taken back would have been considered a "gift-in-kind" to the couple that abandoned their mortgage. The couple would have been expected to pay taxes on that gift, and the mortgage bank would have sent them a 1099 tax form to facilitate the process. So what we now have are two types of incentives: On the positive side, we have the historical appreciation of home prices; on the negative, we have the complete loss of an original investment, coupled with a sudden gift-in-kind tax owed to the IRS.

That, in a nutshell, is why people tend to buy and *hold* through thick and thin—homeowners and stock investors alike.

The Returns: Capital Gains

Something in this story might already be telling you that it pays, in general, to stick with your investments. It does. And now you know the minimum length of the holding period: until the transaction costs are covered. After that, your choices are clear. You can switch to another investment if you feel the new investment will give you a higher rate of return. You will incur new transaction costs if you decide to switch, but. presumably. the new investment will, in time, cover those costs and produce returns to your liking. Alternatively, if no new investment can make such a promise, you can stay the course with your original investment, further minimizing the impact of the original transaction costs and maximizing your net take.

Applied to homeownership, it's interesting to consider that the buy-and-hold formula is largely *induced* by transaction costs: Homeowners generally will not consider cashing in until those costs are covered. And once they are covered, they still might sit on their properties, particularly if they're interested in making hay with their investments. And by "hay," I mean *capital gains.*

A capital gain is the increase in the value of an asset that you realize when you sell that asset. Jennifer and Carlos each sold their properties for $240,000, or 20 percent more than they paid for them. Twenty percent is a nice capital gain over five years.

If you round out the average holding period for homes in the U.S. to 5 to 7 years and look back at the appreciation of homes for the last 45 years, you clearly can see the possible magnitude of capital gains that homeownership offers. It's a pretty wide range: In the 45-year period between 1961 and 2005 (see Table 1.1), people who sold their homes in the five- to seven-year holding period realized a minimum 11.23 percent capital gain, on average, and a maximum 76.28 percent gain. These gains are based on the appreciation of owner-occupied residential real estate in the U.S., with the minimum gain coming in both 1966 and 1967 after a holding period of five years, and the maximum gain occurring in 1980 following a seven-year holding period. Both the low and high results are worlds apart, but, importantly, each leaped an estimated transaction cost of 10 percent and brought additional capital gains, to boot.

TABLE 1.1   Holding Period Appreciation for Owner-Occupied Residential Real Estate

	1 Year	2 Years	3 Years	4 Years	5 Years	6 Years	7 Years
1/1/61	3.74%						
1/1/62	3.93%	7.67%					
1/1/63	1.89%	5.82%	9.55%				
1/1/64	1.82%	3.71%	7.64%	11.38%			
1/1/65	3.45%	5.28%	7.16%	11.10%	14.83%		
1/1/66	0.14%	3.59%	5.41%	7.30%	11.23%	14.97%	
1/1/67	3.93%	4.06%	7.52%	9.34%	11.23%	15.16%	19.09%
1/1/68	4.23%	8.16%	8.29%	11.75%	13.57%	15.46%	17.35%
1/1/69	8.12%	12.35%	16.28%	16.41%	19.87%	21.69%	23.52%
1/1/70	5.36%	13.48%	17.71%	21.64%	21.77%	25.23%	28.68%
1/1/71	7.53%	12.89%	21.01%	25.24%	29.17%	29.31%	29.44%
1/1/72	7.38%	14.92%	20.28%	28.39%	32.63%	36.55%	40.48%
1/1/73	7.92%	15.30%	22.83%	28.19%	36.31%	40.54%	44.78%
1/1/74	10.19%	18.11%	25.49%	33.02%	38.38%	46.50%	54.62%
1/1/75	9.81%	20.00%	27.92%	35.30%	42.84%	48.20%	53.56%
1/1/76	7.63%	17.45%	27.64%	35.56%	42.94%	50.47%	58.01%
1/1/77	11.87%	19.50%	29.31%	39.50%	47.42%	54.80%	62.18%
1/1/78	12.68%	24.55%	32.18%	41.99%	52.18%	60.10%	68.02%
1/1/79	13.43%	26.11%	37.98%	45.61%	55.42%	65.61%	75.80%
1/1/80	11.04%	24.47%	37.15%	49.01%	56.65%	66.46%	76.28%
1/1/81	6.53%	17.57%	31.00%	43.68%	55.55%	63.18%	70.81%

	1 Year	2 Years	3 Years	4 Years	5 Years	6 Years	7 Years
1/1/82	2.09%	8.62%	19.66%	33.09%	45.77%	57.63%	69.50%
1/1/83	3.62%	5.71%	12.24%	23.28%	36.71%	49.39%	62.07%
1/1/84	2.94%	6.56%	8.65%	15.19%	26.22%	39.65%	53.08%
1/1/85	4.19%	7.14%	10.76%	12.84%	19.38%	30.42%	41.45%
1/1/86	6.16%	10.36%	13.30%	16.92%	19.01%	25.54%	32.08%
1/1/87	6.39%	12.56%	16.75%	19.69%	23.31%	25.40%	27.49%
1/1/88	4.23%	10.62%	16.79%	20.98%	23.92%	27.54%	31.16%
1/1/89	0.22%	4.46%	10.85%	17.01%	21.20%	24.15%	27.09%
1/1/90	2.75%	2.98%	7.21%	13.60%	19.77%	23.96%	28.15%
1/1/91	5.40%	8.15%	8.37%	12.61%	19.00%	25.16%	31.32%
1/1/92	2.64%	8.04%	10.79%	11.02%	15.25%	21.64%	28.03%
1/1/93	3.35%	6.00%	11.39%	14.15%	14.37%	18.60%	22.83%
1/1/94	3.90%	7.25%	9.90%	15.29%	18.05%	18.27%	18.49%
1/1/95	3.03%	6.93%	10.28%	12.93%	18.32%	21.08%	23.83%
1/1/96	4.68%	7.72%	11.62%	14.97%	17.61%	23.01%	28.40%
1/1/97	5.05%	9.74%	12.77%	16.67%	20.02%	22.66%	25.31%
1/1/98	5.28%	10.33%	15.01%	18.05%	21.95%	25.30%	28.65%
1/1/99	3.75%	9.02%	14.07%	18.76%	21.79%	25.69%	29.59%
1/1/00	4.19%	7.93%	13.21%	18.26%	22.95%	25.98%	29.01%
1/1/01	6.14%	10.33%	14.07%	19.35%	24.40%	29.08%	33.77%
1/1/02	6.74%	12.88%	17.06%	20.81%	26.08%	31.14%	36.19%
1/1/03	7.26%	13.99%	20.13%	24.32%	28.06%	33.34%	38.62%
1/1/04	7.97%	15.23%	21.96%	28.10%	32.29%	36.03%	39.78%
1/1/05	5.56%	13.53%	20.78%	27.52%	33.66%	37.85%	42.03%

Source: Global Insight

Perhaps more important, for the sample period in question, no evidence exists that the aggregate of home prices ever failed to post positive gains. This means that even if you hold a property for one year, you have a good chance of making a capital gain. (At face value, the data does not reflect local price dips, such as those experienced by Californians in the early 1990s. However, the broad data is more assurance that homeowners should ride out any price-decline storms.)

It would seem that residential real estate is something of a capital gains–generating machine. And the machine still functions when we figure in taxes. Since 1997, single individuals selling their homes have been exempt from paying taxes on the first $250,000 in capital gains they realize.[4] For couples, the tax-free amount is a whopping $500,000. Thus, in most cases, homeowners in America can roll over their investments from one house to another tax-free, quite often increasing their cost basis, or the price they pay for a residence. Put another way, the new home price becomes the new number from which the $500,000 in tax-free capital gains then is calculated.

The Returns: Imputed Income

Homeowners also enjoy the income produced by their properties, which, more technically, is the *imputed income*—an amount that is not necessarily visible in the value of a house, although it does exist. Simply, the imputed income of a home is the amount of money one would have to spend in renting an equivalent residence, had one not owned the home in the first place. Specifically, you can think of this income as the imputed rent. If you own a home and live in it, you essentially act like a renter who is not paying any rent. This sounds like a nice deal, and it is. Under current law, homeowners do not have to report the income attributed to living in their homes, so imputed income is also tax-free. (You also can think in terms of the imputed income that *you* carry around. If you are an electrician and you rewire your house, you performed a service that has a monetary value and cannot be taxed.)

Imputed income is a valuable thing, and you can get a good sense of this by looking at the contrasting situations of renting and home-owning. Let's say a group of renters spends a quarter of their monthly incomes on rent, and a group of owners spends a quarter of their incomes on mortgages. Let's further assume that members of the two groups earn roughly the same amount and live in comparable houses.

Okay, so it's the first of the month, and rent and mortgage payments are due. The renters use their income, which is taxed either paycheck to paycheck or when they file with the IRS, to make their rent payments; those payments are then taxed as income generated by their landlords. Contrastingly, the homeowners can deduct the interest on their mortgage payments when they pay their taxes, while not having to report the imputed rental income that comes with living in their homes. In effect, the homeowners are not paying as high a tax on their home-related income as are the renters.

Calculating Your Total Return

To discover the *total return* generated by any investment, you must account for all the gains (income + price appreciation) generated by the investment, the cost base (the initial price of the investment) to which those gains will be applied, the tax treatment of those gains in all their forms, *and* the transaction costs.

So, in terms of total return, how did Jennifer and Carlos do?

Well, the cost basis in each case was $200,000. Because they each sold for $240,000, they each had a capital gain of $40,000. And because they each lived in their homes rent-free for five years, we can set their imputed incomes at a reasonable $20,000 each (a modest $4,000 a year in imputed rent). This gives us a pre-tax total return on the sale of each unit of $60,000. And now for taxes. The $20,000 imputed (rental) income is not taxed at all. Because single taxpayers can realize $250,000 worth of capital gains every two years tax-free, the $40,000 in gains is not taxed, either. This means that the pre-tax and post-tax total return is the same for each: a full $60,000, which is 30 percent of the original cost base. However, after subtracting 10 percent in transaction costs, or $20,000, based on an original purchase price of $200,000, the total return drops to $40,000. In percentage terms, a 30 percent total return falls to 20 percent, although this is still an attractive number.

And because Jennifer and Carlos finally got married, their total-return story climbs one more profitable notch. Again, for a married couple, the first $500,000 in capital gains on the sale of a home is exempt from taxes. Putting their resources together, if Jennifer and Carlos bought their next home for $400,000 and sold it five years later for $500,000, again moving up in life, they would pay no capital-gains taxes on that transaction.

When it comes to total returns, it's hard to beat homeownership. And the case can be made even better when you look at how homes are financed.

The Impact of Leverage on Your Total Return

As I've noted, Jennifer and Carlos are a lot alike—almost identical. But Jennifer is a lot smarter than Carlos, as I see it. Not yet revealed in their story is that, when they purchased their first homes, Carlos decided to pay the entire $200,000 up front, while Jennifer opted to finance her purchase by putting down $40,000, or 20 percent.

This was a very smart move on Jennifer's part. When she sold five years later, the $60,000 she cleared (capital gains + imputed income) represented a gain of 150 percent because it was based on an original investment of $40,000.

This example shows the impact that *leverage* can have on the total return of an investment (leverage being the degree to which an investor or business uses borrowed money). Borrowing often gets a bad rap because it is thought of as acquiring and spending money that is not yours. But leverage can increase a shareholder's return on investment because it is the use of smaller amounts of cash to obtain assets of greater value. Jennifer was entitled to the total gains of her house, which were applied to only her original investment when calculating her total return. So by putting down only 20 percent, or one-fifth, of the purchase price, she essentially leveraged her investment (or down payment) five times when compared to the purchase price.

Yet by risking only one-fifth, she got control of the whole investment and captured the full capital gains produced by her property.

Now, whether this is a wise strategy depends on what homeowners do with the money they decide to not put toward their homes when they make their purchases. Let's say Carlos had decided to put down only 20 percent of the original purchase price, or $40,000, just like Jennifer. This means he would have had $160,000 to "put to work" in another endeavor. That's a good amount, and to make certain that the new endeavor would generate some additional hay, it would have to pay only in excess of the loan rate of his mortgage.

Let's say that in the five years he held his home, he netted 2 percent over the loan rate by way of a new endeavor (which could have been an investment in the stock market, the bond market, or a business). This means he would have added a 10 percent return (2 percent × 5 years), or a total of $40,000. This amount would be subject to taxes—capital gains, dividend, and/or income taxes—as well as the transaction costs related to the investment. But even when these are factored in, his additional take still would have been worth it.

Of course, maybe Jennifer simply didn't have that $200,000 to put down at the time of her purchase, making her smarter than Carlos only by default. But Carlos proved rather risk-averse, in that he did not leverage the investment in his home and put his available money to work where it could have grown in excess of the loan rate.

Onward and Upward to the Stock Market

You thought this was a book about investing in the stock market, and now you're being led to believe that owning a home might be the best place for your money. Well, there are important twists to this story.

In touring the ins and outs of homeownership, you now should understand how to measure any investment—how to compute your total return while accounting for the transaction-cost effect. Taken together, this should always be your bottom line—it will allow you to assess your investment performance as well as judge how you're doing relative to other investors. You also should have a grasp of the fundamental investing concept known as buy-and-hold, *through thick and thin*. When you think of it, what do you get when you average out the good times (the thick) and the bad (the thin)? Well, you get average performance over time. Add in the fact that home prices appreciate significantly over time, and you have a winning, though average, formula.

So armed, we can now make the case for taking the next step to owning and managing your very own portfolio of stock and bond investments. If you can understand the fundamentals of owning a home as outlined in this chapter, you can grasp the basics of investing in the stock market. But in the next two chapters, we use the same fundamentals to show how the returns generated by stock market investing can soundly beat the returns delivered by homeownership. In doing so, we inch up from average to above-average investing. Perhaps, not surprisingly, transaction costs will again hold center stage: Because these are so much lower relative to stocks than to residential real estate, unlike Jennifer and Carlos, you won't have to hold your investments for five or so years to generate a total return to your liking.

Endnotes

1. U.S. Census Bureau. According to the National Association of Realtors, U.S. homeownership could exceed 70 percent by 2013.

2. Jennifer and Carlos are fictional representations of real-life Americans in terms of the average period of time they held on to their properties before selling and their rationale for doing so (e.g., their mutual desire to profit on their investments,

which required that they hold on to their investments long enough so that their initial transaction costs were covered and their desire for capital gains was satisfied).

3. If you own a home, you might have to move regardless of whether you covered your transaction costs or whether you can get a better return on your investment elsewhere: Maybe your job changes or the size of your family outgrows your living space, and you simply must relocate. But without these pressures, the combination of when you cover your transaction costs and the total financial attractiveness (new transaction costs + the promise of higher gains) of housing alternatives determines when you leave one residence for another. Not only is this stated in terms of a financial best-practice, but it is how most American homeowners behave.

4. Since the passage of the Taxpayer Relief Act of 1997, married couples filing jointly have been exempt from taxes on profits (i.e., capital gains) of up to $500,000 on the sale of their residences. For singles, the exemption cut-off is $250,000. In both cases, sellers need to have lived in their homes for two out of five years prior to the sale.

2

Leaping the Transaction-Cost Hurdle: Sometimes It's Easy, Other Times It's Not

The parallels drawn in the previous chapter lead us to the logical conclusion that a buy-and-hold strategy will work equally well for investing in residential real estate or the stock market. But now we turn to the differences between these activities, to shed a light on the attractiveness of stock investing relative to home-owning. The critical differences have to do with the transaction costs and tax treatments related to each activity—at first glace, the former favors stockownership, and the latter gives the edge to homeownership. However, when we account for the opportunities alternative investments provide, stocks gain a visible edge over residential real estate. Or, perhaps, I should say that the returns that *certain* types of stock market investing generate eclipse those that home-owning generates.

I haven't kept it a secret that I rank my investing strategy—out of the countless strategies available to you—among the above-average performers. In the course of this book, I defend this ranking empirically, historically, and anecdotally. But I like "average," too. I like it for home-owning because if you buy a house and live in it long enough, you will profit from that investment (very likely tax-free) while enjoying the tax-free imputed income that comes with having that roof over your head. At times, I also like "average" for investing in the stock market, but only when sticking with your current investments (or "holding" them) is more prudent than turning them over. Only when holding your investments makes very little sense in relation to selling them, or switching to alternative investments, do I part company with average performance.

Consider these comments a brief introduction to the passive versus active debate. When you invest passively, you buy and hold; when you invest actively, you buy and sell and switch between investments. Toward the end of this chapter, we take a closer (though still introductory) look at passive versus active investing, drawing the conclusion that passive stock market investors have a lot more in common with homeowners than do active investors.

The Long-Run Precedent for Investing in the Stock Market

In the third edition of his seminal book *Stocks for the Long Run*, Professor Jeremy Siegel of the University of Pennsylvania turns in a full 200 years' worth of data to re-emphasize his point that, over time, the stock market will rise—and rise significantly. Siegel's analysis spans the period from 1802 to 2001. Inside that time in U.S. history, there were a civil war, two world wars, several recessions, trade wars, a great depression, more regional wars of smaller scale, hyperinflationary periods, energy shortages—a string of events that predictably pulled down the stock market. Yet Siegel's stock market graph for the period looks like a manageable hike up a mountainside, with no impassible crevice along the way. According to the professor, "One dollar invested and reinvested in stocks since 1802 would have accumulated to $8.80 million by the end of 2001." That's an impressive return any way you slice it.[1]

By now, I think it has been firmly established that every investor can bank on the long-run upside of the stock market—not that *200 years* is a realistic timeframe for any one investor (and Siegel makes this point, too). Investor horizons aren't even half that long and are usually much shorter. The gold-standard long horizon today is about 40 years, a period of time that historically has always beaten a negative return. But 30 years is also a relatively long horizon, although there's no reason not to get in the market for 20 or 10 years, if you shift to less-risky investments the shorter your horizon gets. Right now, I'm speaking purely in a passive manner: Buy a broad range of stocks and bonds, and hold on to them for a while to make some money. In doing so, you will, in fact, be acting just like Jennifer and Carlos, with the strong confidence that you'll come out ahead.

Hurdles and Holding Periods

However, if the idea is to do better than just "make some money," the challenge is to accurately foresee which stocks will exhibit the greatest gains during *each and every* economic period, while at the same time pinpointing which stocks (or asset classes or groups of stocks) are bound to plummet due to the economic circumstances. Importantly, for such a strategy even to exist, the promise of a higher return elsewhere must also exist. For instance, if acting in a financially responsible manner, homeowners *will not* move to new properties if the gains associated with the move are not high enough to compensate them for any new transaction costs over a new time horizon.

Looked at this way, transaction costs affect the length of holding periods on both the back end (from the time an original investment is made) and the front end (in relation to the prospect of a new investment). The higher the transaction costs are on either end, the higher the "hurdle" is for any decision to buy or sell an investment.

Wall Street types talk about *hurdle rates* all the time: Jump over the hurdle (which is what an investment costs you) and you're going to make some money. From this logic, we can make some interesting deductions: The higher the transaction costs are—with all else being the same—the longer the holding period will be. In other words, it will take an investor longer to hurdle his or her transaction costs. The same holds for the *differential of returns* between investments. The lower the differential is—meaning that very little difference exists between the returns of all possible investments—the less likely it will be that people will turn over their investments. Thus, the higher the transaction costs are and the lower the differential of returns is, the lower will be the frequency with which investments are bought and sold.

This is the more precise reason why the average holding period for owner-occupied housing is in the range of five to seven years: The transaction costs are high, and/or the differential of returns between houses in the same localities are not high enough to justify a move any sooner.

But here's the kicker: Due to the respective levels of transaction costs and differentials of return, homeowners are married to their properties *a lot* longer than stock market investors need to be wed to the assets in their portfolios.

Stacking Homes Against Stocks

To quickly review, investing in homes and investing in stocks are extremely similar activities in terms of how these investments perform, the consistency of the upside of returns, and the various ways each rewards participants. These similarities are "key" in the context of this book because they determine the buy-and-hold strategy as practiced by a great many investors (see Table 2.1).

TABLE 2.1   Homes vs. Stocks: The Key Similarities

	Homes	**Stocks**
Average price of investment rises over time.	Yes	Yes
Investors are motivated by secular price increases.	Yes	Yes
Investments produce capital gains.	Yes	Yes
Investments produce dividends.	Yes	Yes
Investments are taxable.	Yes	Yes

But it is in the relative differences between these two activities that we find our opening—our opportunity to transform average into above-average investing (see Table 2.2).

TABLE 2.2   Homes vs. Stocks: The Crucial Differences

	Homes	**Stocks**
Magnitude of transaction costs	Higher	Lower
Holding periods as implied by transaction costs	Longer	Shorter
Incidence of tax payments on investments	Infrequent	Low to high
Differential of returns	Low	Low to high

In hashing out these differences, I begin with taxation because this is the final area where home-owning has a decided advantage over stock-owning.

The Differences: Tax Treatments

Just like homes, stocks generate price appreciation, or capital gains. Also just like homes, stocks produce income, but rather than imputed income, this is true *dividend* income. In stock-speak, a dividend is a cash payment that a company makes to its shareholders. No set amount exists for a stock dividend; it is based on a company's profits and can be distributed quarterly or annually. If a dividend-paying company is doing well, it might very well raise the dividend it pays to shareholders.[2] Like imputed income, the dividend is the extra value implicit in an asset. But unlike imputed income, stock dividends are not tax-free.

Per the Jobs and Growth Tax Relief and Reconciliation Act of 2003, the capital gains and dividends that stock market investments generate are each taxed at a 15 percent rate—something of a high threshold when compared to the taxes on owner-occupied residential real estate: Once more, the tax on the dividend income generated by a house is zero; the tax on the capital gains a home delivers is zero if those gains are below $250,000 for a single person and $500,000 for couples.

Holding transaction costs aside for a moment, let's calculate the total return for a sample share of stock.

Suppose you bought one share of a public company for $100. That $100 was your cost basis. After holding it for some time, the price of your stock increased by $20, or 20 percent, at which point you decided to sell. That 20 percent was your capital gain. But during your holding period, your stock also generated a $10 dividend, which for you was another 10 percent worth of income. So the two sources of income combined to produce a 30 percent gain, before taxes. Under current law, both dividends and capital gains are taxed at a maximum rate of 15 percent. Therefore your after-tax total return when you sold was 25.5 percent.[3]

So, how well did you do—say, compared with Jennifer?

As calculated in the last chapter, her original cost basis was $200,000, and she sold for $240,000, for a capital gain of $40,000. But she also lived in her home rent-free for five years, which, at a modest $4,000 a year in imputed rent, delivered her an additional $20,000 in imputed income. After figuring in taxes—zero for both income and capital gains—her total return was $60,000, or 30 percent.

On a percentage basis, Jennifer and our sample stock each delivered a pre-tax total return of 30 percent. After taxes, however, Jennifer's total return was 4.5 percentage points better.

In this way, you can see that home-owning is a stunningly tax-advantaged activity when compared with stock-owning. The behavioral implications also are important. Every time stock market investors sell shares of assets at a profit or receive a dividend, they have to pay a tax (15 percent) on that profit. Thus, when their sales are profitable, what they have left to reinvest is less than their gross earnings when they sold.

The Differences: Transaction Costs

Though they're very similar activities, the implicit transaction costs related to investing in the stock market are quite often *much lower* than those for investing in a home.

In the last chapter, we set the average home-related transaction cost at 10 percent. Comparatively, what does it cost to buy stocks, or stock funds (the latter being a preferred vehicle for investors)?

Using a rough but instructive range, fund fees might be anywhere from 0.2 percent annually (for a low-cost fund that tracks the actual performance of a stock market index) to 2 percent annually (for a high-cost fund that employs stock-picking managers and must compensate those managers). Because not all the funds charge a load or a transaction fee for early redemption, the total management fee represents an upper-bound estimate of the transaction costs associated with switching funds.

In this respect, the stock range of 0.2 to 2 percent soundly beats the 10 percent home figure. If you are keen, however, you might have noticed the term *annually* in describing the stock market fund fees. Two percent *annually* relative to a stock market investment fund is a lot different than a *one-time* 10 percent cost relative to homeownership across a range of five to seven years. But because I am not advocating that you buy and *hold* a portfolio of stocks and bonds over a long time horizon, I can make the following case: Two percent is a lot lower than 10 percent at any one point in time. And if at that time an investment that will cost you 2 percent a year will quickly compensate you for that amount and generate even more profit, that 2 percent doesn't present that high of a hurdle, does it?

I can say as much for the 0.2 percent fee versus the 2 percent fee. Over, say, a 30-year investment period, any annual fee adds up. And this is one of the key reasons why true buy-and-hold, or passive, investors work so diligently at the outset to keep their fees low, more toward that 0.2 percent. As a quick example of this, let's say you had $100,000 in a fund costing 0.2 percent a year, and the same amount in a fund costing 2 percent annually, and each fund returned 10 percent a year. Well, in twenty years, the lower-cost fund would generate $709,932, while the higher-cost fund would deliver $495,303. You made $214,629 more by way of the lower-cost fund.

But if you chose the more expensive manager, you had better hope that, through his or her actions and investment acumen, that manager will add at least $214,629 of value added over the 20 years; otherwise, the manager will not cover his or her fees, and you will be worse off. The same holds true if you decide to switch among low-cost passive strategies: If the annual transaction costs are 2% per year, you had better hope that, by doing, so you are increasing the investment strategy value by at least $214,629 over the 20-year horizon. Thus, if you are invested in the right fund at the appropriate times, it is possible to make up for the transaction costs. We look into this opportunity more in the next chapter and, indeed, throughout this book.

The Differences: Return Differentials

At most times, the range of expected returns generated by stocks is much greater than the range driven by home prices in the same city or neighborhood. More technically, the differential of returns is higher for stocks than it is for homes. However, and critically so, within the stock market, this range fluctuates, helping open and close the door on opportunity.

The discussion has brought us to the concept of *trading frequency*. By definition, trading frequency is simply the rate at which trades are made, and the term can easily apply to how active investors are at any given time. When trading frequency is high—when the buying and selling of stocks is occurring at a very high rate—one can say that investors are very active. On the other hand, when very little trading is going on, most investors are passively "holding" the assets in their portfolios.

What determines these two environments? Well, when it costs too much to be active, or when there are no gains to be made from being active, investors aren't active. Trading frequency is low. When the average returns of investments move higher, the same reasoning suggests that investors can more quickly hurdle transaction costs and make some money. They get active—sometimes *very* active.

For example, during the bull market of the late 1990s, the differential of returns between investments could be considered high (there was money to be made), transaction costs were suddenly lower than ever, and the resulting trading frequency was nothing short of breakneck. A new classification of investor emerged during this period—day traders, people who buy and sell stocks at severely high frequencies, sometimes holding shares only hours or only minutes. (Looking back, "day" trader may have been a generous term.) In these lightning-fast transactions, sometimes the trader made a buck and at other times only a penny. Although a penny does not seem to equate with a high differential of return, those pennies can add up. Here's how: The advent of low-priced computers and high-speed Internet, coupled with a roaring bull market, essentially lowered the transaction costs enough to make day trading not only possible, but quite often very profitable—at least, for a time. The millennium stock market bubble infamously burst in 2000, and a lot of day traders went "pop" along with it.

Nonetheless, the combination of steady stock market appreciation, the expected differential in returns between separate stocks and asset classes, and the reduction in transaction costs during the late 1990s all clearly favored active trading. And how did the passive-investing crowd do? Some argue that the broadly defined transaction costs imposed by many passive programs (included among these are the popular IRA and 401[k] plans), along with the tax penalties that come with exiting these programs early, restricted or reduced the incentive of participants from shifting to an active-trading mode. This arguably forced passive investors to focus on their longer horizons and ignore the opportunities afforded by many of the active strategies that thrived toward the end of the last century.

This might sound familiar. As you'll recall, homeowners are generally *forced* by transaction costs to hold on to their properties for a minimum amount of time. In the case of the late-1990s stock market, tax treatments and transaction costs arguably *forced* passive investors to focus on longer-term investments instead of shorter-term active strategies.

Are passive investors and homeowners a lot alike? Indeed, they are—although they don't have to be.

The Passive-to-Active Switch

In theory and practice, passive investors and homeowners are restricted from venturing to new investments for two reasons:

1. Transaction costs have locked them in for a certain (and relatively long) amount of time.
2. Based on the long-run data, it is arguably more prudent to bank on long-term historic price appreciation than to act on short-term price fluctuations.

As we've seen, homeowners have no choice in this matter if they want to come out ahead. Passive investors, however—just like active investors—*do* have a choice.

Regardless of the restrictions of various investment plans, transaction costs might often be low enough—and the upside of alternative investments high enough—to warrant a shift from a passive to an active trading mode. In other words, prototypical passive investors do not have to go all passive all the time.

In my experience, stock market investing has a sure hand up on homeownership for this reason: Because the transaction costs are relatively low for stock market investing when compared with homeowning, stock market investors can regularly *shift* between active and passive strategies to get the most out of the market. This is the essence of the "switching strategy," a cornerstone concept I build through this book. And there's only one caveat to this: A switching strategy is warranted only when it promises to deliver an incremental return high enough to more than pay for the transaction costs over an investor's stated time horizon.

In the following chapter, 42 years of stock market data helps quantify just how lucrative a switching strategy can be.

Endnotes

1. Jeremy J. Siegel, *Stocks for the Long Run: The Definitive Guide to Financial Market Returns and Long-Term Investment Strategies* (New York: McGraw-Hill, 2002). In making his calculation about how well $1 would do if it was invested in the stock market between 1802 and 2001, Siegel notes, "This sum can be realized by an investor holding the broadest possible portfolio of stocks in proportion to their market value and does not depend on how many of these companies survive or not."

2. A company raises or lowers a dividend based on the reinvestment opportunities it sees and the current tax rates on dividends.

3. Twenty percent capital gains × 15 percent capital-gains income
tax = 3 percent capital-gains tax liability; ten percent dividend ×
15 percent dividend tax = 1.5 percent dividend tax liability. The
total of the two taxes = 4.5 percent. Subtracting that amount
from the total pre-tax gain of 30 percent = 25.5 percent after-
tax total return.

3

Dressing Appropriately for the Stock Market: The Potential Payoffs of a Switching Strategy

You don't often see bikinis on ski slopes or winter coats on tropical islands. But if you'll allow these landscapes to stand in for contrasting stock markets, you see such unfortunate dressing decisions all the time. Take that millennium stock market bubble, which "popped," as they say, in 2000. Before this correction, to continue the analogy, passive investors were stuck wearing their parkas while the sun was shining—they stood still, frozen in their buy-and-hold investment plans while the money-making action was hot. After the pop, however, many active investors were caught in the cold wearing nothing but their bathing suits, exposed to the nasty elements of a market in abrupt decline.

By "dressing" appropriately for the stock market, I simply mean that investors can accentuate the positives of each market while deemphasizing the negatives, by adjusting the mode in which they invest. In the most basic sense, these modes are passive and active. Passive investors stick with an initial allocation to stocks and bonds over the long haul. Active investors look for superior investment opportunities all the time. And each represents but one style of investment dress—attire that moves both in and out of fashion and function.

When to dress passive? When to dress active? The simplest answer is that you want to invest actively when the hurdles between you and enhanced profit are low and passively when these hurdles are high, or prohibitive. And investing is just this easy. In truth, many investors trip because they incorrectly judge the height of these hurdles—or, worse, they don't judge them at all. To correctly measure any barrier that stands between you and the promise of added profit, you need sound information and direction—about a couple hundred pages' worth, the length of this book. (In other words, you will arrive at this informational and directional plateau soon enough.) But at this point I want to convince you, quantitatively, of the payoffs related to a strategy that is neither all-active nor all-passive—a strategy that can switch between active and passive or land somewhere in between, remaining appropriately dressed for the stock market at all times.

When you come right down to it, why read an investment book about "doing better" than the average investor if you can't put a dollar figure on that promise? How much can a strategy that switches between investment strategies—the approach I set forth in this book—add to your bottom line?

Let's find out.

A Quick Psychological Classification of Investors

This is the payoff chapter. Here you can determine whether it is worth your time and effort to even *attempt* to "do better" than the majority of investors. But first a quick classification: Just who are these passive and active investors I speak about?

One way to sort shareholders, in a psychological sense, is by how long they hold their investments. Active investors can be characterized by short-term holding periods—a year or less, by some standards—because they tend to turn over their portfolios quite frequently. On the other side of the spectrum are the purely passive investors, people who buy and hold until retirement, although they typically add cash to their plans on a periodic basis. In the middle are the intermediate investors, those who tend to hold on to the allocations in their portfolios but from time to time turn them over.

The reasons *why* investors fall into these different categories vary. Passive investors might be smart enough to understand that investing broadly in the stock and bond markets pays very well over time. Yet they might be too inhibited or risk-averse to want to fiddle with an allocation that, based on the historical data, will deliver them sound gains. Or maybe they just don't want the hassles involved with active investing—or the fees; active plans often are managed by brokerages or investment banks that want to get paid for their services.

Active investors, on the flip side, might be attracted to making the most money they can out of the stock market; maybe they have a penchant toward risk-taking and also believe that they possess superior short-term information on which to act. As for the intermediate investors, maybe they change their beliefs about the future direction of the stock market every once in a while, sometimes profoundly enough to drive them to adjust their portfolios.

The upshot of these three strategies is the same: Each seeks to make the most from the stock market based on a given level of risk. So a question: Which style of investment dress best fits your frame?

As you might suspect, the correct answer is a trick answer: Each can be a perfect fit at different times. This is a fundamental concept that I build throughout this book. But for now, here are the basics of why one strategy "size" does not fit all investors for all time: The level of transaction costs related to stock investing is relatively low when compared with other forms of investing, although these costs periodically trend higher or lower (helping increase or decrease the "hurdle" between investments); credible information relative to the expected direction of stocks and bonds exists (*period*); and the differential of returns between current and new investments (or the "extra" return that one investment offers relative to another) rises and falls, depending on the nature of different stock markets. From these considerations, we can derive two general investment rules—in essence, the basics of a switching strategy:

- When the transaction costs are relatively high and/or the differential of returns is low, and you have little or no reliable information on which to base a switch between investments, choose a passive strategy.

- When the transaction costs are relatively low and/or the differential of returns is high, and you believe you possess superior information on which to base a switch between investments, pursue various degrees of active strategies.

Qualitatively, this should sound reasonable: When the costs of taking action are high, stay put; when they are low, take action. But the quantitative argument for a switching formula might strike you as even more persuasive because, I presume, we all are interested in achieving the highest investment payoff possible.

On to the data.

Strategy Analysis: Passive vs. Active vs. Intermediate

In all probability, investors purchase stocks and bonds to add to their net worth, so we can say that any investment plan that generates capital gains in excess of the inflation rate is making its investors richer. In determining the range of possible payoffs of a switching strategy—or a strategy that is sometimes active, other times passive—this is our performance measure. Additionally, to evaluate any investment strategy, we need to assume that the past is a good guide to the future if the data sample is long enough. For this study, I have used data collected from the S&P 500 for the period between January 1962 and December 2004. By the standards of modern stock market analysts, 42 years and 9 months of data easily meets the requirement of being "long enough."

Overall, I calculated 513 one-year and 285 twenty-year holding periods, with the number of intermediate holding periods falling in between.[1] Table 3.1 shows the results. For this argument, you can think of the one-year holding period as the one-year horizon of an active investor. This investor is very active; never does this year's portfolio look exactly like last year's. The 20-year period can be considered the horizon of a passive investor. This investor bought a reasoned allocation to stocks and bonds and held it for two decades. Finally, the 5-, 10-, and 15-year periods correspond to a range of intermediate horizons.

How did the strategies do?

TABLE 3.1   Annualized S&P 500 Inflation-Adjusted Gains for Different Holding Periods

	12 Months (1 Year)	60 Months (5 Years)	120 Months (10 Years)	180 Months (15 Years)	240 Months (20 Years)
Number of Holding Periods	513	465	405	345	285
Maximum Gains	58.26	22.68	13.35	9.85	8.19
Minimum Gains	−76.52	−17.67	−7.96	−5.49	0.14
Number of Negative Returns	175	135	100	60	0
% Negative	34.11	29.03	24.69	17.39	0.00
Average of Negatives	−16.56	−5.49	−3.10	−1.90	0.00

The 20-year horizon produced an average maximum gain of 8.19 percent per year over and above the inflation rate and an average minimum return of 0.14 percent per year. That's a wide range for the passive strategy, but note that *there were no losers:* The number of negative returns was zero. In other words, investors in this crowd *never* lost money.

If past gains are representative of future gains, the 0.14 percent minimum annual return suggests that there is little or no chance of a 20-year holding period ever producing a negative outcome. This may be more firm evidence that stock market investing is worth your time, but can anyone say, "Buy and *hold?*"

Well, *not* holding has its advantages, too.

As the holding periods shorten—moving away from the purely passive strategy, through the intermediate strategies, and then to the active strategy—the upside, as measured by the average returns, also increases. Watch the maximum average inflation-adjusted gains ascend proportionately as the holding periods decline in length: 20 years, 8.19 percent; 15 years, 9.85 percent; 10 years, 13.35 percent; 5 years, 22.68 percent; 1 year, 58.26 percent.

Importantly, however, as the holding periods turn shorter, the number and magnitude of the negative outcomes increase. Now watch the minimum average inflation-adjusted gains *decline* proportionately as the holding periods shorten: 20 years, 0.14 percent; 15 years, –5.49 percent; 10 years, –7.96 percent; 5 years, –17.67 percent; 1 year, –76.52 percent.

Further reinforcing the downside of active investing is the fact that the frequency of negative outcomes increases as the length of the holding periods declines. Negative returns made up 17.39 percent of the returns for the 15-year horizon, 24.69 percent of the returns for the 10-year horizon, and 34.11 percent of the returns for the 1-year horizon.[2] The passive, 20-year negative outcome of zero seemingly laughs at such downside potential.

From this perspective, the data clearly supports the long-term buy-and-hold strategy. Thus, a risk-averse person possessing this data might choose the safe path of passive investing over the long haul. But in doing so, such a risk-averse person eliminates the potential (and potentially large) upsides that partner with the shorter, more active holding periods.

What to do?

Figuring Risk into Your Return

Are you, for instance, willing to give up the potential upsides of an active strategy to protect yourself from the negative returns that can accompany that strategy? Will a 20-year average annual return in the range of 0.14 percent to 8.19 percent, with virtually no chance that you will fall below this range, meet your investing aspirations? Or are you enticed by that 58.26 one-year return, the one that coincides with a 34 percent chance of a negative outcome? According to the data, your prospect of witnessing a negative result are one in three if you take this route—175 out of 513 one-year periods in the sample, with an average decline of 16.56 percent.

Well, what if those negative outcomes can be avoided—at least, most of the time? Theoretically, an investor can use superior knowledge to avoid the down markets and increase his or her average returns to a handsome level, which, based on our data sample, would be approximately 13.39 percent per year—far superior to the best 20-year passive outcome.[3] Such a return is not far-fetched if one believes superior knowledge not only can be acquired, but can steer an investor away from bad investments and toward good ones. Again, this is the topic of the book you are reading, and for now, we are simply interested in the possible payoffs of the most active and passive strategies and those that fall in between.

Table 3.2 should give you a sense of both the risks and rewards that are at stake. In this table, I have calculated the *distribution of returns* for each of the sample holding periods, providing something of a grading system for stock market performance. For instance, if you ranked in the 90th percentile for a holding period, you ran with the top 10 percent of performers for that period. That's an A+ grade.

Where might you fit in?

TABLE 3.2 Distribution of S&P 500 Inflation-Adjusted Gains for Different Holding Periods

	12 Months (1 Year)	60 Months (5 Years)	120 Months (10 Years)	180 Months (15 Years)	240 Months (20 Years)
90th Percentile	34.90	17.20	11.30	8.90	7.63
80th Percentile	27.20	12.90	9.60	8.03	7.00
70th Percentile	20.30	11.20	8.85	7.46	6.50
60th Percentile	15.30	8.98	8.45	7.03	5.96
50th Percentile	7.92	6.34	8.02	6.20	4.87
40th Percentile	2.90	2.74	5.85	4.08	3.89
30th Percentile	-2.00	0.40	2.32	3.05	3.61
20th Percentile	-2.00	-2.70	-1.40	1.26	2.65
10th Percentile	-22.70	-7.70	-3.70	-1.70	1.77

The far-right column in the table provides a sense of the range of opportunities for the buy-and-hold, or purely passive, strategy; the far-left column does the same for the purely active strategy. In the passive strategy, we again see a wide range of results—from 1.77 percent for the 10th, or worst-performing, percentile to 7.63 percent for the 90th, or best-performing, percentile. And there is an implicit randomness to these returns. Simply, because some two-decade stock markets are a lot better than others, how you perform in a passive long-run strategy has a lot to do with the date you start.

Moving leftward across the table, or from passive to active, that scenario changes. In a critical sense, the more active you get, the more your returns are in your own hands because every switch you make between investments presumably is based on the information you possess.

Let's consider the 15-year holding period: Here the range of possible outcomes widens to include a worst-performing return of –1.7 percent and a best-performing return of 8.9 percent. You can do better in this strategy than the pure-passive strategy, and you also can turn in a negative result. But think of this: If you ranked in the 90th percentile of the 20-year strategy, you performed worse than you would have if you had ranked in the 80th percentile of the 15-year strategy. In other words, your performance ranking could have been lower in a slightly more active strategy, and you still could have performed better than the best purely passive performance. In fact, the top performance of the passive buy-and-hold strategy is only slightly above the 70th percentile of the 15-year strategy. Sliding left to the 10-year holding period, you would need to rank only among the top half of performers to eclipse the best 20-year passive-only result.

Obviously, you don't have to be the *best* active investor, possessing the best information, to beat the best passive-investing result. Is this proof somehow that active investing is superior to passive investing? Not quite.

The bolded numbers in Table 3.2 paint an instructive picture. As one moves left, from passive to active, notice how the range of purely passive returns from the 20-year holding period squeezes into a tighter and tighter window. Because the purely passive return is the market-average long-run return, all of these bolded numbers represent the opportunity set for *average* investors—people who possess neither superior nor inferior information on which to act and earn within the range of the average market rate of returns. A question: If there is a tighter window in which to earn the same average returns the more active one gets, why attempt to earn those returns in an active manner? Basically, *there is no reason to do so.* To begin, these average returns will cost you more to earn if you earn them actively. Why? Transaction costs. Simply, the more your strategy switches investments, the more your strategy will cost you. Then there's the incidence of negative returns. The more active you go, the greater your chances are of falling on your face.

Clearly, if you are going to turn in an average result—or if the information you possess will return you only average results—keep it simple and invest in a passive, long-run, buy-and-hold manner.

As for the *unbolded* numbers in the table, those in the bottom range are ugly, to say the least. Basically, these returns apply to active investors with inferior information—each is an incidence of falling on one's face. On the flip side, however, the unbolded numbers in the upper range of the table represent the opportunity set for active investors with superior information. It is a tighter sweet spot than the bolded average returns, but it's certainly a much sweeter sweet spot. To land here—in a range that encompasses several strategies, from very active to mostly passive—one needs only superior information on which to base investment action.

We deal with *how* to acquire that information in the chapters ahead, but now you know what you're aiming for.

Some Random Thoughts about the Availability and Viability of Market Information

Psychiatrists have famously used Rorschach tests to uncover the fixations of their patients, often with wildly dissimilar results. You might easily imagine something like the following: One day, holding up a card with blobs of black ink on it, a psychiatrist asks his patient, "What does this look like to you?" His patient responds, "An onion riding a camel." The next day, the doctor holds up the same card to a different patient and asks the same question, "What does this look like to you?" The second patient responds, "A noose, hanging a coat rack." The realm of responses is probably infinite and hardly predictable without any prior knowledge of what makes a patient tick.

Investors, of course, are attracted by predictability. At the least, when acting passively, they believe the market will inevitably rise over the long run. At the other extreme, when behaving actively, they believe they possess enough information to predict turns in the market and take advantage of those turns—believing that the gains of alternative investments will be large enough to compensate for any new transaction costs while coming in over and above the gains of previous investments.

As I've mentioned, I'm interested in both strategies. I also believe that every stock market environment is predictable based on the economic forces of the day. How predictable?

For fun, and a little instruction in this regard, I've put together a Rorschach test of my own. Figures 3.1 and 3.2 show my two "cards." Rather than think like a patient, think like an investor. What are these cards telling you?

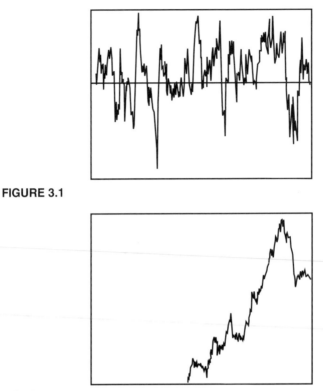

FIGURE 3.1

FIGURE 3.2

If you are thinking like an investor, Figure 3.1 might suggest tremendous volatility—lots of ups and downs, although with a regular passing-through of a middle ground. Contrastingly, Figure 3.2 might suggest a thing that rises over time, although with a few bumps along the way. If you understood each card in such a manner, I'd give you a clean bill of health.

Figure 3.1 is, in fact, the return net of inflation that you would have earned by holding the S&P 500 for one year, starting at various points in time during the period from 1962 through 2005. The volatility and the potential negatives of the one-year holding period are patently evident. As you might now guess, Figure 3.2 tracks the 20-year holding-period returns of the S&P 500 across the same time frame. The long-run result is upward overall and appears highly predictable.

The visual representations of these two holding periods suggest that there will be many fluctuations during the short term and that these fluctuations will wash out over time. This phenomenon is related to the concept of *mean reversion:* What goes up must come back down; what goes down must come back up. However, what if the disturbances that are so evident on the one-year card can be anticipated? If they can, it might be possible to anticipate the mean-reversion adjustment process, in effect, adjusting to a thing that will likely go up and readjusting to a thing that will likely come down.

Let's look at the data in Figure 3.1 again but this time in light of the left axis (the price performance of the S&P 500) and the bottom axis (the years 1962 to 2005)—see Figure 3.3.

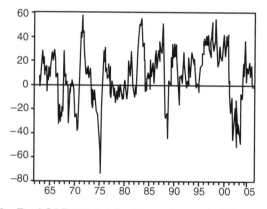

FIGURE 3.3   Real S&P 500 total returns: 1-year holding periods

The fact that the bulk of the worst negative (below-the-line) returns occurs during the high-inflation 1970s and the period after the millennium bubble burst suggests that an understanding of what caused these periods of underperformance would have helped an investor anticipate them. The length of the underperforming periods is also instructive. Roughly, market dips and surges last around five years, which suggests that there is a cyclical, nonrandom, and *predictable* nature to the stock market, just as there is a cyclical and predictable nature to the buy-and-hold home-owning strategy, with the average holding period lasting five to seven years. And practically speaking, five or so years is a wide target, plenty of time for you to adjust your investments toward the profit-making specifics of each stock market.

Indeed, dressing appropriately for the stock market is not an activity that will have you in your closet (i.e., your portfolio) every day. The climate of the stock market generally changes gradually, just like the seasons, and over the course of a season, the weather is usually predictable.

On the first day of winter in Boston, it might be 55°F and sunny, but if you live there, you know with certainty that the chill winds and snow are on their way. You prepare accordingly. In this sense, if a stock market "season" lasts a few years, one or several months of being misallocated (or even a year or so) will not eliminate all the potential gains generated by a proper anticipation of, and allocation to, that season. And when those "natural disasters" occur in the stock and bond markets, there is still no cause for alarm: An adjustment process must occur following every economic shock that will restore the economy to its long-run equilibrium. And like the seasons, those adjustment processes can be anticipated and acted upon.

And *if* you do act upon those adjustment processes, I can guarantee that you will be generating above-average performance more often than not.

What (Strategy) to Wear, and When to Wear It

Risk has risen to a prominent place in this argument: As an investor, you must choose a way to evaluate the trade-offs between the risks and returns offered by the different strategies at your disposal. But I tend to think of risk, or risk aversion, in relation to one's level of knowledge. Simply, I don't think it's chancy to take advantage of your understanding of a certain set of circumstances. If, armed with the knowledge of how markets are likely to react, you adjust your investments to avoid the negative outcomes and accentuate the positive ones, taking advantage of the best strategies for the economic times, you will likely significantly enhance your investment returns over the long run.

At this point, far from stock-picking, we're talking about strategy-picking. When you think of the thousands of possible stocks to choose from versus the relatively few strategies to select, the strategy-picking approach should seem much less daunting—and, hopefully, much more promising. Of course, your results will be based on your ability to predict turns in the market. But if those turns are predictable—or nonrandom—well, they can be predicted.

I sometimes have the sense that risk-averse, stereotypically passive investors think the information necessary to make serious gains in the stock market—to predict those market turns—is attainable only by the greatest minds or the most well connected. But all investors can be the bearers of the right information on which to better their performance. That's not to say good information is foolproof. The best active investors make a few bad calls during their careers, even when they possess good information from which to draw the appropriate conclusions. In other words, risk is always a factor—but risk is justified over time as the correct calls are made more and more often.

How much of a downside are you willing to risk to realize a higher upside? The better your understanding is of the various macroeconomic forces—the theme for the remainder of this book—the easier that question is to answer.

Endnotes

1. Rather than giving an average cumulative return for a period—which you get in the most simple terms by dividing the gains over a period of years by that same number of years—Table 3.1 reports annualized gains, or the performance of investments year to year. The methodology I used was based on the monthly performance of the S&P 500 during the holding periods specified. This staggered the results at one-month intervals, allowing for a high number of holding periods for study. For instance, the one-year holding period was calculated based on the performance of 12 consecutive months, such as January 1962 to December 1962, February 1962 to January 1963, March 1962 to February 1963, and so on. The methodology was the same for the 1-, 5-, 10-, 15-, and 20-year holding periods.

2. By multiplying the average of the negative returns by the percent of negative returns for the one-year holding period, I obtained an estimate of how much the negative returns "cost" the average performance of the one-year holding-period returns. By my calculations, those negative returns reduced the one-year holding-period returns by an average of 5.65 percent per year.

3. I arrived at that number by adding to the average return of 7.74 percent, the additional return of 5.65 percent that would be generated when the negative years are removed from the sample.

4

Catch Elasticity If You Can: An Introduction to Industry Behavior

Economic shocks tend to be a bit more subtle than the shocks that scream at us from the newsstands—rogue tsunamis, the threat of pandemic disease, or the blasts and carnage of war. But they are of equal force when we judge their impact on industries, businesses, jobs, incomes, and profit, or on basic behavioral trends such as those related to saving, spending, and investing. Positive economic shocks—for instance, suddenly lower regulations, tax breaks, or declining inflation—bring about affirmative economic behavior: more saving, spending, and investing. They also can trigger increased national prosperity: higher economic growth, more jobs, fatter incomes, elevated corporate profit. But negative shocks can injure the components of an economy, as well as the stocks, bonds, and other assets that are linked to economic performance.

In this chapter, I introduce economic shocks as they relate to the top of the economic food chain: industries. *Industry* is a rather cold, perhaps abstract word; day to day, most of us think in terms of our jobs, some of which are more warm and cozy than others. But just as we now can say there is value in building an investment plan based on the promise of the most big-picture investment strategies—active *and* passive—we also can say there is value in ascertaining which of our giant industries hold the most investment upside. In a top-down investment strategy, such as the one I offer, industries deserve top billing.

From one economic shock to the next, the separate industries shift and adjust in predictable ways; the very composition of each industry determines these movements. By *composition,* I mean that which determines behavior, with behavior being a crucial arbiter in life. When Action A occurs, Person A might respond quite differently than Person B because each has a different behavioral makeup. Psychologists discuss the dynamic of "fight or flight." In times of adversity, some of us put up our fists; others of us head for the exits. Similarly, when economic shocks manifest, some industries stand tall, whereas others shrink under the new weight. A specific type of shock might spark higher profitability in the travel, health care, and software sectors, yet the same shock might mean decreased profitability in another set of industries. With each industry representing dozens to hundreds of publicly traded stocks, the industry response to economic shocks cannot be overlooked if you are to invest in a responsible, above-average manner.

In the pages ahead, government regulations very often become our pandemics, fluctuating levels of inflation our tidal waves, and technological innovations our more creative forces of destruction—midnight firebirds that, after torching a forest, presage a morning of new growth. But in discussing the behavior of industries in relation to shocks, our investment lexicon needs to expand. Key terminology includes *elasticity* and its close relative, *beta,* words that are linked not only to each other, but to the behavior and profitability of industries.

At this point in your journey toward becoming an above-average investor, you must act something like a behavioral scientist—someone who can judge the behavioral response of an industry when an economic shock occurs. You gain profit in this: Which groups of companies will fight the hardest when the economic environment turns sour? Which will lose these bouts? In the good times, maybe all companies will stand tall. But which will stand the tallest?

Your portfolio wants to know.

Shock Terminology: Beta and Elasticity

Beta and inelasticity go a long way toward deciding these answers. We begin our industry study with some definitions.

The risk inherent in a stock (or asset class) in relation to the overall market is technically known as its *beta*. Every stock has a beta, a numerical value that can be positive or negative (or even zero), with a beta of 1 representing the benchmark average. For instance, if a stock has a beta of 1, it is in sync with the market, meaning that it will move with the market in either direction, up or down. When the stock market is going up, an asset with a beta of 1 will likely rise with the market; in a declining market, it likely will fall. Think of a beta of 1 as a seatbelt that secures an asset to the average performance of the market, and a beta of any other number as pulling an asset either toward above- or below-average performance. For instance, in a rising market, the beta of an asset that is less than 1 will likely underperform the market; a beta of greater than 1 might well outperform the market.

Obviously, beta is a neat little investment tool. And as a general rule, you don't have to calculate beta for every stock or asset class out there. Financial analysts do this work for you: Go to any online stock-tracking site and type in a company name, and you will likely find that company's beta (listed alongside a range of other stock fundamentals). For example: Dow Chemicals (DOW), beta 1.17; Hilton Hotels (HLT), beta 0.89.

Critically, however, beta *is not* to be viewed on its own. That is, beta must be partnered with additional economic concepts if you intend to use it as a profit-generating investment tool. Beta, you see, can change, and often the historical beta of an asset is not its true beta. Again, you won't likely ever have to calculate beta yourself—this is an involved mathematical equation—but subjectively, you will want to forecast its direction with the changing economic times. As I see it, beta must be understood in relation to the supply-and-demand realities within every economy, as well as the ability of the separate industries to respond to these realities.

We pursue this line of reasoning shortly, but first, we turn to another new term: *elasticity.* By *elasticity,* I very simply mean the ability of an industry to adjust to economic shocks. An elastic industry shifts and alters and transforms when an economic "tsunami" envelops it, thereby helping to guarantee its very own survival. In supply-and-demand terms, when an economic shock brings about a shift in the demand for an industry's product, an elastic industry has all options at its disposal: It can either raise or lower prices to meet that demand and/or increase or decrease output, performing all the necessaries to bring about these appropriate shifts: hire or fire employees, put up new plants or close some, keep production where it is or move it elsewhere, hold a sale or quietly raise sticker prices. But the adjustment options for inelastic industries are very limited when economic shocks arrive. Often they can only move prices higher and lower because they have a narrow ability to alter levels of production or output. As you will see, this sometimes leads to outsized profitability; at other times, it can lead to bankruptcy.

Taking all this together, the behavioral response of an industry to an economic shock goes a long way toward determining its profitability and the related direction of its stock price, up or down. Admittedly, this is a very quick interpretation of beta and elasticity, and witnessing each in real-world action might be the best way to understand their importance relative to your portfolio.

So, on to our first case study: In what follows, government regulation is our shock of choice—our thematic tidal wave, with swells of inflation thrown in. And our victim is the airline industry, an inelastic behemoth for much of its history.

High Beta, Which Strategy?

Another, and perhaps better, way to understand beta is to think of it as the *sensitivity* of an asset in relation to the stock market. For example, some stocks might move in line with the market, others might increase at a faster rate than the market (say, by 20 percent), and still others might exhibit an even greater sensitivity to the market, beating it by 30, 40, or 50 percent—or even more. Clearly, in an upward-trending market, investors like to own the stocks or groups of stocks with the greatest sensitivity—those with the highest betas. In this way, they will maximize their returns. However— *and this is a big however*—you do not want to own high-beta stocks when the stock market is going down. The market will take you down with it.

An argument can be made (and is often made in certain corners of Wall Street) that high beta and the long-run buy-and-hold strategy work together. Say that the world of stocks is expected to gain 8 percent over a period of time. In this environment, a stock that is 20 percent more sensitive to the market will theoretically gain 9.6 percent, eclipsing the market by 1.6 percent. (1 percent [the market] + 0.2 percent [the extra beta] × 8 percent [the expected market rise] = 9.6 percent.) Because there is little or no chance that, over a long horizon, stocks will generate negative returns, by buying and holding the most sensitive stocks, investors will maximize their returns over a long horizon.

But a better-performing alternative exists: If you ride high beta during uptrending markets and avoid it when the market turns down, your return will be all high-beta upside. In high-beta terms, a switching strategy also makes sense.

The Friendlier Skies of Industry Profitability

A few decades before it died an old, beaten, dismembered thing, Pan American Airlines got a lot of respect—not only for being one of the original great airlines, but for representing something far more alluring than what one finds in everyday life. The 2002 film *Catch Me If You Can* puts a bright shine to this image. From the pilots' perspective, that blue Pan Am jacket with the gold stripes on the sleeves meant autograph requests from children, gazes and winks from adoring women, and that extra bit of attention in each business hour of the day. It was a powerful uniform, one that elicited respect and awe— and not just for the pilots, but for the luxury planes they steered to far-off destinations. Pan Am blue meant palm trees and gold sand, romantic cafes up cobblestone streets, après-ski at an Alpine chateau. Pan Am meant possibility.

This is a Hollywood illustration. But in spirit, I believe it is an accurate rendering of Pan Am during the golden era of the big commercial airlines. This was not the airline business of crowded terminals and flight delays, of 40 planes stacked on the runway and a bag of pretzels for a meal. The carriers were rich, the passengers were well heeled, and the sky was the limit.

Pan Am boomed during the 1960s. For much of the decade, it ordered planes at a clip that suppliers couldn't match, served a passenger base that was growing exponentially, *and* made money. In 1961, the airline earned $26 million on $460 million in revenues, both new highs; in 1963, profit was $79 million on $561 million in revenues.[1] In 1965, Pan Am was serving about 6 million passengers; by 1969, it was serving more than 10 million.[2] Such growth indicated that Pan Am had a bright future, and by most indicators, it did. In particular, Pan Am brass believed that not only would its future be one of passenger-filled cabins, but that an investment in the biggest commercial planes money could buy was warranted. Acting on this conviction, Pan Am became the first carrier to purchase the vaunted Boeing 747, ordering 23 of the jumbo planes (each carried nearly 500 passengers) in 1966 and putting the first one in the air commercially in 1970.[3]

These were high times for the airline, which begs the question: If you were just starting out investing in 1970, would you want to own a piece of Pan Am or, in general, other airline stocks?

Not a chance.

The Pitfalls of a Beta-Reliant Strategy

Let's start our investment analysis of the airlines industry at the very top by identifying the overriding macroeconomic forces of the day.

First, the 1970s were a notoriously high-inflation, high-interest-rate decade. One result was that the price of travel increased as the value of every dollar decreased. *Higher air-travel prices, less air travel.* Second, these were the OPEC oil-shock days, with the cost of flying airplanes climbing with the rising price of fuel. *Higher air-travel prices, less air travel* once more. So very quickly, we have two big negatives that warned against investing in the airlines industry.

And what would beta have told us? Well, airline stocks have been notorious for their high betas, which, again, are the most sensitive stocks to market movement. And how did the stock market do in the 1970s? It floundered for much of the decade, meaning that those high betas would only pull stock prices below the market average.

Without question, smart investors would have wanted to avoid airline stocks during the 1970s. But how about when the economic and stock market situations turned around? Would smart investors have been correct to jump back into airline stocks?

Again, not a chance.

During the 1980s, the stock market soared, oil prices declined, and eventually interest rates and inflation both came down—a seemingly perfect environment for those high-beta airline stocks. So let's say you understood each of these variables well and put your investment dollars into the airlines early in the decade; let's say you were an astute forecaster of the economic trends and just knew that an airline-favorable environment was in the making. How did you do?

Well, at least your forecast was correct: During the 1980s, much of what was anticipated—a rising stock market coupled with declining interest rates and oil prices—came to pass. However, despite the bull market of the 1980s and the high betas of the airline stocks, you underperformed. Airline stocks gained only 36.07 percent during the ten-year period between 1983 and 1992, well below the average of all industry groups, which came in at 180.91 percent (see Table 4.1).

TABLE 4.1   Performance of Selected S&P 500 Industries, 1983–1992

Industry (Alphabetical)	Appreciation	Industry (Worst to Best)	Appreciation
Aerospace/Defense	153.87	Machine Tools	−53.66
Aluminum	45.65	Transportation: Railroad	−48.92
Auto Trucks & Parts	104.1	Financial: Savings & Loan	−47.94
Automobile	−9.47	Oil & Gas Drilling	−43.7
Auto Parts After Markets	74.54	Financial: Banks: Major Regional	−23.94
Beverages: Alcoholic	472.46	Coal	−17.39
Beverages: Soft Drinks	825.94	Gold Mining	−12.41
Broadcast Media	225.88	Homebuilding	−10.95
Building Materials	65.68	Automobile	−9.47
Chemicals	293.2	Computer Systems	−7.53
Chemicals: Diversified	157.08	Financial: Banks/ Money Centers	3.76

Industry (Alphabetical)	Appreciation	Industry (Worst to Best)	Appreciation
Coal	−17.39	Transportation: Misc.	9.39
Communication Equipment	286.56	Transportation: Truckers	26.2
Computer Software & Services	391.89	Financial: Misc.	27.66
Computer Systems	−7.53	Oil Well & Equipment Services	33.86
Containers: Metal & Glass	717.37	**Transportation: Airlines**	**36.07**
Containers: Paper	329.88	Publishing	43.75
Cosmetics	359.97	Aluminum	45.65
Electrical Equipment	197.68	Financial: Insurance/ Prop. Cas.	49.09
Electronics: Instrumentation	56.19	Electronics: Instrumentation	56.19
Electronics: Semiconductors	130.03	Utilities: Natural Gas	56.96
Entertainment	361.83	Machinery: Diversified	58.2
Financial: Banks: Major Regional	−23.94	Building Materials	65.68
Financial: Banks/ Money Centers	3.76	Hospital Management	67.63
Financial: Insurance/Life	182.43	Retail: Food Chains	68.29
Financial: Insurance/Multiline	289.2	Manufactured Housing	73.03
Financial: Insurance/Prop. Cas.	49.09	Auto Parts After Markets	74.54
Financial: Misc.	27.66	Leisure Time	76.91
Financial: Personal Loans	223.81	Steel	79.63
Financial: Savings & Loan	−47.94	Metals: Misc.	85.33
Foods	406.02	Toys	89.48
Gold Mining	−12.41	Household Furn. & Appliances	95.35

continues

Industry (Alphabetical)	Appreciation	Industry (Worst to Best)	Appreciation
Health Care: Drugs	592.51	Auto Trucks & Parts	104.1
Health Care: Medical Products	165.25	Publishing: Newspapers	115.39
Homebuilding	−10.95	Paper & Forest Products	116.4
Hospital Management	67.63	Utilities: Electric	127.58
Hotel/Motel	228.93	Retail: Department Stores	128
Household Furn. & Appliances	95.35	Electronics: Semiconductors	130.03
Household Products	217.59	Aerospace/Defense	153.87
Leisure Time	76.91	Chemicals: Diversified	157.08
Machine Tools	−53.66	Health Care: Medical Products	165.25
Machinery: Diversified	58.2	Textiles: Apparel Manufacturers	176.98
Manufactured Housing	73.03	Financial: Insurance/Life	182.43
Metals: Misc.	85.33	Shoes	191.6
Oil: Domestic Integrated	204.97	Electrical Equipment	197.68
Oil & Gas Drilling	−43.7	Oil: Domestic Integrated	204.97
Oil: International Integrated	309.4	Household Products	217.59
Oil Well & Equipment Services	33.86	Financial: Personal Loans	223.81
Paper & Forest Products	116.4	Broadcast Media	225.88
Pollution Control	531.11	Hotel/Motel	228.93
Publishing	43.75	Communication Equipment	286.56
Publishing: Newspapers	115.39	Financial: Insurance/ Multiline	289.2
Restaurants	326.05	Chemicals	293.2
Retail: Department Stores	128	Oil: International Integrated	309.4

Industry (Alphabetical)	Appreciation	Industry (Worst to Best)	Appreciation
Retail: Drug Stores	443.38	Restaurants	326.05
Retail: Food Chains	68.29	Containers: Paper	329.88
Retail: General Merchandise	403.64	Cosmetics	359.97
Shoes	191.6	Entertainment	361.83
Steel	79.63	Computer Software & Services	391.89
Textiles: Apparel Manufacturers	176.98	Retail: General Merchandise	403.64
Tobacco	970.2	Foods	406.02
Toys	89.48	Retail: Drug Stores	443.38
Transportation: Airlines	**36.07**	Beverages: Alcoholic	472.46
Transportation: Misc.	9.39	Pollution Control	531.11
Transportation: Railroad	−48.92	Health Care: Drugs	592.51
Transportation: Truckers	26.2	Containers: Metal & Glass	717.37
Utilities: Electric	127.58	Beverages: Soft Drinks	825.94
Utilities: Natural Gas	56.96	Tobacco	970.2
Industry Average	*180.91*		

What went wrong? In a nutshell, you relied too heavily on beta.

The Promise of Beta Plus Elasticity

The broader explanation for this underperformance is rooted in the forces of supply and demand. Before 1978, the airline industry was tightly regulated. The federal government—specifically, the Civil Aeronautics Administration—totally controlled fares, route structures, and the like. The airlines industry could barely sneeze without the approval of the CAA, making it the textbook *inelastic* industry. Again, an industry is deemed *inelastic* when it cannot easily shift modes of production (supply) to meet changes in demand. For instance, if Pan Am wanted to fly more routes in the U.S. but was told it could not—which, indeed, was often the case—the supply of its service (which was to fly people around the globe) was severely limited.

Taking this to the next level, what happens when an industry cannot easily increase supply when the demand for its product or service increases?

The only way to satisfy demand in this case is to raise prices. Here's the reasoning: If the price of a product goes up, a business or industry will receive more money per unit sold, although consumers will purchase less of that product. And the amount the sales volume declines depends on the flexibility of the consumer. If the consumer is quite flexible, volume will fall a lot; if inflexible, volume will fall very little.

These two opposing effects—price and volume—lead to different results: When the price effect dominates, revenues will increase. When the volume effect reigns supreme, revenues will fall. Thus, when the price effect is on and demand increases, businesses in an inelastic industry can survive—and even prosper—when the higher price of its goods or services compensates for its inability to increase supply. Basically, if you can sell more of what you have at a higher price without having to make any more of it, you're sitting pretty.

This was the idealistic world of the super-regulated airlines. Largely due to government restrictions before 1978, the airlines were unable to easily expand their supply when there was an increase in demand. As a consequence, when the economy performed well and people traveled more, the *regulated and inelastic* airlines raised prices, an action that increased their profitability in exaggerated proportions relative to the economy. In this respect, the industry's high betas were well earned.

But everything changed for the airlines beginning in 1978. With the passage of the Airline Deregulation Act that year, new carriers could freely enter the market, and all carriers could select their own routes. By 1982, the airlines could determine their own fares. This dramatically changed the shape of the airline industry's supply curve:

Where the spigots of supply had been tightly monitored, essentially opening or closing only by the hand of government, now the airlines could determine the flow of supply. This is not to that say the spigots could be opened all the way at this point; several factors still limited supply in the industry (for instance, airport gates and runways are not so flexible). But with the advent of deregulation, an inelastic industry suddenly became more elastic.

And by the early 1990s, Pan Am was bankrupt—which is not so surprising from the perspective of industry elasticity.

Fine-Tuning Your Stock Market Indicator Lights

Viewed in isolation, beta can be misleading. But when observed in terms of elasticity, it can be extremely directional, letting you know exactly how to invest.

In a way, what I'm talking about are the indicator lights—like those in the cockpit of an airplane—that flash when it is time to buy or sell a stock or group of stocks. Back in 1982, a few years after deregulation hit, my indicator lights would have blinked for airline stocks such as Pan Am, telling me to *sell*. However, someone else's indicator lights might well have been signaling the complete opposite: "Buy Big Air."

Why the disparity? From my seat in the cockpit, if you bought airline stocks in the early 1980s, your indicator lights were primarily reading historical (or backward-looking) *beta*—an important reading, but potentially a false indicator if it doesn't take into account both the big economic picture and the forces of supply and demand. Back in the early 1980s, when the Airline Deregulation Act was working its magic (or voodoo, depending on your point of view), the betas of the big airlines were declining as the industry shifted elastic. That meant, very simply, that the airlines would not participate in the forthcoming bull market as much as they might have in the past.

In the first blush of deregulation, the airline industry lost most, if not all, of its pricing power in the mass market. With the arrival of new airlines, the race was on to fill the marginal "empty" seat. And because the best way to fill an empty seat is with a lower price, the prices of coach tickets went down. (In theory, there is no incremental cost to filling the empty seat. Hence, all an airline needs to do is lower prices enough to induce consumers to fly. How low prices need to go depends on the price sensitivity of consumers.) Imagine, for a moment, big, bold, brassy Pan Am attempting to reach down low for the marginal-seat scraps. It did reach; it knew it had no other choice. But the big carrier couldn't adjust at the speed or accuracy of the new and smaller carriers. Before deregulation was a decade old, Pan Am was no more.[4]

So if you invested in the airlines industry in 1982, here's why you got short-changed: Fluctuations in demand following airline deregulation were satisfied primarily by an increase of supply without the industry experiencing significant changes in profitability. An inelastic industry turned more elastic, those high betas plummeted, and the list of macroeconomic variables that once favored airline stocks—low inflation, low energy prices, and a rising stock market—were, to a degree, neutralized.

The investment lesson here is to be sure your indicator lights are forward looking: Use an industry's historical beta as a guideline, but be sure to view that beta in relation to any current economic shocks that might be changing the elasticity (and, hence, the beta) within that industry.

Rethinking Industries That Suddenly Go Elastic

If your indicator lights are functioning properly, you will want to own inelastic, high-beta stocks during the good times and abandon them during the bad. But a company does not necessarily fall out of favor when its business turns from inelastic to elastic. And the same holds for a stock that sees its high-beta decline. As we move between levels of elasticity and beta, all that changes are the investment rules.

To make this case, we can continue with the airlines saga.

In the decades since deregulation hit, the airlines industry as a whole has morphed along with its newfound elasticity. In particular, the airlines have become very deft at predicting the demand for each flight and each seat by passenger class, particularly with the aid of computers.

Just like industries, consumers can be considered either elastic or inelastic, a delineation the airlines now make all the time. Inelastic passengers might be the business travelers, people who need to be in a certain place at a certain time and are less concerned as a group about ticket prices. Elastic passengers, on the other hand, might be the vacationers who can adjust times of travel to when traveling is more affordable. With different price structures for elastic and inelastic passengers, the airlines are now better able to fill each flight—a profit-generating strategy in an industry whose margins of profit are quite small.

As noted, Pan Am flew high and far as a regulated bird but was unable to adapt its business fast enough or well enough to an explosion of elastic free-market activity. Other big airlines also went out of business, while still more acquired, merged, and expanded with skill to prolong their survival. That said, the few big airlines left standing—such as Continental, United, and American—continue to deal with the aftershocks of deregulation, if only because the low-cost provider still drives the market. The older airlines—specifically, the airlines with unionized workforces—have not been able to lower their cost structures enough to compete on a level with the nonunionized, fleet-of-foot upstarts.

JetBlue, for example, was hardly a blip on the airlines map at the turn of the new millennium. But with rapid speed, it became a darling of the business. A *60 Minutes* news story began this way only a couple of years ago: "With most of the major airlines cutting back or

even going bankrupt, Jet Blue, the new guy on the block, keeps turning a profit and expanding."[5] Excellent management, service, and
marketing have gone a long way toward making the airline successful.
But in good part, JetBlue has operated in a low-cost, highly elastic,
and efficient way because it is a nonunionized airline. Elastic and
inelastic are not necessarily polar opposites; grades of elasticity exist
within industries. Unions will always handcuff businesses by making
the cost of doing business less elastic. Pay scales, pensions, and benefits, in particular, are shaped less by the unionized businesses than by
the unions themselves. And when a business cannot adjust its cost
variables to economic realities, it is put at an immediate competitive
disadvantage to the businesses that can.

To borrow from another popular film, an industry is not like a box
of chocolates. It's more like a box of assorted rubber bands, with each
business in an industry able to "stretch" to a different degree. As an
investor, if you look hard at elasticity, you will always know which
company or groups of companies you're going to get.

Catching Elasticity: Rules of Engagement

Investors who "catch elasticity if they can" will see superior results.
And the example of the airlines industry instructs that catching elasticity depends partly on your ability to understand the effects of government regulation on industries overall, partly on your knowledge of
how macroeconomic forces act on separate industries in unique ways,
and partly on your ability to detect the winning innovators within
each industry (such as those companies that can provide the most to
consumers at the lowest cost). But catching elasticity will not have
you micromanaging your portfolio. The changes in industry elasticity
that economic shocks bring on—such as regulatory changes or technological advances or shifts in the tax burden—have, in general, been
gradual.

It took Pan Am more than a decade to succumb following airline deregulation, a period of time in which the carrier attempted, unsuccessfully, to become more elastic through mergers, sell-offs, and strategic adjustments to routes and pricing. At the same time, it took the low-cost carriers time to perfect the art of filling that empty seat. Changes to industry elasticity are also *predictable* because similar shocks have caused the same reactions within individual industries throughout history.

Taking all of this into account, any investor will want to apply this set of elasticity rules:

Elasticity Rules of Engagement

Investing in Inelastic Stocks

- *Hold or buy stocks in inelastic industries that are facing rising demand (or during bull markets).* In this case, prices will increase to satisfy higher demand. This is a win–win situation: Price increases coupled with more consumers who are willing and able to pay a higher price will be reflected in increased profitability.

- *Sell or avoid stocks in inelastic industries that are facing decreasing demand (or during bear markets).* In this case prices will decrease to satisfy lower demand. This is a lose–lose situation: Price decreases coupled with fewer willing consumers will be reflected in decreased profitability.

Investing in Elastic Stocks

- *If you must hold stocks in your portfolio when economic conditions are unfavorable (or during bear markets), hold or buy stocks in elastic industries.* When the economy is doing poorly, the most elastic companies will be the best able to outperform the market. This is a win–lose situation in which you can favor the win: Here you will want to find the elastic businesses that are most able to efficiently adjust their cost structures to increase profitability.

- *Reduce exposure to elastic industries when economic conditions are favorable (or during bull markets).* When the economy and the stock market are doing well, elastic companies will generally underperform the least elastic (or most inelastic) companies because the latter will rise high with their high betas. As a general rule, investors will want to take extra care to choose elastic companies that can provide the greatest value to their customers at the lowest cost. (This brings up the concept of "uniqueness," which we discuss in Chapter 5, "Putting High-Beta to Work: Industry-Based Portfolio Strategies.")

An Outperforming Strategy

As I've noted, industries are big-picture items, with each industry representing a large bucket of stocks. It follows that if we correctly separate the winning industries from the losers, we will, in all likelihood, be able to allocate our portfolios to many outperforming companies. When people say they invest in sectors, this is just what they are attempting to do. These investors often buy sector funds that represent stocks within individual industries, or sector funds that have grouped several industries under a common heading (such as a "consumer" fund that includes stocks from the retail, food, and leisure industries).

Obviously, this should be a profitable activity when it is performed correctly. Flip back a few pages to our industry chart for the 1983–1992 period: Tobacco (+970.2); Beverages: Soft Drinks (+825.94); Containers: Metal & Glass (+717.37). How lucrative, one imagines, to have "caught" these industries during the 1980s. Alas, I cannot offer a formula that will locate, say, the top three or five performing industries over a future ten-year period. But I do offer a strategy that will have you selecting most often from the outperforming industries in relation to the economic environment.

Beta *plus* elasticity will get you to this level of outperformance. In the following chapter, we develop some practical measures of beta and elasticity, which will help simplify the process of catching (or avoiding) true high beta while you can.

Endnotes

1. George E. Burns, "The Jet Age Arrives," *Pan Am World Airways History* (Pan American Historical Foundation, www.panam.org).

2. T. A. Heppenheimer, *Turbulent Skies* (New York: John Wiley & Sons, 1995).

3. "Pan American: The History of America's 'Chosen Instrument' for Overseas Air Transport," U.S. Centennial of Flight Commission.

4. The troubled history of the big commercial airlines has been well documented. It is a tale of arrogance and overspending and bad management converging with the Airline Deregulation Act of 1978 for a perfect storm that spelled eventual doom for Pan Am. To set the hinge for downfall in 1978 is correct: That act changed everything. Where government once set the rules for its pedigreed airlines, it now let the carriers fight it out among themselves in the free market. Big, tough, and once dominant Pan Am just couldn't cut it—and, yes, arrogance, overspending, and bad management assuredly played a part. But I see the demise of Pan Am and the stormy history of commercial airlines overall a bit differently than most business and flight historians. What happened to Pan Am and several of its competitors (at least, for a time) was that the cost structures of these big airlines could not easily adapt to the increase in competition that deregulation suddenly ushered in. If you knew

this 20 or so years ago, you might have looked at a Pan Am pilot with sympathy rather than reverence—every indication showed that his company was caught in a tailspin from which it couldn't pull out. For thoughtful accounts of the effects of deregulation on the airlines industry, see Heppenheimer's *Turbulent Skies* (referenced earlier) and Alfred E. Kahn's *Lessons from Deregulation* (Washington DC: AEI-Brookings, 2003). For an up-front and personal account of the demise of Pan Am, see Robert Gandt's *Skygods: The Fall of Pan Am* (New York: William Morrow & Co., 1995).

5. "Jet Blue: Flying Higher?" *60 Minutes II/CBS News*, 18 June 2003. No matter how much of a Wall Street "darling" JetBlue quickly has become, there is no way the carrier can escape the macroeconomic shocks that are specific to the airlines industry. Crude oil prices began surging in 2004; in 2006, JetBlue announced its first quarterly loss, in good part attributing this performance to high fuel prices.

5

Putting High-Beta to Work: Industry-Based Portfolio Strategies

Any number of different economic shocks can deliver the same economic results. For example, a tax cut might initiate a sustained increase in the stock market, or what is commonly known as a bull market. So might lower inflation. So might a string of interest-rate cuts from the Federal Reserve. But each of these bull markets is not the same. In particular, the shocks that generate these markets draw out different responses from individual industries. And elasticity is the reason why.

In a way, shocks seek out sensitivity—or high-beta, or inelasticity, which are all interchangeable terms in this discussion. Our challenge, then, is to connect specific shocks with their most sensitive industry counterparts. In doing so, we will know just which industries deserve our investment dollars—and those we should avoid at all costs.

To this end, I focus on two shocks in this chapter: a fundamental shift in Federal Reserve monetary policy and the technology explosion ushered in by the personal computer. The Fed example is instructive in its own right: Inflation and the level of interest rates influence all investors. For instance, low future inflation means your future dollars will retain most of their value, and low interest rates translate to lower costs for all sorts of financial transactions. Here, however, the Fed discussion leads us to a historical method for selecting the best industries shock to shock. Correspondingly, the computer example helps us develop criteria for selecting the best-performing companies within *elastic* industries. Each approach is based on common sense, but I also introduce what we can call, well, the common-sense approach to industry selection: Often the simplest data can steer you in the right direction.

With our strategies in hand, we move to putting high-beta to work in a portfolio, developing elasticity-based investment rules for active, passive, and intermediate investors.

Shock Study: A Federal Case

A little electricity always blows in the financial air when the Federal Reserve Board meets to determine interest rates. This is the day eight times a year when the investment community learns the destiny of the *federal funds rate*. Technically, this is the short-term interest rate at which the Fed lends to banks, but in a broader sense, it is the rate on which so many real-world rates are based—business loans, adjustable-rate mortgages, and on down the line. Changes to the fed funds rate also indicate where the Federal Reserve believes the inflation rate is headed and what it intends to do about it.

In theory, when the Fed raises interest rates, it believes inflation needs to be cordoned off. Meanwhile, interest-rate cuts theoretically signal a noninflationary, or perhaps deflationary, environment. I say "theoretically" because not all the people who are appointed to the Federal Reserve are the same or view the world the same way; Fed policy, right or wrong, depends on the personalities guiding the operations. It is reasonable to assume that the Fed always has its eye on inflation and, thus, the value of the dollar. But Feds notoriously watch all sorts of economic indicators, some of which have nothing to do with inflation. This adds to the "electricity"—and sometimes the heartburn—that surrounds every Fed meeting.

In the early 1980s, however, I was feeling increasingly sure about the direction of Fed policy. I remember that a lot of writers, including myself, were watching interest rates very closely—and not just the Fed's stated policy rate, but the rates of securities selling in the market. During 1980 and 1981, many of us argued that interest rates on low-risk, long-maturity securities (such as ten-year Treasury bonds) were lofty relative to inflation and that the resulting yields of the securities were near all-time highs. Based on historical experience, I argued that such high real yields could not persist and that the gap between inflation and interest rates also could be expected to narrow. (You need not worry here about what economists see when they look at the "gap" between inflation and interest rates. The early moral of the story is to keep your eyes open.) At the time, the question was, how would the gap close? By way of interest rates falling, or inflation rising?

To determine this, I kept my eyes pinned to the Fed.

Paul Volcker took over the chairmanship of the Federal Reserve in mid-1979 with the stench of that decade's hyperinflation still thick in the air. Volcker had a couple of false starts, but in the early 1980s, I fell under the impression that the Fed was changing its operating procedures—and for the better. (I note here that the Fed does not necessarily announce what these procedures are; it is usually up to economists to discern them, by way of experience and a little mind-reading.) My indicators suggested the Fed was moving toward a *price rule,* which, in the simplest terms, means it would let real-world prices indicate the direction of inflation and adjust the money supply accordingly. If prices were going up, it would raise interest rates (which, in effect, pulls excess inflationary money out of the system). If prices were going down, it would lower interest rates (returning cash to the economy).

Volcker seemed to have begun the price-rule attack in earnest in October 1979 when he began to significantly hike the fed funds interest rate. By reading the newspapers, I reinforced my belief that the Fed was indeed on a new policy course: When President Ronald Reagan took office in 1980, he appointed a string of price-rule advocates to the Fed board—Martha Seger, Manuel Johnson, Wayne Angell, and Robert Heller among them. These were still inflationary times, so I knew the Fed was going to continue raising interest rates—and it did, fiercely: The increase in the underlying inflation rate during the 1970s led to a 10 percent federal funds rate by the end of 1978. However, as Paul Volker changed gears, the fed funds rate rose to 15.5 percent by October 1979 and 20 percent by March 1980. After a brief decline that year, the rate touched 20 percent again in December 1980.

And the high rates did their work on inflation. By the end of 1981, when the fed funds rate dropped back to 12 percent, inflation had suffered a severe blow, and the economy was poised to recover. For the decade ahead, I argued that both the U.S. inflation rate *and* the Fed's target interest rates would decline even further. With the price rule working its magic, I knew that inflation would at last be tamed and that interest rates would come down.

As I mentioned, any investor benefits from an understanding of Federal Reserve policy, simply due to the gravity of the policy results. High inflation, in particular, can destroy the economic good times, while low inflation often equates with smooth economic sailing. But this particular Fed interlude leads us to a fundamental strategy for industry selection: In looking backward, we can sometimes know just how to look forward.

Industry Selection: The Historical Method

If you read the newspapers in the early 1980s and understood a little bit about Federal Reserve policymaking, a future economic shock became knowable: Inflation and interest rates were both headed down. But how to take advantage of this insight? Well, my first inclination was to look back a few years and isolate periods of rising and falling interest rates. I show these results in Table 5.1—information that, on its own, would not have done any investor much good.[1]

TABLE 5.1　Periods of Rising and Falling Interest Rates, 1968–1981

Falling	Rising
June 1970 to March 1971	October 1968 to April 1970
April 1974 to December 1974	January 1972 to August 1974
November 1975 to March 1987	January 1975 to October 1975
	January 1977 to December 1981

Source: Federal Reserve Bank of St. Louis

However, in these interest-rate periods, I had a baseline for comparison. Which industries, I wondered, performed the best, or the worst, in each of these timeframes? I show these results in Table 5.2.

TABLE 5.2　Performance of Selected S&P 500 Industries, 1983–1992

Industries Benefiting From:			
Falling Interest Rates		*Rising Interest Rates*	
Industry	**Appreciation**	**Industry**	**Appreciation**
Automobile	–9.47	Aluminum	45.65
Broadcast Media	225.88	Gold Mining	–12.41
Electrical Equipment	197.68	Hospital Management	67.63
Financial: Insurance/ Life	182.43	Machinery: Diversified	58.2
Financial: Insurance/ Prop. Cas.	49.09	Oil & Gas Drilling	–43.7

continues

Industries Benefiting From:

Falling Interest Rates		Rising Interest Rates	
Industry	**Appreciation**	**Industry**	**Appreciation**
Financial: Personal Loans	223.81	Oil Well & Equipment Services	33.86
Financial: Savings & Loan	–47.94	Steel	79.63
Foods	406.02		
Leisure Time	76.91		
Manufactured Housing	73.03		
Pollution Control	531.11		
Publishing: Newspapers	115.39		
Restaurants	326.05		
Retail: Department Stores	128		
Retail: Food Chains	68.29		
Retail: General Merchandise	403.64		
Retail: Drug Stores	443.38		
Textiles: Apparel Manufacturers	176.98		
Tobacco	970.2		
Average	238.97	Average	32.69
Average of All Industries	180.91		

My methodology here was simple: The industries that outperformed the market during periods of declining interest rates, and the ones that underperformed the market during periods of rising interest rates, were defined as those that would benefit from falling interest rates.[2] Similarly, the outperformers during periods of rising interest rates and the underperformers during periods of falling interest rates became the industries that would most benefit from rising interest rates. Just as I might look for the high-beta sensitivity of stocks or industries, I was now looking for interest-rate sensitivity. My elasticity rationale was, and is, the same: The most sensitive stocks in relation to any economic shock can be said to have high-betas in relation to that shock. And high beta, as we know, pulls a stock disproportionately upward in the good times and disproportionately downward during the bad.

The potential upside of such a historical strategy is obvious: In the Fed example, the industries that had benefited from falling interest rates in the past gained an average of 238.97 percent in the 1983–1992 period. If you did your historical homework and invested in the industries projected to do the best in this environment, you would have beaten the industry average by 58.06 percentage points (238.97 – 180.91 = 58.06). In other words, if you "caught" those sectors with the greatest sensitivity or (highest betas) to falling interest rates, you would have eclipsed the average industry gain by a noteworthy amount. Avoiding the groups that benefited from rising interest rates also would have added to your strategy performance because this group gained a mere 32.69 percent for the period.

This is how one properly looks backward to properly invest forward. Here's the historical industry-selection process, step by step:

Step 1. Determine a shock—whether one that is in process or is likely to occur.

Step 2. Measure the stock performance, good and bad, of industries when the shock occurred in the past.

Step 2 (Alternate). Measure the performance of industries when the mirror-image shock occurred and reverse the results. (For example, if all you can find is historical data showing the impact of higher interest rates, it is safe to assume that many of the winners in this situation will be the losers when interest rates fall.)

Step 3. Favor the stocks in those industries that have historically benefited from the shock, and avoid those that have not.

This method isn't perfect. In the case of the interest-rate shock, you might have noticed that a few losers mingled with the winners, while some industries "won" by much greater margins than others. Still, had you selected all the historical industry winners, you would have beaten the industry average decisively during the period.

And beating the average is what above-average performance is all about.

Industry Selection: The Common-Sense Approach

Over the years, I have examined the levels of employment and profitability within separate industries when economic shocks occur. From this study, I am able to pull two general rules for identifying whether an industry will behave in an elastic or inelastic manner following the arrival of an economic shock.

First, inelastic industries respond to positive economic shocks with below-average employment increases and above-average profit gains (example: the airlines industry preregulation). Second, elastic industries respond to positive economic shocks with above-average employment increases and below-average profit gains (example: the airlines industry post-deregulation).

Common sense is your guide here.

In the first case, no increase in employment takes place while profits go up. Thus, higher prices must be meeting demand, rather than an increase of supply meeting demand. This is *classic inelastic.* You want to own these stocks (and/or industries) when profits climb and employment gains are below average, and avoid them in the converse situation.

In the second case, an increase in employment takes place, although profits come in slightly below or slightly above average. This indicates strong competition and that demand is being met by greater supply at lower prices. This is *classic elastic.* Sometimes you'll want to own these stocks; other times not. (We discuss why shortly, in the next section.)

If you can understand the general rules for selecting industries using historical data and/or jobs-and-profitability statistics, I'd say you are well on your way to becoming a certified inelasticity catcher—or avoider. Whatever you want to call these stocks—inelastic, high-beta, or sensitive—you want to own them when they are the beneficiaries of positive economic events and avoid them when shocks turn negative.

As for selecting stocks within elastic industries, your investigative skills might need to mature, although the payoff can be worth it.

Industry Selection: The Separation Method

In the last chapter, I stated that an industry is more like a box of assorted rubber bands than a box of chocolates. Here's a closer look at why.

The ultimate burden of any given macroeconomic shock finally comes to rest on an industry's supply-and-demand elasticities. Inelastic companies face rigidities that restrict their ability to adjust production during periods of shifting demand. These rigidities are central to an active investment strategy because they determine which industries will experience above- or below-average rates of return when the demand for their products rises or falls.

Critically, however, there's nothing static or constant about this approach: Sometimes an inelastic industry goes elastic, as the airlines example showed, starkly changing how it can adjust to shifts in demand. Inelastic and elastic components also exist within the same industries, company to company, although some elastic industries or companies have been able to generate what we might call *unique* inelasticity, giving them a decided competitive advantage.

Think of how the computer industry developed. When personal computers first arrived, they were high-priced and accessible by only a few. However, as the technology advanced and competition in the category increased, prices came down, making PCs available to the masses. The market expanded rapidly, and computers quickly became standardized products in offices and homes—which is another way of saying that computer manufacturing turned elastic. When the benefits of this technology became known to consumers, increased competition for those consumers forced a price reduction. This also meant that one PC would soon be about as good as another PC at the same price.

So what we have is a classic example of a once unique product turning into a *commodity,* which here can be defined as any standard bulk item that can be freely bought and sold.

That's the hardware story. But the PC explosion has had a well-documented "spillover" effect: What company or industry has not benefited from the computer revolution? PCs have spawned several tributary industries, such as software. But unlike keyboards or monitors or hard drives, with one about as good as another at a similar price, PC software is task-specific. "Costs" also are associated with learning a particular program—for instance, time—and copyrights have restricted the entry of clones to the category. In short, *unique* factors in both supply (copyrights) and demand (such as the time invested in learning programs) have made the PC software industry less elastic than the PC hardware industry.

The art of industry selection often requires that an investor follow innovation from the source to the extremities. To stick with this example, the computer revolution has had far-reaching implications that have shifted elasticities within many industries. For instance, just-in-time inventory—the technique by which factories produce certain goods right when they are needed and only in the amounts needed—has been greatly enhanced by computerization, which, in turn, has greatly reduced the cost of doing business industry-wide. This is an elastic event from the point of view of all manufacturers, bettering their just-in-time capabilities thanks to the computer. However, high-tech developments applied to the production process also can give rise to economies of scale that make it difficult for small competitors to enter a category. Witness Wal-Mart: In the sense that it dissolved much of its competition in becoming one of the most efficient low-cost operators in the history of chain-store retail, it can be considered *uniquely* inelastic.

The investor challenge becomes to separate the elastic commodities (the standard "bulk" goods, such as PCs or TVs) from the unique inelastic factors company to company within industries (i.e., software, MP3 players, etc). The elastic/inelastic rules of engagement from Chapter 4, "Catch Elasticity If You Can: An Introduction to Industry Behavior," still apply—in particular, buy or hold those high-beta inelastic companies in periods of high demand. But looking company to company, we now have a nuance:

> During rising markets, delete industries or companies from a portfolio that can be classified as commodities.

Companies usually can be classified as commodities for a good reason: They do it just as well as most everyone else. Within industries, the true gems are those businesses that have been able to become uniquely inelastic. Such companies often energize a portfolio.

High-Beta Portfolio Strategies for the Short and Long Run

At some point, all investors must decide who they really are. Are they low-risk, long-run passive investors? Are they higher-risk active players? Are they somewhere in the middle? Putting aside my strong position that an investor can be all of these at different times, or at the same time, each of these strategies can be geared to capture as much high-beta as possible.

Active Industry Selection

Obviously, if you follow my general investment guidelines for elastic and inelastic stocks, you will find yourself investing in a more active mode. Good for you—you'll find a lot of upside profit in being correctly allocated (or unallocated) to inelastic, high-beta stocks at the right times. As a general rule, you will want to own as much high-beta as you can during bull markets and avoid that high-beta during bear markets. But watch out: Historical stock beta is not always the true stock beta, so make sure your beta indicator lights are also reading industry elasticity, which we now know can change shock to shock.

Undoubtedly, the frequency of negative returns increases over shorter (more active) horizons. The active-investor challenge is to anticipate the positive and negative cycles that occur during relatively shorter periods of time and act on that information. In high-beta terms, the active strategy is as follows:

- During positive-return periods—when the economy, stock market, and/or consumer demand are rising—increase your exposure to inelastic (and hence high-beta) industries.

- Avoid inelastic industries that are undergoing or projected to undergo adverse or negative shocks, such as a falloff in demand.

- During negative-return periods—when the economy, stock market, and/or consumer demand are falling—if you must hold stock in these industries' portfolios, switch to elastic low-beta stocks.

On this last point, low-beta is your safety net: These stocks are considered low risk and will protect you, to an extent, when market conditions turn sour.

Passive Industry Selection

As for passive, buy-and-hold investors, high-beta is more of a no-brainer. Using history as our guide, the stock market will always post a positive return over a long horizon of 30 or 40 years. Hence, passive investors will want to identify the stocks with the greatest sensitivity to the market—high-beta stocks that will capture all the market upside over a long horizon. The only downside to this formula is that you have to take the good with the bad because high-beta stocks drop conspicuously during bear markets. But again, this is the reason for the buy-and-hold formula. Over the long haul, both the high-beta upside and downside will average out, giving passive investors solid performance.

However, the ideal for investors wedded to the passive long-run approach is to make a determination to readjust portfolio allocations in the event of *major* thematic changes in the business and economic environment. The computer, for example, has transformed the way business is done and has altered the betas of nearly all companies and industries. By adjusting to such changes, passive investors might have to relabel themselves as "intermediate" investors, but this is a relatively painless process:

From time to time, as the thematic winds change, you should follow these guidelines:

- Add stocks to portfolios that become inelastic as a result of economic or policy shocks.
- Delete stocks from portfolios that become more elastic as a result of economic or policy shocks.

Lifecycle Industry Selection

Nonprofit organizations and some trust funds are set up as infinite-horizon, or infinitely lived, institutions (they don't necessarily invest for lifetimes, but for generations), and a strong argument can be made that these entities should invest in high-beta stocks exclusively. This is the realm of Professor Siegel's 200-year stock market, from Chapter 2, "Leaping the Transaction-Cost Hurdle: Sometimes It's Easy, Other Times It's Not," which we know will always chart as a proud upward slope with just a few bumps along the way. However, individual investors do not have infinite horizons, and the horizons they do enjoy shrink with each passing year. Meanwhile the possibility of negative returns becomes more likely as these holding periods shorten. With this in mind, the passive buy-and-hold strategy has been modified to minimize the downside risks that increase as we age. The result is the *lifecycle* strategy, which automatically adjusts the split between stocks and bonds across an investment career, essentially lowering the risk factor as an investor nears retirement.

Young investors employing lifecycle strategies might start with an allocation of 80 percent stocks and 20 percent bonds. This original allocation is considered low risk and high gain because even though stocks have inherent risk and bonds are basically risk-free, young workers can dissipate this risk over their long horizons. Over time, however, this lifecycle strategy will adjust the stock/bond split until a retirement-ready allocation of, say, 20 percent stocks and 80 percent bonds is reached. But the stock/bond split need not be the only risk-lowering adjustment in the lifecycle portfolio. As with the passive strategy, the lifecycle strategy can adjust over time in relation to beta:

Rather than simply lessen the stock exposure and broaden the bond exposure over time, reduce beta exposure—and the potential downsides of that exposure—as your horizon shortens.

In doing so, lifecycle investors might witness better performance because lower-beta (and hence lower-risk) stocks could well return more than bonds when horizons shorten.

Beta of 1, for Everyone

And what about those middle-of-the-road stocks with a beta of 1? Again, these stocks will always be market performers; with their seat-belts fastened securely, they will move with the market, up or down. But they play an important role in an industry-selection strategy, in that they provide insurance against the accuracy of a forecast that predicts shifts in demand.

For instance, if you incorrectly forecast the demand reaction to an economic shock, you just might put the worst-performing industries in your portfolio. Hence, it might always be prudent to allocate a portion of your portfolio to average, beta-of-1 stocks. This guarantees you some level of market performance at all times, while protecting you from the downside of making a bad call.

The Above-Average Investor Mandate: Think Elastically

Across each of these industry-selection strategies, I note that my message remains the same: Elasticity-minded investors are empowered investors—people who are adept at selecting the assets that will earn them superior portfolio returns in the event of any economic shock. Indeed, if you take anything away from this book, I want it to be an elasticity mindset. This is not a static world. The winds of change never stop swirling: a light breeze of change here, a gale-force transformation there. Shocks come and go, and businesses change with them.

To track all this, you need to keep your eyes and ears open—although not a shock goes by that the media doesn't report. And to act on all this, you now have some simple procedures at your disposal.

Investigate how industries performed when a shock occurred in the past and capture (or avoid) that performance when the same shock returns. Separate unique businesses from commodity businesses and invest in that uniqueness. Detect and invest in inelastic industries based on the simple recipe of high profitability and low employment gains.

Because elasticity asserts itself everywhere, the applicability of these strategies is sweeping. In the next chapter, we investigate the elastic responses of businesses within distinct geographical locations;

in so doing, we fine-tune our ability to invest properly across all sorts of economic shocks. The old business phrase is that location matters. In terms of investing with an elasticity mindset, it matters a lot.

Endnotes

1. In Table 5.1, I report the interest-rate cycles as they were identified using ten-year bond yields monthly averages. On the basis of mean monthly excess returns, the returns over and above the S&P 500 were classified according to their interest-rate sensitivity. Industries that display no systematic pattern during the cycles were identified as ambiguous.

2. On the basis of mean monthly returns, the returns net of the S&P 500 were classified according to their interest rate sensitivity during the cycle. Industries that displayed no systematic pattern during the cycle were identified as ambiguous.

6

California Is a Country: An Introduction to the Location Effect

If the state legislature of Rhode Island enacts a draconian law whereby businesses must pay a 50 percent tax on earnings produced within the state, will that law affect a company based in Peoria, Illinois? Well, if the Peoria company has factories in Rhode Island, that legislation will matter. If not, it probably will care less. Meanwhile, all the companies with operations in Rhode Island will have a significant shock to deal with—one that is location-specific, locked within 2,000 square miles of American turf.

When an economic shock lands on a specific geographic area, we can say the *location effect* is on. The Peoria example reveals this in a blatant way: If you don't do business in Location A, the policies of Location A likely won't affect you; if you do perform business there, the policies of Location A will matter greatly. Simple enough, but there is a good deal more to the location-effect story. In particular, the nature of a shock and the economic makeup of a region combine to determine the *different behaviors* of the assets *within* that region.

The elasticities of each company in relation to a geographic area will cause the winners to separate from the losers—a phenomenon that begs our attention because picking the winners is what above-average investing is all about.

The elasticity theme continues, but this is a flexible term (if you will forgive the pun). In this chapter, you can think of elasticity as the extent to which a company can *physically* escape a bad shock or embrace a good one. In hashing out this elastic nuance, our lexicon needs to expand, with new terminology, including *economic integration, transportation costs, arbitrage,* and *mobility.* I also make use of a recent economic shock that hit close to home (my home, that is)—a contagion of rolling blackouts. In this one example, policy blunders delivered an outsized shock that challenged all businesses within California's borders in 2000 and 2001. But some companies were challenged more than others, and I use this example to show how the separate responses of public companies to localized shocks can be quite predictable.

The Location Lexicon

I state in the title of this chapter that California is a country. Technically, it is not. It is one of 50 states in a union, a political determination. But as I see it, California is a giant and a true player on the world stage. As a territory, it ranks consistently among the top countries in the world in terms of economic output. California also is an open, free-market society that does business not only with other states in the U.S., but with countries around the globe. Considering all this, I see California as a country, one with an *integrated economy.*

Increasingly, countries worldwide are considered integrated within a global economy. When economies are integrated, trade, information, and capital flow freely, although to different degrees, from one location to the next. The U.S. itself is an integrated economy. So is California, on its very own. A nonintegrated economy, on the other hand, can be characterized as one that is, to a degree, self-sufficient and in which trade flows to it or from it in a limited or restricted way. Before the collapse of communism, the Soviet Union could have been considered a nonintegrated economy, as can Iran and Cuba today, although to differing degrees. The U.S. and the "country" of California rank among the most integrated.

In good part, economic integration is all about the flow and the ease of flow, of goods, information, and capital between locations. An air hockey table might help describe this. When the table is turned on, a layer of air forms over it, making air hockey a low-friction game. Simply nudge your puck, and it glides (or flows) to the other end of the table; lessen or remove that air, and moving the puck takes much greater effort.

This example is an ideal, and, unquestionably, the real world is not always ideal: *Grades* of friction exist between locations. Sometimes the "puck," or product, flows almost effortlessly between points A and B, as if across a cushion of air. Sometimes it labors to move or gets stuck, as if someone pulled the plug and shut off the air.

In practical terms, the friction that plays on the free flow of goods is in large part the cost of moving those goods from one place to another. Just as we discussed transaction costs in previous chapters, now we're talking *transportation costs*. In the past, I've gone to the orange to illustrate this concept: If it generally costs 5¢ to transport an orange from California to New York, that 5¢ becomes the accepted level of friction for the flow of that good. If the friction increases and it costs 6¢ to transport that same orange, New York might turn to Florida, which can deliver the fruit for 5¢. This introduces another investment term: *arbitrage,* the process of attempting to profit by exploiting price differences of identical or similar financial instruments on different markets or in different forms. By looking elsewhere for cheaper oranges, New York involves itself in "arbitraging," or taking advantage of the difference in prices between locations. (Economists would refer to that 5¢ as the *protection shield* New York enjoys. If California can't deliver at 5¢, New York is protected because it can maintain that 5¢ cost by going elsewhere.) Conversely, if the friction lowers and it costs less than 5¢ to transport an orange between California and New York, the supply of oranges between the localities will increase. At the same time, New York will not have an incentive to arbitrage or go elsewhere for its oranges because it would not be profitable to do so. This latter situation also protects California's orange growers against foreign competition: If it is not profitable for New York to arbitrage the difference in the price of oranges, foreign competition (which here could mean Florida or South America) against California will not arise.

As we turn to the California energy shock, try to think in terms of pucks and oranges—in terms of the flow of energy into California and the differences of energy prices between regions. Jumping ahead a little bit, certain California "pucks" weren't gliding so well, while the price of "oranges" it was forced to buy was too high.

Shock Study: Rolling Blackouts

In March 2001, the sun pulsed over California with a bit more muscle than usual for that time of year. The mercury, which in a more normal spring might slide between 60°F and 70°F, pushed through the 80s and even into the 90s in parts of the state. High summer had come early to the West Coast, and as one might expect, the air conditioners went on—an annual event that in most other years would mean cooler Californians and business as usual. But this year was different: When the ACs powered up, California fell deeper into crisis.

Signs of a crisis first asserted themselves in 2000 when it was announced that rolling blackouts might be enacted in the state. Rolling blackouts are typically unique events that occur when the supply of energy falls to a certain level below demand, forcing power companies to unilaterally shut off customers town by town and sector

by sector for a period of 60 or 90 minutes. In June 2000, rolling blackouts went into effect in San Francisco, and in January 2001, they
again rolled through the north of the state. But the March 2001
episode marked the first time they crept into Southern California. No
longer was this an inconvenience; it was a sustained statewide crisis.

Media reports that March described the damage: People got
stuck in elevators, teachers moved classes outside, store workers led
shoppers through aisles by flashlight, drivers went to hand signals at
darkened intersections—all problematic but manageable events. On
the more serious side of the ledger: fatalities occurred, businesses
came to a complete stop, workers idled, technicians delayed research,
chain stores turned away customers, factories came to a pause, deliv-
eries fell behind, and clients—those companies that purchased goods
from California's firms—began looking for alternatives.

All this added up. And even when the blackouts were not in
effect, the wrath of the energy crisis was still being felt. For instance,
many California companies were given incentives to save on power
use, such as discounted rates if they cut their energy consumption.
The idea here was to "play team ball" while the state grappled with
the power crunch. But companies complained that the productivity
losses that came with reduced energy use negated any savings that
showed up on their monthly energy bills.

California-wide, productivity, sales, and profits were all taking a
hit. And when these drop, economies suffer.

The San Diego Regional Chamber of Commerce is one of the
most influential forces in local government and regional economic
development. With more than 3,000 members, the Chamber of Commerce is actively involved in public policy and providing valuable
resources to its members. The chamber economist for San Diego
County, Kelly Cunningham, took the March 2001 episode seriously.
He had been bullish on the area's prospects coming into the year, but
when the lights rolled out for the first time in Southern California, he

knew he had to alter his projections. Rather than stick to his forecast of 3.5 percent growth, he began to contemplate recession.[1]

Would you as an investor have made the same call? And what would you have done if you had companies in your portfolio with operations based in California during the energy crisis of 2000–01?

Detecting and Dissecting a Location Shock

If you *had* owned stocks of California companies at the time of the blackouts and you feared for their performance overall, your gut reaction would have been correct. The energy crisis was a particularly bad one. Lost productivity, sales, and profits infected thousands of California's businesses. If you were uninvested in California during the period, you would have considered yourself lucky.

Of course, you don't need to rely on luck when you can see a shock coming.

My crisis indicators were flashing well before March 2001, the point at which we can say the shock fully manifested in California. As the media reported it, the statewide blackouts were the result of a confluence of factors: reduced energy imports by the major utility companies, power plants unable to supply energy because they were offline for repairs, alternative-energy plants shutting down operations because they hadn't been paid, and those summer temperatures that arrived in earliest spring. The root cause, many concluded, was a combination of energy deregulation in the state and the rate "ceilings," or caps, that were placed on California's utility companies. Those ceilings were below what it cost the utilities to purchase the energy they were to supply customers, which is hardly a good way to do business. (Another source of the crisis can be traced to Enron, the pariah of all pariah companies these days. But this connection wasn't made in the media until the crisis period in question had ended.)[2]

Each of these factors played a part in the March 2001 wave of rolling blackouts, but I and a few others look at the origins of the crisis a bit differently. For years, environmental groups had pressured California's politicians to mandate a reduction in the use of conventional "dirty" fuels, such as coal and oil, or new-age "dangerous" options, such as nuclear power. That pressure worked, and environmental regulations were passed that made it difficult for companies in the state to build plants that burned anything other than "clean" natural gas. It follows that the demand for natural gas increased in the state, as did the price of a fuel that had historically sold at a discount to light crude oil.

Added to this, the state could acquire the energy it needed at the time of the crisis in basically two ways: import the energy itself or import the fuel to generate the energy. The problem in California in 2000–01 was that the pipelines transporting natural gas were running at full capacity. Hence, it was virtually impossible to increase that supply. Energy itself needed to be imported, which came at quite an expense.

From here the energy crisis boils down to an instance of supply not meeting demand. When the temperatures soared in March 2001, the demand for the energy needed to keep people air-conditioned, refrigerators operative, and factories powered outpaced the ability of suppliers to deliver. If you lived in California, read the papers, watched the local news, and were tuned to the forces of supply and demand, you might have been among those who predicted the arrival of this shock.

But questions remain. In this instance, with supply not able to meet demand, don't we have a classic inelastic situation in which price increases will restore equilibrium?

Not necessarily—or, at least, not automatically.

As discussed, the delivery mechanisms for the preferred fuel, natural gas, were running at capacity. Buying and bringing in suddenly expensive natural gas and pure power from out-of-state suppliers wasn't working that well because California's utilities had trouble paying their bills. And why couldn't they pay? Because California's government had put caps on what its utilities could charge customers.

Arbitrage—specifically, the practice of taking advantage of differences in prices between markets or regions—ultimately lessened California's energy crisis. California needed energy, so energy became a profitable enough endeavor to mobilize (or incentivize) market forces to solve the problem. Politicians also started to wake up to the fact that California could not function in a modern world if it could not adequately power its inhabitants. This movement, currently ongoing, is working to reduce regulations in the state. For instance, to the extent that an easing of regulations will put the various fuels on a more even playing field, markets naturally gravitate toward the cheaper fuels—perhaps more coal in the near term and nuclear power in the longer term (because nuclear facilities take longer to build).

In the short run, however, the delivery mechanisms for the supply of power had constricted enough to put the "country" of California at a disadvantage to its neighbors in an integrated economy. Arbitrage would cure the situation, but before it could, California's companies were left to manage the crisis on their own. This begs another question: If a state or location can arbitrage price differences between regions, why can't a company?

Our investment opportunity is founded in this answer.

The Location Effect and Mobility: Perfect Together

We've discussed flow and friction in terms of the supply of fuel and energy to California. These variables exist for companies, too, and can be considered in terms of the *mobility* of factors of production.

Many factors of production exist, and some are more mobile than others. If you work in a company, you are a factor of production. In a free society, you can stay or go as you choose, and most likely, you'll go if you can get a better paycheck elsewhere. Capital is a factor of production that displays much mobility in free societies; by nature, it migrates to where it will see the highest return. A company with several factories spread across different locations also exhibits mobility in terms of production—it can shift operations to low-cost areas or away from high-cost ones, with a great incentive (i.e., the lure of increased profits) to do so. This might sound like arbitrage, and it is.

At this point, we can begin focusing on the location effect from an investment perspective.

Size and location are among the "pair-wise" decisions that must be made in constructing a balanced portfolio, and these should be considered together in terms of the location effect. Size-wise, larger-cap stocks represent the biggest public companies, smaller-caps the smallest, and midcaps those companies that fall in between. Companies are usually classified as either large cap, medium cap, small cap , or micro cap, depending on their market capitalization, but the dividing lines are usually arbitrary. As a general guideline, the market capitalization is $5 billion or more for large caps, $1 billion to $5 billion for medium caps, and less than $250 million for micro caps. The market capitalization is based on the value of the outstanding shares. Location-wise, the choice is between international and domestic assets. This is a pretty clear-cut decision when thought of in terms of whether to invest in U.S. companies or businesses based elsewhere around the globe. But the distinction gets a little muddier when you think of, say, a large-cap stock such as Procter & Gamble.

P&G is based in Cincinnati, Ohio, although it has operations throughout the U.S. as well as nearly 80 countries worldwide. Will an economic shock in Ohio—or the U.S., for that matter—affect P&G the way it does a small-cap company that can boast only one plant in that same state? Not at all. Because of its size, P&G can adjust to a shock by sliding operations either toward that shock (if it is a positive one) or away from it (if it is a negative one). The one-plant company in Ohio, meanwhile, must ride out every shock that lands on its location, good or bad.

This idea further extends the concept of elasticity: The inelastic company, this time in terms of its production being fixed in a certain location, will feel the full effect of an economic shock on that location. Conversely, an elastic company, with plants in multiple locations, can move its production either toward good shocks or away from bad ones. In the preceding example, Procter & Gamble, the large-cap company, displays elasticity in terms of location. The one-plant small-cap company exhibits inelasticity.

Sometimes big *is* better. And sometimes small is stuck.

A single-plant company exhibits *immobility* in that it cannot easily relocate its operations to take advantage of a better economic environment. It can and will do so in extreme cases, such as when the negative effects of an economic shock in a location threaten to persist for a very long time. But extremes are not the norm, and often businesses by their nature have few options but to operate right where they are. Think again in terms of an orange. If you were a grower in California during the energy shock, you needed that sunshine (i.e., you weren't about to move your farm elsewhere), although you might have worried about your irrigation systems, which required power to operate.

The basic rules for how companies behave in terms of mobility are similar to those we determined for elasticity:

- Mobile, multiple-plant companies can shift production toward positive shocks and away from negative ones, thus arbitraging differences between prices and regions to their advantage.

- Immobile, single-plant companies must ride out any shock in a location, good or bad, for as long as they decide to operate in that location. Unlike mobile companies, they will realize all the downside of a negative location shock, although they also will realize all the upside of a positive one. (Sometimes small is better.)

Know your shocks, the *locations* they touch, and the *size* of the companies they touch, and you will be well on your way to implementing a successful location-based strategy. Maybe you can begin implementing it now. If you discovered companies in your portfolio with operations based in California at the time of that state's energy crisis, which ones should you have abandoned first, large-caps or small?

Testing and Acting On the Location Effect

If you answered "small," you are correct.

The California energy shock was clearly a negative one, so, in theory, the single-plant small-caps would have underperformed the multiplant large-caps headquartered in the state. Back in 2001, in an attempt to quantify this expected result, my first chore was to separate California's immobile, single-plant businesses from its mobile, multiplant operations. But I was faced with a practical dilemma: How could I determine the number of plants operated by each of California's public companies without spending countless hours on research?

Well, I used a shortcut.

I first looked to the entire S&P 1500 universe—that is, the 1,500 public companies tracked by Standard & Poor's—and from there I extracted all the companies with headquarters in California, 247 in all. After that, I separated the California companies by size (or market capitalization), the idea being that a large-cap company would likely be a multiplant operation (with some out-of-state facilities) and that a small-cap would operate only one or a few facilities (most of which would be anchored in-state). In my California stock basket, I identified 77 large-caps, 106 small-caps, and 64 midcaps. And what did I find out?

Before I show the results, I need to point out that not all economic shocks happen independently. In fact, shocks rarely happen in
isolation. In the California example, while the energy crisis was
spreading mayhem, the stock market was attempting to recover from
the shock of the Internet bubble going "pop." In other words, back in
2001, many tech companies in California had a lot more to worry
about than the lights going out. Thus, if my analysis was to concen-
trate on the impact of the energy crisis on California's public companies, I would have to separate out the tech companies. If not, they
would infect the sample.

With this in mind, Table 6.1 shows what I uncovered for January
to April in 2001 (when the energy crisis was at its height): All of California's companies, tech included, underperformed their respective
benchmarks. (In other words, California large-caps underperformed
the greater universe of large-cap stocks; California small-caps underperformed the greater universe of small-cap stocks; etc.) But company performance, after weeding out the tech companies, worsened
the smaller you went on the size scale: California's *nontech large-cap*
firms performed almost on par with their benchmark (the S&P 500),
while California's *nontech small-cap* firms underperformed their
benchmark (the S&P 600) by more than double.

**TABLE 6.1   Performance of Size-Related Portfolios of Companies Head-
quartered in California During the California Energy Crisis (January 2001
to April 2001)**

	All	**Nontech**	**Benchmark**
Large-cap	−26.15%	−9.53%	−9.73%
Midcap	−8.58%	−11.12%	−7.99%
Small-cap	−10.54%	−12.52%	−5.69%

Source: Research Insight

Taking these negative results together, investors clearly would
have been smart if they had avoided all California companies for the

duration of the energy shock. But the study also confirms the predictability of the location effect: As expected, California's nontech *small-caps* suffered the most.

From these results, we can draw some general investing rules:

The Golden Rules of a Location-Based Investment Strategy

- When a negative shock hits a specific location, most likely all public companies in that location will suffer. However, small-caps very likely will underperform large-caps because they will capture the full downside of the shock.

- When a positive shock lands on a specific location, most likely all public companies in that location will benefit. However, small-caps very likely will outperform large-caps because they will capture the full upside of the shock.

Because you can use a stock's size designation (e.g., large-cap, small-cap, etc.) as a stand-in for whether that stock represents an immobile, single-plant operation or a mobile, multiplant business, this strategy is relatively painless to apply.

A Note on Elasticity (or Flexibility, or Mobility, or…)

Often mitigating factors arise—such as the tech-stock decline in relation to the California energy crisis—when you apply any one investment strategy at any given time. So the idea should be to keep your eyes wide open—but not necessarily for a host of diverse variables. In my opinion, as a good investor, much of what you should be on the lookout for will be similar in nature. You need to identify a location shock, be it a natural disaster, a tax increase, or an energy crisis etc. and then use the multiplant and location approach to identify the companies that will be affected and those that will not be affected by the shock.

I've stated that I am an extreme advocate of the simple, and there's no reason we can't reduce much of what has been discussed so far in this book to a common denominator. The concept of mobility is much like that of elasticity, which I've equated to the idea of flexibility. At this point, I argue that all these terms are, to an extent, interchangeable. Call it what you want, but in the big investing picture, the flexibility, mobility, or elasticity of companies and/or industries most often determines their ability to adjust to, circumvent, or benefit from an economic shock. A bird watcher might look for color, plumage, and shape in identifying a species. But a bird watcher might also take note of how well a bird can fly. In my opinion, this latter case is how a good investor should proceed: Shock to shock, attempt to judge which companies can fly and which are grounded. The investment world will appear somewhat symmetrical, or balanced, when you proceed in this manner.

In economics, as in nature, every shock must have a resolution. A wind blows and a tree bends, but maybe a wind blows and a tree breaks. In the first situation, we have flexibility; in the second, we do not. Companies and industries have a few ways of responding to the economic winds, but the sum of responses is symmetrical—balanced within the larger macroeconomic picture. Sometimes companies reach out with supply to meet a sudden increase in demand, a situation that often means plenty of new competition and a downward pressure on prices. Sometimes companies cannot reach out to meet an increase in demand, but because demand still must be satisfied, prices will rise. In each case, the elasticity (or flexibility or mobility) of any one company in relation to the competition forces it to pass along (either forward to customers or backward to suppliers) the benefits or costs of adverse or positive shocks. In each situation, there is a resolution—and a predictable one when you can grasp the supply-and-demand conditions underlying each movement in price.

Endnotes

1. As described in "Outages Darken Economic Outlook in State, Some Say," *San Diego Union-Tribune,* 22 March 2001.

2. For a detailed account of the Enron debacle, see *Smartest Guys in the Room: The Amazing Rise and Scandalous Fall of Enron,* by Bethany McLean and Peter Elkind (New York: Penguin, 2003).

7

...And France Is a State: How to Invest Internationally in the Age of Globalization

I have argued over the years that markets in the age of globalization are becoming more alike and that prices between localities are coming into balance. That's good news for the world and not-so-good news for investors. We investors like differences. With difference, there is opportunity. Opportunity suggests a chance—a chance to win, or to try to win. But a world in balance smells of everybody doing the same thing all at once, an odor of equal and average performance.

And what's to blame for this global sameness? Two things, predominantly: the emergence of the large-cap multinational corporation and the global push for freer trade. As more locations seek to be competitive in the world marketplace—attracting those mobile, elastic, multiplant large-caps—global tax and regulatory policies are trending lower. This is happening more or less in a coordinated fashion. Across the planet, this means the transportation costs that long divided localities are coming in line, an event that is reflected in an increased parity between global prices.

Parity. There's not much opportunity in that. For starters, if no price differences exist between locations A and B, any prospect for arbitrage between these regions evaporates. Why chase something far away that you can get at home for the very same price? In the age of parity, the same thinking applies to stocks. Why look over an ocean for an investment opportunity that you very well might find at home?

Well, for a couple of reasons.

First, and most importantly, attractive international investment opportunities still can arise when parity is *interrupted*. Markets are not perfect, and shocks do occur—in regions, countries, and individual smaller localities. Basically, these shocks raise or lower transportation costs, causing a disparity between the purchasing power of currencies and the relative value of assets between regions. As I see it, this is *the* case for investing internationally in the age of globalization, and it's from here that we can build a prudent international strategy.

However, a second, and certainly more fashionable, rationale exists for investing around the globe. If today you opened an account with a reputable financial-management firm, at some point your advisor would discuss the importance of international diversification. By diversification, the advisor here refers to the practice of international investing as a way of reducing risk in a portfolio. Just as you want to be invested in different classes of stocks and bonds, so as never to feel the full downside when one asset class performs poorly (a topic we address in greater detail in Chapter 8, "Pipelines to Our Investment Returns: How We Get What We Want, in the Amount We Want, and When We Want It"), international investing arguably provides one more level of diversification, or risk reduction.

I agree with this, but only to a certain level. Unlike the typical financial advisor, I argue that international investing provides *opportunities* for risk reduction. As stated, with trade barriers dropping and economic integration on the upswing, prices are equalizing across the globe. This clearly means that, in the bigger picture, the diversification effect of international investing is on the decline. However, in the smaller picture—region to region and shock to shock—the international diversification story is alive and well.

Here we switch from defense to offense in terms of the location effect. In the last chapter, we developed a defensive play: A negative shock occurred, one that generally would bring down all stocks in the infected region. The defensive move was based on the idea that the smaller, less-mobile, location-fixed companies would suffer the most. Playing defense, we would avoid these stocks at all costs. The difference in prices between regions, however, switches us to the offensive mode—in effect, turning us into arbitragers who take advantage of price disparities whenever they arise and wherever they exist.

That said, I hope to simplify the international investment process in the pages ahead. Our new phrase is *purchasing power parity* (PPP), which basically is a measure of the relative purchasing power of global currencies. PPP is something of a dry acronym, but it comes to life when thought of in terms of hamburgers. Yes, hamburgers. Flashing forward, when parity exists between the prices of Big Macs in different regions, we can say there is no investment opportunity. But when a Big Mac in Location A is pricier than one in Location B, we can go on the offense.

International investing can be just this straightforward, but only if you track the shocks that bring about differences in price.

Countries versus States: An Alternative Perspective

In the last chapter, I was able to separate California from the rest of the U.S. not just because of its size and integrated economy, but also because the government in that state acted independently by placing a large regulatory burden on its power utilities. In other words, California determined California's behavior.

This is an important point. As investors, we are interested in the behavior of stocks. In terms of location, we are interested in the behavior of locations. Sometimes a location acts just like a country; it asserts a level of independence whereby it holds its economic fate in its own hands. And sometimes a location acts just like a state, beholden to the policies of a larger governing union. Such a location can, by definition, be a state, but it also can be a country or a group of countries.

Take France, for instance.

France ranks as the fifth-largest country in the world in terms of economic output, while the "country" of California ranks eighth.[1] But this does not necessarily mean that France is any more of a country than is California. Over the past decade, France increasingly has acted more like a state within a larger governing region: the European Union. The EU now lists 25 members, all of which must abide by a certain set of economic rules. This development in general has been a positive for EU members. Trade barriers have lowered, and individuals, companies, and factors of production within the EU territory have displayed increased mobility.

In this scheme, France—a cog in a larger machine—exhibits stateness. In the last chapter, California—large and integrated, yet independent—exhibited countryness.

The lesson here is that to fully understand and react to location-specific shocks, you should erase the borders on your globe as they are currently drawn. From there, you want to redraw borders based on the levels of transportation costs (or the levels of friction) that exist between regions when economic shocks occur.

Because these costs are readily knowable, redrawing borders is not much of a chore.

Hamburgers and the Power of Prices

In the introduction to this book, I asked, "What can an increase or decrease in the price of something tell us about the profits that thing is generating or the quantities of it that are being transacted?" And my answer was, and still is, "Not very much." However, in the context of the location effect, important information is embedded in the *differences* in prices between regions. Without transaction costs, you would expect that identical commodities would fetch the same price in different localities; if they don't, a profit opportunity will occur. Arbitrage will ensure that the differences are eliminated and the prices will be equalized. This is known as the law of one price.

When economists or financial analysts measure purchasing power parity, or "the law of one price," they are gathering price information using a very simple method: comparison. Because countries use different currencies, PPP measures the relative purchasing power of the various world currencies. Parity fails to occur when the purchasing power of currencies differs—when, for instance, the U.S. dollar and the British pound (adjusted into dollars) can purchase differing amounts of a given good.

Consider, for example, a hamburger.

In a very clever article two decades ago, *The Economist* magazine introduced an innovative measure of purchasing power parity. This indicator, an index that has been published annually since its inception in 1986, is the price in local currencies of a McDonald's Big Mac hamburger.[2]

Here's the theory: In an idealized, frictionless world—one without transportation costs, regulations, taxes, and the like (think of an air hockey table that's on full blast)—the price of a Big Mac is the same everywhere. In reality, however, transportation costs, taxes, and regulations alter the friction between regions and bring about differences in the price of a Big Mac. Thus, Big Mac prices, at differing times and to various degrees, must be different location to location across the globe.

How different? For a sense of scale, here's a recent (and partial) snapshot of the Big Mac index (see Table 7.1):[3]

TABLE 7.1   The Big Mac Index

Region/Country	Big Mac Price
Switzerland	$4.93
Denmark	$4.49
Sweden	$4.28
Euro Area	$3.51
Britain	$3.32
United States	$3.15
New Zealand	$3.08
Turkey	$3.07
Canada	$3.01
Chile	$2.98
Brazil	$2.74
Hungary	$2.71
Mexico	$2.66
Czech Republic	$2.60
South Korea	$2.56
Australia	$2.44

When this measure was first conceived, the authors argued that, given the standardization of a McDonald's Big Mac (two all-beef patties, special sauce, lettuce, cheese, etc.), price differences between the burger, location to location, would give investors a quick and reliable measure of the differences in PPP across locations. This indicator thus could be used to identify the overvalued and undervalued economies of the world. However, what interests me is what *causes* these differences in prices. For instance, at the time this Big Mac snapshot was taken, I'd have wanted to know why Switzerland was cooking up such an expensive hamburger, or why Australia could do it at half the price.

In asking the "why" questions, we are inquiring about economic shocks. And in answering them, we'll know just how to invest.

The Search for Expensive Big Macs

Markets are not perfectly correlated, nor are prices; the price of a Big Mac is not, and likely never will be in our lifetimes, fully equalized across regions. In formal terms, this means that PPP is not complete and that international investing will still produce some additional diversification within a portfolio.

To take advantage of this opportunity, our guideline for success again combines the location effect and the size choice. Interestingly, in the example of the California energy crisis, the correct defensive move was to lean away from small-cap stocks. But when playing offense in terms of location, you want to lean *toward* small-caps, which exhibit the least physical mobility of all public companies.

This process has you gathering two pieces of information. First you want to know the nature of an economic shock: Is it positive or negative? Second, you want to know the price of a Big Mac: Is it high or low relative to Big Macs in other locations?

Here's how the process breaks down: In most cases, countries (or global locations) that adopt lower levels of taxation and regulation witness higher economic growth and higher rates of return.[4] This is a positive event that, for a time, results in a violation of PPP. Because a reduction in taxes and/or regulations represents a positive shock, the violation of PPP will be upward in the location that underwent the shock: *The price of a Big Mac will climb.*

And here's a closer look at why: In prosperous places, the demand for immobile factors of production is high and the returns for those factors tend to be above average. The Big Mac is not necessarily an immobile factor because it is a food source that technically can be imported. However, locally and logically speaking, the Big Mac has to be cooked somewhere, a fixed place where rent and wages have to be paid. Meanwhile, rent and wages in prosperous areas are likely relatively high because people have a strong desire to live and work in such places. Over time, these higher prices will attract investment, which, in turn, will increase supply. Finally, when that new supply is established, prices will return to their long-run trajectories.

Such is the cyclical nature of arbitrage: After an initial shock brings about a disturbance in prices, an influx of capital restores the long-run equilibrium of prices. In Big Mac terms, a location undergoing a positive shock will experience an increase in prosperity that will be reflected in greater earning power, particularly for the least mobile factors of production. This violation of PPP is a window of opportunity for the international investor, and a rule we established earlier again can be applied:

> When a positive shock impacts a specific location, most likely all public companies in that location will benefit. However, (immobile) small-caps very likely will outperform large-caps as they will capture the full upside of the shock.

But this rule takes on a nuanced flavor when described in hamburger terms:

> Invest in places where the price of a Big Mac is high and considered expensive, favoring (immobile) small-caps in these locations.

Internationally, these windows of opportunity open and close all the time. Capital is mobile and tends to flow to areas where it will see the highest return. If a positive shock makes the return for capital higher in a location, capital will stream toward that location. Eventually, however, as capital flows change to bring about economic equilibrium, higher rates of return will be eliminated and PPP will be restored.

But the window of investment opportunity (the temporary deviation from PPP) will remain open for as long as policy shocks make one region more attractive for investment than another. At this point, you'll want to play offense with the location effect, chasing down those pricey Big Macs.

When to Own International Stocks, Large and Small

At this point, capturing the location effect appears to be a small-cap investor's activity. To a good degree, it is. Looking internationally, you want to shift toward small-caps undergoing positive economic shocks and away from small-caps experiencing negative shocks. But that doesn't mean you shouldn't have international large-caps in your portfolio.

As noted, professional financial advisors often recommend international investing as a way to reduce portfolio risk. And a big reason for this is that large-cap international stocks are an insurance policy against negative localized shocks. Because they are so big and so mobile, they feel the good and bad of economic shocks worldwide, although they will never experience all of the bad or all of the good.

I agree that this is a good argument for an investor to have some exposure to international large-caps. But when selecting from this asset class, you want to be thinking elastically: Choose large-cap international stocks by focusing on the industries they are in and the elasticities and betas of those industries in relation to the economic environment (as discussed in Chapters 4, "Catch Elasticity If You Can: An Introduction to Industry Behavior," and 5, "Putting High-Beta to Work: Industry-Based Portfolio Strategies").

I always stress that there is a time and place for everything. Sometimes you want those international large-caps in your portfolio, and at other times not. The same holds for small-caps. But if the boon of international investing, as it is discussed today, is to add another level of risk reduction to a portfolio, shouldn't investors always own *some* international stocks, whether large-cap or small?

Not necessarily. For instance, if your home stock market is reasonably diversified and a level of purchasing power parity exists between major world currencies, why would you look to invest elsewhere? Markets in this case would be somewhat correlated, at which point you can make things a little easier on yourself by simply looking for the best domestic industries in which to invest your money. Conversely, when PPP does not hold, turn back to international. Just be sure you are identifying the shocks (positive or negative) that cause those violations to PPP.

Putting together everything we've discussed so far in terms of the location effect, we can draw some international investment rules relative to the size of stocks:

When to Own International Small-Cap Stocks

- When positive shocks impact locations, buy small-cap stocks in those locations. This will put you in the best position to gain all the upside a positive location shock has to offer.

- When PPP does not hold—meaning disparity exists between the exchange rates of currencies and the markets are not correlated—favor small-cap stocks in the regions where the local currency has strengthened.[5]

When to Own International Large-Cap Stocks

- Investing in international large-cap stocks should be based on an analysis of industries that are abundant across nations. (If not abundant, meaning their facilities are concentrated in only a few areas, they might be inescapably tied to a region that could be infected by a negative shock.) Choose these stocks based on an understanding of the elasticities and betas of industries in relation to the economic environment.

- Do not go out of your way to buy international large-cap stocks when owning large-cap domestic stocks will offer you just as much diversification. This will be the case when PPP holds (or, in other words, when markets are highly correlated).

Playing Offense on the Pacific Rim

Little in this book isn't shock-based. Shocks are the starting point from which you should make all your investment decisions. There's work involved in this: You need to understand the nature of each shock you encounter while grasping how different shocks affect different industries. And there's no getting off the hook when it comes to an international strategy: Because the location effect alters the performance of small-cap stocks to the highest degree, you have to keep track of changes to tax, regulatory, and monetary policies (the shocks themselves) region to region across the globe. This *is* work, but it's not *that* much work.

Other than natural disasters and other unpredictable events, the great thing about economic shocks is that they're so easy to anticipate—even from the point of view of you, sitting in your chair, a solitary speck on the surface of this planet. To see an international shock coming, all you usually need to do is read the newspapers—or surf the Internet, or do whatever you do in the digital age to stay informed. Here's an example:

Not so long ago, the news was that Japan was going to lower marginal tax rates. This information was in the newspapers and on the Internet, and was a topic of conversation on financial TV. As I've noted, a suddenly lower tax burden most likely will represent a positive economic shock. In Japan's case, marginal tax rates were being lowered from about 65 percent to 50 percent, which is a very strong incentive for Japanese companies to change their behavior. In particular, they could take advantage of higher after-tax cash flows by increasing production and therefore profits. This is exactly what happened, and it was easily predictable if you 1) kept current on world events and 2) understood that lower marginal tax rates bring about increased economic activity.

Here's how a savvy investor would have taken advantage of this situation. Theoretically, a Japanese large-cap company with, say, 20 percent of its operations in the country would see 20 percent of its total operations benefit from a positive shock. Meanwhile, a Japanese small-cap company with 100 percent of its operations in the country would benefit by 100 percent. That's the theory, and did it hold up? Indeed. In 1999, following the arrival of the tax cuts, the total Japanese stock market climbed near 50 percent. The Japanese small-cap market? It soared *by more than 100 percent.*

The Rewards of Doing Your Homework

It took some effort to understand that small-caps were the way to go in Japan in 1999. You had to read the newspapers and know that small-caps and positive economic shocks go together—say, like burgers and buns. But in doing so, you would have separated yourself from those who invested broadly in Japan—the crowd that climbed 50 percent with the market. That's pretty good, but a 100 percent gain is worlds better. You also had to do some work to understand that small-caps were going to tank in California in 2001. You had to read the newspapers and know that small-caps and negative shocks go together more like oil and water. If you did so, however, you would have been able to weed out some ugly underperformance from your portfolio.

Applying the location strategy, or any strategy outlined in this book, requires you to be well informed on current events and have a sound understanding of the inherent elasticities of industries and companies shock to shock. Whether you are playing defense or offense, the extra effort is decidedly worth it.

Endnotes

1. The Los Angeles County Economic Development Corp. set the gross product (in billions of dollars) for France at $2,018.1 and for California at $1,524.9, as per 2004 data. The U.S. ranked first, at $11,733.5.

2. *The Economist* magazine publishes its Big Mac index annually, and throughout any year, many world publications reference it. Indeed, the index, conceived as an informal way to discuss PPP, has become a widely accepted tool for measuring the purchasing power of currencies location to location around the globe. A more advanced way to apply the location-based strategy, in regard to temporary deviations from PPP, would be to take advantage of changes in real rates of return across countries: Use real (inflation-adjusted) exchange rates as the appropriate framework of analysis during a fixed-exchange-rate period (or a period when one currency is fixed, or pegged, to another). That said, in your search for PPP and violations of PPP, you won't go wrong if you stick with hamburgers.

3. "Big Mac index," *The Economist*, 14–20 January, 2006, p. 102.

4. The macroeconomic analyses contained in this book are not dependent on a person's political leanings; correct big-picture viewpoints will lead all investors toward enhanced net worth, regardless of political stripe. For example, you might not

advocate reducing the tax burden on all taxpayers, preferring instead that taxes be reduced on lower-wage earners and held in place for higher-wage earners. This is fine if this is your political and/or economic position. But if your aim is to rank among the most successful investors, you need to accept things simply as they are. For example, tax increases in general lead to lower economic growth; tax cuts bring on higher economic growth.

5. Large-caps, such as Procter & Gamble, capture some of the upside when positive localized shocks occur, as well as a degree of the downside when localized shocks are negative. But importantly, in arbitraging these differences between regions, they help bring markets back toward equilibrium, or PPP. In this way, large-caps help close the investment windows that open for small-caps in the wake of positive regional shocks.

8

Pipelines to Our Investment Returns: How We Get What We Want, in the Amount We Want, and When We Want It

Why are you reading this book? I assume it's because you want to make money through your investments, and perhaps more money than the average Jane or Joe. That's good, and it shows decisiveness. And if you don't mind, I'd say it reveals an admirable distance from emotion. Our emotions have their place, but they can get in the way of an investment strategy. When purely thought of in terms of our motivations, investing is a pragmatic venture. Pragmatism focuses on the ends, not the means, and emotions need not apply. At this point, you should have a grasp of just how important those means can be. But let's be honest: We involve ourselves in investing because we desire the ends, because we want results. We want money, wealth, financial independence, a sound retirement, prosperity—whatever you want to call it. We want returns.

In this chapter and the two that follow, we focus specifically on those returns. Working backward, in Chapter 10, "Your Benchmark Portfolio…and Beyond," we construct a benchmark portfolio, the starting point and hub of activity for all investors, from the beginner to the most expert. Here we act sensibly: If we seek above-average performance or above-average returns, average is a good place to start. In Chapter 9, "Who Are You? Investor Profiles and the Case for Asset Allocation," we usher in a little psychology. As an investor, who are you and what do you want to be? To answer this, we must weigh risk against return. At this point, I offer a formula that puts these two in the most advantageous balance for the long run.

As for now, we act like good pragmatists in this chapter, focusing specifically on the return. Returns, simply, are the dollars we earn through our investments. And you know what? Within the limits of the law, we really don't care how we get 'em. We just want 'em. This is an obvious, though significant, truth. At the outset, we want the price of the investments that will generate our returns to be low, with the idea that the price will move higher. But how much do we really care about these investments that will deliver our returns? Pragmatically, we shouldn't care all that much. This brings us to the concept of *derived demand:* Our demand for the vehicles we invest in is really a demand for the returns these vehicles can generate. And what about the flow of these returns? In the best-case scenario, we want that flow to be *uninterrupted.* And how do we guarantee that this flow, to the greatest degree possible, will be uninterrupted—or, to use another investment term, that it will arrive in the most *efficient* manner possible? Simply, we *diversify.*

I've waited until this point of the book to discuss the return because I wanted you, the reader, first to be grounded in the laws of supply and demand. Returns—and their delivery vehicles—are subject to the same rules that apply to the trade of material goods and the prices of those goods. With this in mind, over the years I have found that the best way to discuss the investor return, the various return-generating vehicles, and the flow of these returns is to talk energy, discussing many of the supply-and-demand dramas that go on behind the scenes of this sector. I employ this analogy to full extent in this chapter and the next two, with the idea of placing our pursuit of the return in a very pragmatic light.

Here's a quick parallel to get us started: What if one day you were driving along just fine with a full tank of gas, but the next day you were stuck on the road with an empty tank? Would you say this describes an optimal situation? I would hope not. Similarly, I don't think it's optimal to have a large sum of money in a portfolio one day, only to lose a good portion of it the next. And yet, year to year or cycle to cycle, this happens all the time, if only because, in adhering to the long-run upward trend of the market, most of us understand that today's loss will be tomorrow's gain. But I argue for more; I argue for a smoother and more regular flow of returns into our lives, a process that will generate returns sufficient enough to maximize both our well-beings and the quality of our lifestyles.

Can this be achieved? I'm certain of it—and a quick tour of the fuels that power our lives and the energy sector at large provides unique and ample evidence that it can.

Our Pragmatic Relationship with the Investment Return

Throughout history, mankind's relationship with fuel has been quite rational. Early man was drawn to fire, and thus to wood, which cooked well and warmed well. Then in the middle 1800s, when technology made it feasible to burn other fuels efficiently, mankind turned to coal, an abundant fuel that was soon joined by natural gas and oil.

In a mere 150 years, coal, oil, and natural gas have taken over. Today these three account for roughly 80 percent of the world's total fuel consumption. Yet nothing intrinsic changed as we adapted to new fuel technologies. Whether we burn wood, coal, oil, or gas, we're doing the same thing: We're creating energy—or, more specifically, BTUs. The BTU, or British Thermal Unit, is the amount of heat it takes to raise the temperature of 1 pound of water 1° F. A BTU is energy, a thing modern man cannot do without. And one BTU is about as good as another.

As consumers of energy, we are less concerned about what generates it as we are with how much it costs and how readily available it is. Some of us choose the direct on-site burning of the fuels that will produce our coveted BTUs, while others opt for the indirect method of buying the BTU-making electricity that is generated from various fuels. Either way, this is derived demand. We desire the BTU, the final product, which is reflected in the demand for the source of that product: fuel.[1]

Technology is a wonderful thing. It allows us to burn a wider variety of fuels while also increasing our ability to produce more goods and services with that energy. If our relationship with energy were irrational—and, hence, addictive in nature—why, as a country, would we use less energy the larger we grow?

There's a *downward* secular trend in the ratio of total BTUs consumed in the U.S. per unit of gross domestic product (see Figure 8.1). This trend has accelerated since the 1970s, with our BTU consumption plummeting across the OPEC decades that have been marked by higher energy prices. Importantly, this reflects a steady improvement in the energy efficiency of the U.S. economy. What's more efficient than getting more (growth) out of less (energy)?

FIGURE 8.1

This efficiency is evident not only over time, but each time there is a periodic shift in energy prices. For instance, real (inflation-adjusted) changes in the price of oil have shared a negative (or oppositional) relationship with the consumption of BTUs per unit of GDP (Figure 8.2).[2] In particular, as the price of oil has risen, the energy efficiency of the U.S. economy has improved. This is clear evidence of an economy and a populace that responds appropriately to market signals: We will squeeze more out of less when it is economical for us to do so.

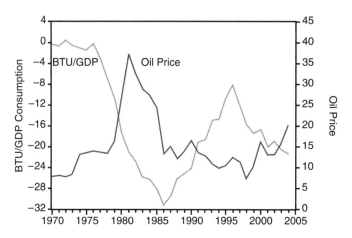

FIGURE 8.2   Percent Change in the Inflation Adjusted Price of Oil Versus Percent Change in the Decade-Long BTU/GDP Ratio

The data confirms our very rational relationship with fuel in general and with the BTU in particular. Not surprisingly, this is the same level of rationality exhibited by many an investor. Think of it: Any way it is derived, the BTU is the result—it is energy, what consumers want and need and will rationally acquire by way of a number of fuel sources. Similarly, think for a moment about the investment return. If you invest $1 and it becomes $2, you earned $1, which was the return that drove you to invest in the first place.

But to get that return, you had to rationally select from a broad number of return-generating investment vehicles, just as modern man selects from a wide menu of fuels. Any one stock or bond can produce a return, and investors have several thousand of these available. Then there's the return-generating world of investment funds, such as mutual funds, exchange-traded funds, and hedge funds, all of which are built in terms of specific investment styles and mandates and are attached to varying degrees of cost and risk.

But which ones are for you? Pragmatically, you want to purchase the ones that will get you what you want, in the amount you want, and when you want it.

As investors, we attempt to organize our portfolios so that returns—convertible to real money—can flow to them in an uninterrupted way. Additionally, the higher and less volatile the flow of these returns, the better the quality of our lifestyles—that is, if we equate enhanced wealth with a better lifestyle. But the key term in this comparison is *uninterrupted*. We don't really care how our returns get to us—just that they get to us. So when it comes to building a responsible investment portfolio, the mandate from the outset must be to mitigate the potential for the flow of returns to be interrupted—to lessen the risk of not having enough at any one time, to minimize the volatility of delivery, to maximize the amount delivered.

Interruption, as one well-known BTU carrier explains it, can be disastrous.

The Case for Diversification

The term *diversification* has become synonymous with investing. It simply refers to the practice of purchasing many different types of assets across many industries and countries as a sure way of reducing risk within a portfolio. Being undiversified, on the other hand, can be a formula for failure.

The Trans-Alaska Pipeline describes this very well.

Basically, this pipeline is an 800-mile tube that moves a commodity from Point A to Point B, from Alaska's North Slope to the state's southern Port of Valdez. And the process involves risk—namely, supply has been vulnerable to disruption. For instance, an October 4, 2001, an intoxicated man shot a hole through the pipeline with his .338 caliber rifle, creating a "geyser" that spit 260,000 gallons of crude oil onto the tundra. The pipeline had been built to withstand many shocks—among them earthquakes and even the occasional errant rifle shot—but that October, all it took was one well-placed bullet to put it out of service for a long three days.[3]

At the time, the pipeline accounted for 17 percent of domestic oil production, so the disruption was not insignificant in relation to the domestic portion of the U.S. oil "portfolio." However, that portfolio also has a very large international component, famously (or infamously) fed by the OPEC nations, among several other oil-endowed countries. Thus, back in 2001, the Alaska pipeline disruption was but a blip inside the total oil portfolio of the United States. However, had the U.S. been dependent on Alaska oil—that is, had the U.S. oil portfolio been highly *undiversified*—a three-day disruption would have been catastrophic. The investing equivalent might be a portfolio built of shares of one stock, or a group of stocks in one industry that originate from one location. (As discussed in previous chapters, the latter tend to move in unison and are highly susceptible to negative local shocks.)

Politicians have long discussed the need for America to reduce its dependency on foreign oil, but the Alaska incident makes a slightly different point. To employ the cliché, it is never good to put all your eggs in one basket.

In Search of Your Efficient Frontier

Two questions, or themes, arise out of this. First, how do investors build truly diversified portfolios, ones that will best connect to the various sources of returns while mitigating the effects of those adverse shocks—those random-bullet or wear-and-tear corruptions—that will interrupt the flow of those returns? Second, how can investors adjust their portfolios when adverse shocks threaten to puncture their return-carrying pipelines?

This latter question regards the central theme of this book; answering it is a lifetime story, whereby investors adjust to the macroeconomic events that cause predictable shifts in the return performance of the various asset classes. The former question addresses the starting point to this process: To capture returns in a responsible manner, each investor must construct a portfolio that connects to several of the various return-generating sources.

Elementary? Yes. But you might be surprised by the number of investors who get this initial step wrong. Looking up at a stock board, long-term investors should never really have moments when they scream "Argh!" and begin pulling out their hair, moments when a single "bullet" has interrupted the flow of their returns. A well-diversified portfolio protects against such events.

To extend the pipeline analogy, the well-diversified portfolio that seeks long-term gains must be built of *many* pipelines that connect to *several* alternative sources of returns. These sources are our fuels— from the single stock to the specific asset class—while those pipelines are our investment strategies. A portfolio built in this manner not only attains diversification—and, hence a reduction in the chance that the flow of returns will be interrupted—but also has the unique capability to maximize the flow of returns, which I believe is possible (and probable) by switching between investment strategies at the appropriate times.

The numerous and distinct pipelines to our investment returns are attached to varying levels of risk and, hence, different levels of potential disruption. Importantly, above a certain level of return flow, the higher the potential *rate* of flow is, the greater the likelihood of disruption is.

Modern financial advisors understand this well, and for the benefit of clients, they often map out all the possible combinations of return-carrying pipelines that can be positioned within a portfolio. In doing so, they come up with what they deem to be the most efficient tradeoff between the potential flow of returns and the potential disruptions. They call this compromise the *efficient frontier.* Specifically, financial advisors choose a point that represents the tradeoff between return flow and return disruption, personalizing this decision by weighing the costs associated with disruption and the marginal benefits of the higher flow of returns. In the end, they present their clients with an efficient path to their investment goals over time.

This *is* an efficient process. But to understand how a thing functions in the best of times, we often need to reflect on how it performed during the worst of times. Energy narrates the diversification story very well, but it does so particularly well in the context of the 1970s. At few times in American history has the free flow of energy been more at risk.

Shock Study: That '70s Show

In his television address of April 18, 1977, President Jimmy Carter, outfitted in his trademark cardigan sweater, told the nation that the world was running out of oil. He said the call of the moment was akin to a "moral equivalent of war" and said that disaster would ensue if Americans did not alter their energy-consuming ways dramatically. To the economist, it was clear that Carter perceived a consumption problem and thus suggested a consumption solution. To most everyone else, Carter's message was nearly equal to the one we now attribute to President George W. Bush: Americans were "addicted to oil."

But by 1977, as anyone who sat in a gas line during that decade can attest, Americans were all too familiar with the rhetoric of energy-crisis wartime.[4]

Oil, among other fuels, was a highly regulated commodity in the U.S. in the 1970s, subject to strict price caps, or ceilings. In economist terms, price ceilings inevitably lead to shortages because they lower the incentive to produce the goods that are capped. Put another way, there's little motivation for companies to chase profits that do not exist. As the demand for a commodity increases in this environment, the ceiling becomes binding and no supply is forthcoming from the regulated suppliers. The only way for incremental demand to be satisfied, or the shortage to be resolved, is for another supplier to be willing and able to produce.

In the 1970s, energy-price controls in the U.S. restricted domestic supply and inadvertently diverted all the incremental supply to that willing and able supplier: the foreign producer and, in particular, OPEC. As OPEC became aware of the supply-and-demand realities in the U.S., it figured correctly that there would be no alternative to OPEC oil in the short run. The U.S. would simply have to pay up or do without the oil.

Once again, this is a single-pipeline story. For instance, oil makes gas, which makes cars go. When there is a major oil shortage and, hence, a major gasoline shortage, drivers can either not drive or deal with the realities at the pump (long lines, high prices, etc.). But the plot thickens when we move to the home, business, and industrial fronts.

Back in the 1970s, oil came by way of the oil truck (as it still does), which fed the fuel into the storage tanks that attached to the individual boilers in the basements of American homes and businesses. As mentioned, domestically produced oil was a price-capped commodity, which only made a scarce commodity that much scarcer. Meanwhile, natural gas was fed via pipelines from the wellhead source to distribution plants, which then sent the gas via smaller pipelines to individual properties. (This is still the case.) But the free flow of natural gas was inhibited by artificially low price ceilings on sales of the fuel across state lines. To make matters worse, the artificially low price created demand in excess of the forthcoming supply.

As a result, to "ration" the available supply, the government set moratoriums on the number of homes and businesses that could "hook up" to natural-gas lines. By the mid-1970s, for example, there were restrictions on residential hookups in nearly half of all gas-utility franchise areas. Such non-price-rationing schemes, in the name of conservation, blocked an alternative source of energy from feeding homes, businesses, and factories alike.

However, none of this meant consumer demand for energy had lessened.

Demand would also be met, if not *directly* via the fuel pipeline that fed the individual boiler, then *indirectly* via the generation of electricity, a prepackaged and highly versatile source of power.

Coal, oil, natural gas, hydropower, and nuclear power—a menu not available to any one end consumer—could all feed the generating facilities. On the demand side of the equation, this meant *risk reduction:* Several fuels could now produce the same energy for the end consumer. It also meant *guaranteed service* at a competitive price: Unlike the end consumer, the electricity facilities could burn multiple fuels, could arbitrage the costs of generating power across fuels, and were freed from the curse of being shut out of any one fuel market. If they could not buy Fuel A, they would simply shift to Fuel B. And unlike the vast majority of end consumers, they could burn coal, an abundant fuel limited to only the largest industrial generators and boilers.

The ultimate result of all this? Between 1970 and 1980, consumption of electricity increased from 24 percent to 31 percent of the nation's total (see Table 8.1).

Table 8.1   U.S. Energy Consumption by Sector (in Quadrillion BTUs)

	1950	1960	1970	1980
Residential and Commercial	7.70 (22%)	9.4 (21%)	12.5 (18%)	11.6 (15%)
Industrial	13.8 (40%)	17.0 (38%)	23.0 (34%)	22.7 (29%)
Transportation	8.4 (24%)	10.6 (23%)	16.1 (24%)	19.7 (25%)
ELECTRICITY	4.7 (14%)	8.2 (18%)	16.3 (24%)	24.4 (31%)

	1990	2000	2004
Residential and Commercial	10.5 (12%)	11.4 (12%)	11.1 (11%)
Industrial	21.2 (25%)	22.8 (23%)	22.1 (22%)
Transportation	22.4 (27%)	26.5 (27%)	27.7 (28%)
ELECTRICITY	30.7 (36%)	38.2 (38%)	38.9 (39%)

Source: Energy Information Administration, Annual Energy Review

However, energy demand—broken down by the transportation, residential/commercial, and industrial sectors—held relatively *constant* throughout the period (see Table 8.2). This is a central point: Although regulations altered 1) the way consumers obtained their energy, 2) the prices paid for that energy, and 3) the methods of delivering that energy, they did not in any significant way alter the amount of energy being consumed.

Table 8.2   U.S. Energy Demand by Final Consumers (in Quadrillion BTUs)

	1970	1975	1980	1985
Residential and Commercial	22.1 (**32%**)	24.3 (**34%**)	26.4 (**34%**)	27.5 (36%)
Industrial	29.6 (**44%**)	29.5 (**41%**)	35.2 (**41%**)	28.9 (38%)
Transportation	16.1 (**24%**)	18.2 (**25%**)	19.7 (**25%**)	20.1 (26%)
Total	67.8 (**100%**)	72.0 (**100%**)	81.3 (**100%**)	76.5 (100%)

	1990	1995	2000	2004
Residential and Commercial	30.4 (36%)	33.4 (37%)	37.7 (38%)	38.7 (39%)
Industrial	31.9 (38%)	34.1 (37%)	34.7 (35%)	33.2 (33%)
Transportation	22.4 (26%)	23.8 (26%)	26.6 (27%)	27.8 (28%)
Total	84.70 (100%)	91.30 (100%)	99.00 (100%)	99.70 (100%)

Source: Energy Information Administration, Annual Energy Review

In the end, by buying electricity, consumers let the electricity-generating facilities worry about the availability of the different fuels. Consumers wanted their power, just as the electric utilities wanted to deliver it to them. In each case, pragmatic pursuits of an end result won the day.

The Energy-Return Parallels

Pragmatism accounted for, this shock study elevates in usefulness because of the near one-to-one relationship between mankind's acquisition of energy and the investor return.

The case can be made, however, that we are much more efficient in our pursuit of energy than we are of the return.

> **Energy:** As consumers, we adjust to ensure that our desired ends (energy) continue to flow to us in an uninterrupted (as well as cost-efficient) way.

Returns: It is safe to say that most investors desire an uninterrupted flow of returns. It's also safe to say that, as a group, we show a variable degree of willingness to adjust our allocations to maintain a steady flow of returns.

Energy: The persistent demand for energy has had the net effect of continuing the trend toward the indirect burning of fuel—i.e., electricity generation—as opposed to direct burning.

Returns: In recent decades, investors have turned decidedly "indirect" in their pursuit of the return. Much of this has to do with the arrival of *modern portfolio theory,* which basically is the idea that investor risk is lessened through the purchase of diverse assets or asset classes. Importantly, not all indirect schemes are built alike.

Energy: On the production end, energy providers will arbitrage the cost per BTU across different fuels and thus maximize profits per each BTU delivered.

Returns: On the management end, financial professionals strive to maximize profits for their funds and clients by assembling what they deem to be the optimal mix of return-generating vehicles. However, the levels to which they strive, as well as the levels to which they succeed, can vary greatly.

Energy: Cost is inextricably tied to the level of demand for each possible energy-generating vehicle. For instance, the small use of coal for heating the home or office is easily explained by the fact that, due to economies of scale, coal-burning is more expensive than the direct burning of natural gas or oil.

Returns: Cost is inextricably tied to the level of demand for each possible return-generating vehicle. For instance, investments with higher relative costs of entry will attract relatively few participants, although the returns these investments generate can be quite substantial.

Energy: Production costs (which include the costs associated with implementing various technologies), transportation costs, and the costs related to government regulation all play a major role in the levels of demand for different fuels.

Returns: On the investing stage, these very same costs go a long way toward determining not only how we as investors behave, but also how the demand for the various vehicles we invest in fluctuates over time.

Energy: The substitutability of the various fuels increases when regulations and/or environmental controls are relaxed, as does the attractiveness of the cheaper fuels (e.g., crude oil) over the cleanest (e.g., natural gas). Basically, when transaction (or transportation) costs lower, our menu of options expands. And because as a populace we exhibit a pragmatic relationship with fuel—we desire most of all what it gives us (energy)—as a group, we will choose the cheapest fuel options.

Returns: When the transaction costs attached to investing are relatively low, investment activity (and the substitutability between the various return-generating vehicles) will increase. In other words, we get "busier" when investing is a lower-cost activity.

Energy: Although coal and natural gas are substitutes for oil in industrial, residential, and commercial applications, they cannot substitute for oil in the transportation sector. Simply, most cars run on gas. Not surprisingly, the price of gasoline is much more volatile than the price of other final fuels (as we saw in the 1970s and witnessed again through the early part of the new century).

Returns: Restrictions go a long way toward limiting the substitutability of the various return-generating vehicles. Think of a fund manager who is limited to investing only in large-cap stocks. This manager's fund will exhibit a great deal more volatility than funds that have no such asset-class mandates.

I could build more parallels between energy and the return. And I make several of the parallels drawn here more specific in the next chapter, when we discuss the several ways modern investors go about obtaining their returns. But you get the idea. When it comes to getting what we want, in the amount we want, and when we want it, we tend to act very pragmatically—substituting different means to attain our ends. But again, investors overall have a lot to learn from the typical consumer of energy.

"Addicted to Asset Classes?"

The next time a politician says you are "addicted to oil," I hope you will understand this accusation to be patently false. Indeed, as automotive technology advances, "addicted to hydrogen" or "addicted to ethanol" might enter the political lexicon. But these statements also will ring artificial. When it comes to energy, consumers have proven that the ends matter, not the means.

Truth be told, however, investors too often show an allegiance to the means.

Imagine, for instance, that someone said American investors were "addicted to large-caps" or "addicted to ETFs" or "addicted to bonds" or addicted to "Microsoft." At this point, I would hope such accusations would sound bizarre to you. If anything, we are, or should be, addicted to the return. However, in each of these fictional accusations, there is some truth. In the pursuit of getting what we want, in the amount we want, and when we want it, we often make compromises. Some of us do so willingly, while others of us do so because we don't know any better.

From here, we shift our study of the return from the theoretical to the practical level. Few investors act alike, but most fall into distinct behavioral groups. Which group is for you? In the next chapter, I steer you toward the optimal answer.

Endnotes

1. Victor Canto, "Fuel Use Patterns in the United States: The Outlook for the 1980s," *Oil and Gas Journal* 80, no. 34, 23 August 1982, 125–143. "The Shape of Energy Markets to Come," co-authored with Charles W. Kadlec, *Public Utilities Fortnightly* 117, no. 1, 9 January 1986, 21–28.

2. Figure 8.2 shows a negative correlation between the real increase in the price of oil and the decade-long change in the BTU/GDP ratio. A decade-long, or ten-year, horizon was used to allow for the implementation of new technologies.

3. Associated Press, Maureen Clark, 5–6 October 2001.

4. The American gas line—sometimes built of 40, 50, or more cars—was one of the most visible aspects of the 1973–74 energy crisis, which can be sourced to multiple and converging macroeconomic events. The most expedient was the Yom Kippur War, which broke out between Israel and Arab forces in October 1973. Because the U.S. was allied with Israel in the Middle East struggle, the OPEC cartel of Arab nations seized the opportunity to restrict the supply of oil coming to the U.S. by way of an embargo. (OPEC was also motivated by profit.) But before this affair, all the seeds of the American gas line had been planted and well fertilized by the regulatory hand of government.

9

Who Are You?
Investor Profiles and the Case
for Asset Allocation

Investors are bound by the common decision to make money in the stock and bond markets. And from here we diverge in a thousand and one ways. Any investment decision we make should be based on information, but the information that can direct our actions is varied and various. This greatly disperses our behavior. Still, strong forces, often outside our control, work on the investment decision-making process. In particular, transaction costs and risk considerations each greatly influence the investment choices we make.

As for the costs, if we don't believe we can afford or overcome the fees related to certain investments, we will steer clear of those investments. At other times, the costs attached to certain investments will simply restrict our access. Linked to this, if we feel that certain investments are too risky, we will avoid them.

In life, we often act based on deep-seated ideas of who we are and what we believe we can be. Every investor wants to maximize his or her returns while taking into consideration the risk or volatility attached to those returns. But some of us stick to the safer routes to what we deem acceptable returns. Others of us throw caution to the wind in the pursuit of break-out gains. And many more of us fall somewhere in between, walking both the safer and riskier paths that lead to the return.

The question is, as an investor, who are you and what do you want to be?

To help you answer this, I have classified the predominant investor types in relation to the most common investment vehicles available today. The parallel between energy generation and return generation continues, and here it enables me to show how investors embrace different levels of risk and cost—sometimes with full knowledge and other times not—in pursuit of their returns. As you will see, this pursuit can be quite primitive. It also can be very sophisticated. It can be relatively cheap. It also can be costly, in terms of both fees *and* risk. Ultimately, however, I believe this pursuit can be well balanced as well as flexible.

By your nature, you might fall in with one of the following groups, or you might gravitate toward several. In the end, I hope that each serves as a reference point for distinct types of investor behavior. Although the following investor types are presented in an absolute sense, I believe that each of their functionalities has value when accessed at the appropriate times.

The Wood-Burning Investor

Wood always will keep you warm. It is a renewable resource that can be counted on to be available in good times and bad. The cost of entry to wood burning is low; you can perform this function by way of an impromptu fire pit or a built-in fireplace. Wood burning might not be the most efficient way to generate warmth, particularly on a large scale, but it is the old standby that will do the job when you need it done.

The investing equivalent to this is bond investing—more precisely, money-market investing. Just as wood will be the zero-risk fuel as long as there are trees, money markets always will be the low-risk investment alternative. Not surprisingly, when America has grappled with oil and natural-gas shortages, there has been a spike in old-fashioned wood-fired home heating. Comparatively, when the stock market has entered periods of decline, investors have flocked to money-market instruments, such as "cash" positions or short-term government securities.

A well-diversified portfolio should always have some exposure to short-term instruments, but for this discussion, we're dealing in absolutes: The wood-burning investor is the one who makes a career out of investing in short-term fixed-income securities.

Treasury bills, as you might know, are debt securities; they are I.O.U.s whereby you lend money to the government at a predetermined rate of interest for a short period of time, such as three months. Given the brief duration of the loan, it is more convenient for the government to sell these securities at a discount equivalent to current interest rates. For example, if the annual interest rate is 4 percent, then the 3-month interest rate on the T-bill is 1 percent. In this case, a bill that pays $1,000 at maturity will sell for $990. Investors receive a certificate for that loan and cash it in at maturity. Because the loan is only for three months, the risk of setting the rate too low in relation to the level of economic activity or the underlying inflation rate is well below that of longer-maturity instruments. In addition, T-bill rates are reset every three months. So in effect, the borrower (the government) refinances every three months.

This is all low-risk stuff. In contrast, the rates for ten-year Treasury bonds are set for ten years. If the market interest rate changes during that time, the price of the ten-year bond must adjust to reflect the new rate. Longer-maturity bonds are thus subject to principal risk, or the fluctuation in the price of the bonds.

Just as many types of wood will burn well in the fireplace, a variety of dependable short-term fixed-income vehicles are available to investors. Risk does fluctuate across this menu, with the short-term debt of businesses and corporations (or commercial "paper") typically promising higher returns along with higher risk, and lower-yield T-bills offering the converse. Yet, as a group, the returns promised by short-maturity fixed-income instruments usually do not approach the potential gains offered by stocks.

This is how the money-market investor becomes the wood-burning investor: Burning wood will provide you with warmth, but many of your potential BTUs will escape out the chimney. (Modern high-efficiency wood stoves are not part of this comparison.) Likewise, the wood-burning investor will enjoy low risk and, for the most part, guaranteed returns, but also will exhibit low return-generating efficiency relative to the overall market.

The Single-Hook-Up Investor

Most of us know someone who has said something to this effect: "If I only had bought such-and-such stock 20 years ago, I'd be sitting pretty right now." The ones we hear from less, if only because they have little to boast, are those who might say, "If I hadn't put all my money into such-and-such back then, my current financial situation wouldn't be so dismal."

These statements are based on extremes, but either might be attributed to single-hook-up investors, those who specialize in a single investment or investment style.

These are the investors who would put all their investment eggs in one investment basket, presumably with the intent of turning a good profit. Such a basket might include multiple shares of the stock of one company or a group of stocks in one industry. It also might include shares of one or more funds that are biased toward a group of stocks, shares that tend to move together (or behave in the same manner) as a result of the preferences of a fund manager toward certain size, style, and/or location characteristics (or other asset attribute).

For instance, if you owned shares of a fund that invested in, say, all growth stocks during the latter half of the 1990s, you probably did very well. However, if you held shares of a value-biased fund during that period, you likely did poorly. Or maybe you owned a 401(k) that was invested entirely in the stock of the company you work for. If that company was Microsoft or Google, you probably did very well. On the other hand, if your company suddenly went belly-up, your retirement nest egg dissolved. (Many an Enron employee can explain this heartache.) Such is the ultimate downside of investing in a small number of stocks or single-interest funds.

Single-hook-up investors are not uncommon, and they are bound together by the common trait of being undiversified. As the BTU story teaches us, this is a position fraught with risk.

For example, if in the 1970s you lived in the northeastern U.S. and your house was hooked to a natural gas line, you likely experienced a disruption in the flow of your BTUs when you needed them most. In the same way, the risks for single-hook-up investors always will be elevated. In the absolute sense, this practice is best suited to the extreme risk taker and well-informed market dabbler, both of whom are poor models for the responsible investor. However, when you believe you have excellent information on the direction certain assets will move and have a high degree of confidence in the certainty of your forecast, you might have every reason to put all or most of your eggs in one basket—but only if you are willing and able to remove them at the appropriate time.

Unfortunately, being confident does not mean you will be correct. Investors who make allocation decisions with conviction but do so without the guidance of an appropriate time-tested framework for making those decisions almost always pay a high price for their mistakes in the long run. It's like playing Russian roulette: You might win a round or two, but someday you're going to end up on the floor.

Single-hook-up investors who own only a handful of stocks or single-interest funds might see high returns when things go their way, but they nevertheless expose themselves to high risk and the potential misfortunes of individual companies.

The Multiple-Hook-Up Investor

Do you know these people? There are a few in every neighborhood and probably a lot more.

The oil truck used to come to their houses before they had lines put in for natural gas. Since that time, they grumble that they should have stuck with oil, which currently is the cheaper fuel in their state, although they hope their investment in clean and efficient natural gas will at some point pay dividends. In the meantime, they attempt to take the edge off their high natural gas bills by firing up their wood stoves on those not-too-cold winter nights. In the summer, they seek out fuel economy as well. When the mercury climbs, they often cook outside on their propane-fueled grills, enjoying the "free" cooling breezes and bypassing the need to turn on their air conditioner and natural-gas oven. They're the kind of people who prepare for emergencies, too. In their garages, they store gasoline-run generators, which sit beneath the shelf that holds the kerosene-fueled lanterns. They sleep well at night knowing they can rely on alternative fuels when warranted by events.

These people manage their own portfolios of fuel-burning strategies. They can predict which fuels they will burn based on the recurring weather cycles, and they take advantage of the random variations in temperature day to day. In this way, they perform two types of fuel management: long-term and passive, based on the cyclical fluctuations of the seasons, and active, based on the randomness of the weather. By storing portable generators, they also lower the potential high cost of their energy supply ever being interrupted. But because they understand that producing BTUs in this way is a relatively expensive proposition (due to economies of scale), the generator is but a last resort.

These people have spread risk around nicely, although they have done so in a very hands-on way. Similarly, spreading investments across many companies and/or funds is a common way investors mitigate risk and lower the costs associated with disruption.

Buying stocks, company to company, requires great diligence if diversity is to be achieved, making it an activity best suited to the most hands-on investors. However, many multiple-hook-up investors strive to achieve diversity by buying mutual funds that are invested in a range of stocks and bonds, and/or exchange-traded funds (ETFs), which mimic the performance of individual stock indexes. Such funds do lower risk, although investors need to choose these vehicles with care.

ETFs are baskets of securities traded, like individual stocks on an exchange. They can be bought or sold throughout the day, they tend to have lower expenses than mutual funds, and they can be bought or sold on margin.

As mentioned in the single-hook-up example, mutual funds tend to have mandates whereby they purchase "like" assets, such as mostly value, growth, small-cap, large-cap, or international stocks. Mutual funds, which are active investment vehicles, also can be attached to high management fees that must be hurdled before even a dollar in profit can be counted. Meanwhile, because ETFs aim to replicate the performance of stock indexes, they can be biased toward the "like" assets contained in the individual indexes. (In Chapters 14, "Ending the Never-Ending Debate: Active vs. Passive Investing and Why You Can Take Both Sides," and 15, "A Rational Walk Down Wall Street: Darting Between Passive and Active When the Odds Are in Your Favor," we investigate whether actively managed mutual funds are superior to passive ETFs.)

ETFs and mutual funds also buy assets in bulk; thus, a "herd" or "all-aboard" characteristic can arise that reduces the potential diversity of these funds. Logically, when people in a group all do the same thing, diversity of action ceases to exist. That said, because mandates are attached to mutual funds and ETFs (making them analogous to the different fuels), combining them based on the cyclical nature of the economy becomes a viable way to maximize long-run returns while minimizing the risks or volatilities associated with those returns.

In terms of achieving diversification that maximizes returns for a given level of volatility, the best multiple-hook-up investors are those who are most diligent about identifying the characteristics of the stocks, bonds, and funds they place in their portfolios.

The Big-Burner Investor

In the cellars of old homes, you can still sometimes find those rooms where the coal was stored before it was fed into the furnace. For many years, coal was king of the cellar, the workhorse of home heating before cleaner-burning oil and gas nudged it aside. But coal as a fuel source did not disappear; in a way, it concentrated on bigger things.

Today, although coal represents only about 20 percent of the fuel used in the U.S., it is by far the number-one fuel source for the nation's industrial boilers and electricity generators. In electricity production, coal fires the enormous boilers that create the high-pressured steam that powers the giant turbines that create the electricity. That's not the kind of thing that goes on in today's cellar; because of economies of scale, coal-burning is an activity best suited to the biggest of burners. Likewise, the relatively low energy needs of most houses are not compatible with the economies of scale offered by the giant coal burners.

In this way, hedge funds are analogous to big-time coal-burning facilities. Hedge funds are unregulated, highly autonomous vehicles that invest in just about anything—stocks, bonds, futures, etc.—but often by way of high-risk techniques, such as short-selling (the practice of trading in unowned securities with the expectation that they will decline in price) and the use of leveraging techniques (or borrowing). These are highly managed investment vehicles that are designed to be uncorrelated with the market and seek to outperform the market. And they are very restrictive, partly because of government regulations: Each fund sets limits on the number of investors it allows in (typically less than 100), requires high minimum investments (normally more than $250,000), mandates that investors meet net-worth requirements (often $1 million or more), and sometimes, largely as a result of the nature of the investments, does not allow investors to redeem the value of their shares all that frequently.

Related to this, just as the coal-burning industrial boiler is costly to operate, hedge funds are attached to high fees: Hedge-fund managers characteristically claim 20 percent of profits in addition to management fees of 1 or 2 percent. But just as coal-burning facilities can generate a massive amount of energy, hedge funds can produce lofty returns.

For most investors starting out, hedge funds are off limits. But in time, as their net worths grow, they can and should look to hedge funds as viable and high-powered sources of returns. The golden rule, however, is to look hard before committing: The big-burner hedge fund can be a risky place to put your money. (In Chapter 16, "Alpha Bets: The Case for Hedge Funds and a Greek Letter You'll Want in Your Portfolio," we more formally weigh the pros and cons of hedge-fund investing.)

The Electricity-Generation Investor

For a very long time in investment history, an asset was simply a stock or bond. But in the latter part of the twentieth century, investing underwent an information revolution. At this juncture, all available assets began to be grouped into *asset classes*.

Generally speaking, no longer were there merely different stocks and bonds to choose from, but different classifications of each based on their inherent and identifiable behaviors over time. The three major classifications became stocks, bonds, and cash. Within these breakdowns, important delineations were made. For instance, within stocks, modern portfolio theory gave us breakdowns by size (small-cap, midcap, and large-cap), style (value and growth), and location (domestic and international). These categories all seem rather intuitive, but once popularized, they transformed the way we invest.

In a way, we were presented with the distinct types of fuels that could power our portfolios, with all the fuels having predictable natures, insofar as they will very likely perform a certain way over a certain period of time. From this point on, we also could attempt to develop the "optimal fuel mix," one that would deliver the highest possible returns for a given level of risk.

That optimal mix is partly based on *mean* performance—the long-term trend-line of asset classes, the future slope of which is predicated on past performance as well as on the historic correlation between the different asset classes. (An understanding of the latter enables us to reduce the chance that the flow of our returns will be disrupted.) Put in the simplest of terms, if an asset class performed a certain way over the past 30 or so years, it can be expected to perform in a similar way over the next 30 or so years (market conditions, in general, remaining the same). Under this assumption, the optimal mix of the past provides us with the optimal mix for the future.

When the financial community began targeting asset classes, the process known as *asset allocation* was born. And energy is to the return as electricity generation is to asset allocation.

By buying electricity, individual consumers *indirectly* burn the different fuels that will ultimately provide them with the energy they seek. The advantages of this are several. When buying electricity, consumers indirectly take advantage of the economies of scale of multiple fuel-burning processes and often extend their reach to the energy produced by the nuclear, hydropowered, and coal-burning processes. In doing so, consumers greatly reduce the possibility that the delivery of their BTUs will be interrupted for any prolonged period of time.

Meanwhile, the generating facilities can attempt to anticipate fluctuations in the prices and availability of the different fuels, a practice that reduces both risk and cost. They also can combine the use of different fuels to minimize the long-run cost of electricity generation. They *also* can take advantage of geographic differences on the fuel map, determining which fuels are easiest and most cost-effective to transport and which facilities are best suited to burn certain fuels. Clearly, electricity-generation facilities have many more fuel-purchasing and fuel-burning options at their disposal than any one end consumer.

Comparatively, by combining different asset classes and formulating alternative asset mixes, the process known as asset allocation could increase the chance that investors receive their returns in the amounts they desire and when they need them. The assumption, and a proven one, is that although asset classes at times deviate from their long-run trends, they will return to those trends. Investment managers call this phenomenon of returning to this long run trend *mean reversion*. Thus, by allocating to asset classes over a *long* period of time, investors reduce the chance that those temporary deviations will cause too much damage to their portfolios.

Electricity-generation investors are asset allocators, which is another way of describing many modern investors. They both have to develop a process of dividing the investment among the different kinds of fuels/asset classes to optimize the risk/rewards trade-off based on the institution-specific situation and goals. By purchasing and switching between asset classes, these investors mimic the functionality of the electricity-generation facilities that substitute between fuels. Importantly, the extent to which this substitution process occurs separates one asset allocator from the next.

The Asset-Allocation Starting Point

As an investor, who are you, and what do you want to be? In the preceding classifications, you might find your answer.

Again, I believe there is value in each of these behavioral models, although I admit that I'm partial to the final classification—at least, as a starting point. Asset allocation is today an extremely viable way for investors to both lessen risk and meet their goals. The theory rests comfortably on the predictable nature of groups of assets over time. But I depart from a strict allegiance to static asset allocation: I believe asset classes *diverge* from their long-run trends in a predictable manner instead of only *following* long-run trends that are predictable.

In this way, *cyclical* asset allocation can offer an investor much higher returns than traditional asset allocation. The cyclical asset allocation strategy is a strategy that deviates temporarily from the long-run optimal allocations to take advantage of predictable fluctuations in the market. The former switches between asset classes periodically and when warranted by events, whereas the latter might switch only occasionally or never. The better or more reasoned those switches are, the better an investor will perform.

All endeavors, however, must have a starting point, or a point of reference. So before a cyclical asset allocation can be performed, a traditional asset allocation must be constructed. This allocation (should you choose to copy it, and I recommend that you do) is the starting portfolio from which you will switch, or *tilt,* throughout your investing career.

10

Your Benchmark Portfolio ... and Beyond

You can think of a traditional asset allocation as a benchmark portfolio in terms of the central argument of this book because there are confirmed ways to improve upon this allocation from time to time. A benchmark is a reference point, and for our purposes, it is a beginning. If you are cyclically inclined, a well-thought-out beginning portfolio that's allocated to the range of asset classes—such as bonds, large-cap stocks, international stocks, etc.—can serve you throughout your investment career. At times, you will switch or adjust your allocations within this portfolio; at other times, you will leave your allocations just as they are. And although at times your portfolio will look very different from the one you started with, at other intervals it might be an identical match.

So where to begin?

The Market-Share Shortcut

My answer is to start in the best risk-adjusted position possible—a point at which, if you never even touch your portfolio again, you will still stand to gain handsomely over the long haul.

Intuitively, an ideal starting point is one where your costs are the lowest in relation to the gains you hope to realize. As discussed, electricity-generation facilities are naturally inclined toward maximizing profit. And because one way to generate profit is to keep costs down, they tend to purchase the fuels that will provide them with the lowest cost per unit of energy. Presumably, the cheapest fuels relative to other fuels will deliver this low-cost advantage, so we can conclude that fuels will gain or lose attractiveness in the market based on their cost-effectiveness. This is a valuable nugget of information.

Let's say you are just starting out in the electricity-generation business and you have all your burners ready to go. All you need to do is purchase your fuels. Which ones will you buy and in what amounts? To answer this, you could perform an intense fuel-optimization study, determining conclusively which will give you the best bang for your buck. Or you could simply look at what your profit-maximizing competitors are doing.

Clearly, an undervalued fuel is more attractive than an overvalued one, so it is safe to assume that fuels that are gaining in market share are, at the time, considered undervalued and, hence, are most cost-effective. Symmetrically, overvalued fuels are the ones losing market share in the total energy-generation market. Furthermore, when all fuels are fairly priced, the various market shares will remain constant: No fuel will gain or lose market share. So if you are an electricity-generating facility and, thus, able to burn all possible fuels, to minimize your long-run energy production costs, all you need to do is allocate to fuels based on their long-run *market shares*, information that is readily available from any number of industry sources.

My rule about free lunches is to eat them when they're served. If you agree, instead of performing a complicated optimization analysis of all possible assets when constructing a benchmark portfolio, you simply can act like the electricity-generating facility and purchase asset classes based on their world market shares, or allocations. In purchasing assets in the proportions that the rest of the world is buying assets, you essentially are accessing the current sum-knowledge of the investment world. That's not a bad place to start. Because the global market share of the different asset classes arguably constitutes an allocation that will maximize the long-run returns of all investors, there seems little reason not to want to own that allocation.

Constructing a Winning World Allocation

Determining the world allocation to the different asset classes is not a complicated exercise, in that it can be based on any of a number of benchmark indexes in the market.[1] In what follows, we build the equity portion of a benchmark portfolio by referencing indexes compiled by Morgan Stanley Capital International (MSCI), the Russell Investment Group, Standard & Poor's, Citigroup, and Barra. These entities are well known in the financial community, and their indexes are referenced and mimicked regularly.

Step 1: The Stock/Bond Choice

Really only one portfolio choice should not necessarily be based on what the rest of the world is doing: the stock/bond (or equity/fixed-income) split. This is a personal decision, and I consider it the most important one an investor can make. In essence, the stock/bond split is the risk/no-risk split, so age is often the prime factor in determining it. For young investors starting out, the proper split might be 80/20, favoring stocks. Risk tends to dissipate over longer periods, so young

investors can lean heavily toward stocks, the riskier yet higher-pow-
ered investment class relative to bonds. Meanwhile, time is less on
the side of older investors, making a 20/80 split favoring bonds more
prudent for those who are closer to cashing out of the market.

That said, investors as a group cannot avoid the global constraints.
Collectively, all investors own all the stocks and bonds in the world.
Thus, the average investor must own stocks and bonds in the same
proportion as the market capitalization of the stocks and bonds in the
world financial markets. The different global indices tell us that the
market caps of the global equity and bond markets break down to
around 60 percent stocks and 40 percent bonds, plus or minus a few
percentage points. Thus, in constructing a sample starter portfolio,
we begin with the now classic 60/40 split. The long-run market capitalizations of stocks and bonds tell us that such an allocation is neither
too conservative nor too risky:

Stocks: 60%

Bonds: 40%

Step 2: The Location Choice

According to the Morgan Stanley Capital Index, MSCI, U.S. stocks
account for about half of the total equity markets worldwide. This
makes for a very neat allocation in terms of the location choice: 50
percent U.S. stocks and 50 percent international stocks. Because our
total portfolio allocation to stocks is 60 percent, the location split here
becomes 30 percent U.S. stocks and 30 percent international stocks:

Stocks: 60%   U.S. Stocks: 30%

                   International Stocks: 30%

Bonds: 40%

Step 3: The Size Choice

Stocks today are grouped by their market capitalizations—the total dollar value of the outstanding shares of public companies—giving us the delineations of large-caps, midcaps, and small-caps. According to the Russell Investment Group, the U.S. equity markets consist of approximately 70 percent large-caps, 20 percent midcaps, and 10 percent small-caps. Applying this breakdown to our portfolio's domestic equity allocation of 30 percent, we get 21 percent large-caps, 6 percent midcaps, and 3 percent small-caps:

Stocks: 60%	U.S. Stocks: 30%	Large-Caps: 21%
		Midcaps: 6%
		Small-Caps: 3%
		International Stocks: 30%
Bonds: 40%		

Step 4: The Style Choice

Stocks can be further subdivided by their styles: value and growth. In brief, value stocks are considered relatively cheap, and growth stocks indicate companies with higher-than-average sales and earnings. According to Barra, roughly half of U.S. stocks are value and half are growth. Thus, all we need to do is split each size allocation down the middle, giving half to value and half to growth:

Stocks: 60%	U.S. Stocks: 30%	Large-Caps: 21%	Large-Cap Value: 10.5%	Large-Cap Growth: 10.5%
		Mid-Caps: 6%	Mid-Cap Value: 3%	Mid-Cap Growth: 3%
		Small-Caps: 3%	Small-Cap Value: 1.5%	Small-Cap Growth: 1.5%
	International Stocks: 30%			
	Bonds: 40%			

This exercise can be continued across the international and fixed-income portions of the portfolio, but it should now be obvious that constructing a world allocation is an uncomplicated process. Importantly, if you believe the world allocation is determined by the collective global effort to maximize profit over the long run, there is every reason for you to own that allocation. By owning the world, you are guaranteed to do as well as the world.

And how good is that? In essence, it's as good as average.

The Global Barnyard Known as Average

Believe it or not, average has become very popular over the past two decades. Investors have herded into mutual funds, ETFs, and other broad-based investment vehicles, and in so doing, they have popularized the indirect pipeline to the return. By going indirect, investors let their investment vehicles sort among the range of return-generating assets. As mentioned, this does not always produce diversification; if diversification is to be achieved through indirect investment, the characteristics of each investment fund must be fully understood. The process of asset allocation can take care of this. In the domestic equity string of our world portfolio, we determined an optimal and diversified mix of assets based on the world allocation to these assets:

Stocks:	U.S. Stocks:	Large-Caps:	Large-Cap	Large-Cap
60%	30%	21%	Value: 10.5%	Growth: 10.5%
		Mid-Caps:	Mid-Cap	Mid-Cap
		6%	Value: 3%	Growth: 3%
		Small-Caps:	Small-Cap	Small-Cap
		3%	Value: 1.5%	Growth: 1.5%

Investors can own this breakdown by purchasing any of a number of funds built to these specifications in the proportions we determined. For instance, you could assign 10.5 percent of your portfolio to a large-cap value fund, 10.5 percent to a large-cap growth fund, 3 percent to a midcap value fund, and on down the line. Mutual-fund and ETF monoliths such as Fidelity, Vanguard, Schwab, Janus, Wilshire, and many others offer funds with the characteristics you need to construct an efficient benchmark allocation. By setting up your portfolio in this manner you indirectly link to the range of return-generating "fuels" that will provide your portfolio with both diversification and long-run cost efficiency; by buying the market mix of assets, you are the electricity-generation investor and thus can be assured of doing about as well as all the other electricity-generation investors. You *will* do about average.

And that's not bad. The benchmark asset allocation is an efficient and desirable allocation, insofar as it minimizes the costs per return over the long run. But importantly, because this allocation is based on the world allocation, it can generate performance only on par with the world.

When discussing average performance, it is always understood that there also can be above- and below-average performance. So, yes, as an investor, you can certainly do better than average. However, to do better, a counter party must be doing worse. This is the cold bottom line of investing: There will be winners and there will be losers. There also will be a giant herd that will mingle in the global barnyard known as average.

Above and Beyond the Benchmark

My philosophy about investing is rather simple: When you do not have strong feelings about the future of the economy or any one asset class, you should fall in with the average investor and buy the world allocation shown here as Figure 10.1. However, when you think you know something about the future of the economy or any asset class, you might want to act on your conviction. Importantly, regardless of the information you possess, you want to act conservatively. For instance, you could make the wrong deduction about the information you hold, or the information you hold could be wrong. Hence, you do not want to put all your eggs in one basket. Instead, you want to *tilt* away from the world allocation in direct proportion to the level of your conviction. The better you think your information is, the more you want to deviate from your benchmark.

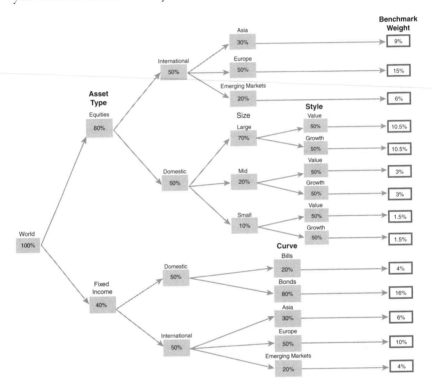

FIGURE 10.1   Starter World Application

I don't believe above-average performance is an elusive objective. To achieve it simply requires some skill or insight that other investors might not have. If one knows the long-run asset-class trends or long-run allocations, as we now know is easy to uncover, an opportunity for above-average gains arises when the market shares of individual asset classes deviate from their trends. To take advantage of this, you must first determine whether these deviations are random and short-term or longer lasting. The more random and short-term they are, the more difficult it is to take advantage of them. The reasons for this are twofold: First, when economic or market cycles are short, your timing has to be close to perfect to capture temporary asset-class divergences. Second, the high turnover related to short-term reallocations generates transaction costs that could eat all or most of your short-term gains.

However, if these deviations are longer lasting—say, a couple years—knowledge of the macroeconomic environments at the times these fluctuations occurred in the past could confirm the direction different asset classes will move in the months or years ahead. In applying this strategy, in particular, you want to determine which asset classes are over- or undervalued in the near term based on how they behaved in similar (or converse) economic environments in the past. In short, patterns in the data guide the cyclical asset-allocation process. What makes them patterns instead of mere deviations is that they are brought on by economic shocks, such as government policy actions, technological breakthroughs, and/or unanticipated natural events. (More on this in the chapters to follow.)

Decisions in life are best made when based on the truth, which is not always common knowledge. This is very important for investors to understand, particularly for those who hope to apply their knowledge of macroeconomic and world events to their portfolios.

Putting a Premium on Simplicity

A wise professor of mine once said, "Most things in life that are true are quite simple once you understand them." I have taken this to heart. I believe that if people cannot articulate their arguments in simple and understandable terms, it is because they do not truly understand their arguments.

Within the modern financial literature, very sophisticated and elaborate terms—such as *alpha, beta, the Capital Asset Pricing Model (CAPM)*, and *the Sharpe ratio*—are used to describe elements of the investment process.[2] As an economist and an investor, I spend a lot of time calculating around this vocabulary, yet there are common-sense and amazingly simple elements behind each term. In building a well-constructed portfolio, marked by diversification and cost-efficiency, you simply lay out pipelines that attach to the various sources of the return. Common sense and a little bit of straightforward analysis can go a long way toward understanding, formulating, and implementing a successful cyclical asset-allocation strategy. By keeping it simple, you help guarantee that you know exactly what you are doing each step of the way.

In the following chapter, I set forth a program for extracting the valuable information that is embedded in all prices. By focusing on the common apple, I hope to keep the analysis as simple and accessible as possible.

Endnotes

1. One of the most watched indexes is the Dow Jones Industrial Average (DJIA), which is made up of a handful of blue-chip, high-quality U.S. companies. Yet rather than a tool for benchmark comparison, the Dow is more of an indicator of the health of the U.S. economy. Standard & Poor's however, generates a good many indexes that serve as benchmarks for portfolio, asset-class, and fund performance. Among these are the S&P 500 (large-cap), S&P 600 (small-cap), and S&P 400 (midcap). The Nasdaq Composite Index is a broad-based benchmark, listing more than 5,000 companies. This is an important benchmark, although it is skewed toward newer and tech-heavy companies. Wilshire and Russell also produce several popular benchmark

indexes, such as the broad-based Wilshire 5000 Composite Index and the Russell 1000 Index (large-cap). Popular style benchmarks include the S&P Barra Growth and Value Indexes. For a snapshot of global equity and bond performance, investors and analysts often turn to the Morgan Stanley Capital International (MSCI) indexes. For fixed-income performance in general, a popular benchmark is the Lehman Brothers Aggregate Bond Index. The "world" of equity and bond indexes has grown quite large, and any investor in search of benchmark comparisons has a broad menu from which to select.

2. In *Understanding Asset Allocation* (Upper Saddle River: Financial Times/Prentice Hall, 2006), I perform a more indepth study of the Sharpe ratio and the Capital Asset Pricing Model (CAPM), both of which are much utilized by the modern professional investment community. The Sharpe ratio is a formula by which the risk premium of an asset is divided by the risk of that asset. It is useful for evaluating alternative investments and determining when to add additional assets to a portfolio. The CAPM looks at the relationship between an investment's risk and its expected market return.

11

Turning Smoke into Signals: How to Make the Most Out of Price Data

Centuries ago, natives in North and South America communicated over long distances by deftly working blankets over small fires. This process sent puffs of smoke into the air; the number, size, and intervals between these puffs varied in relation to the message being sent. These smoke discussions might have concerned the movements of prey, the position of the enemy, warnings of illness or danger, or the details of upcoming events. And although it was a crude technology by today's standards, the system worked well enough: Information in the form of smoke moved across the sky, with the only stipulation being that both sender and receiver needed to know the code behind the smoke for it to have any meaning.

The same dynamic holds true for the smoke that rises out of the stock market and the economy each month, day, hour, and minute. Such "smoke" becomes a signal only if you know how to decipher it, and to do that, you need to put it into context. Context is the code. Without it, the great amount of smoke—or raw data—that rises from the market might, at best, have you performing with the great herd of average investors and, at worst, have you making some very poor investment decisions.

We now have visited several economic shocks, and in each case, we have developed strategies that will have us investing "above the herd" when shocks occur. So far, the analysis has centered on the industries and locations that are the victims or beneficiaries of economic shocks. But in this chapter, we focus on shocks as they relate to the very important market smoke known as price.

In the cause of simplicity, we recruit the apple for our study. It doesn't get much simpler than an apple. Apples are grown on trees, are picked and shipped to market, and are sold at the going (or market-clearing) price—a price that sometimes goes up and at other times goes down. In isolation, the apple price is meaningless—at least, as far as investors should be concerned. If last week the local supermarket sold apples for $3 a dozen but today is selling them for $6, all we know is that the price of apples doubled. In what follows, however, I set forth the procedures for determining when you want to invest in those $6 apples and when you want to steer clear.

Of vital importance to this discussion is the role of the media. Even though I have stressed the value of doing your homework and tracking the news over whichever medium you choose, I convey an important warning in this chapter: Very often the media doesn't have a clue what it's talking about when discussing movements in price. And the reason is that it often looks at prices in isolation: "Apples Double in Price!" That might be an important headline for shoppers, but for investors, it is meaningless unless the price movement is put into context.

And that context is supply and demand.

What can an increase or decrease in the price of something tell us about the profits that thing is generating or the quantities of it that are being transacted?

Once again, the answer is not very much. But it's a starting point that leads to critical information that gives you a decisive edge as an investor.

Apply the code, and price smoke becomes an extremely valuable signal.

Follow That Apple: Demand Shift

Formally, any story must have a beginning, middle, and end. In the marketplace, a price movement is, in many respects, the end of the story. To take advantage of price movements, investors must read backward to the beginning, to the forces of supply and demand that underlie shifts in price. Once there, you must determine the *nature* of those shifts. You must ask, is the response of an industry or a company to a shift in demand elastic or inelastic? On the flip side, you can ask, are the responses of consumers to shifts in supply elastic or inelastic?

Uncovering these answers is critical to this investment strategy because it is the way in which companies and industries adjust to shifts in demand, as well as the supply of commodities that are necessary to production, that largely determine their profitability. And profitability, as we know, is a dominant factor in the direction of share prices.

We can begin our study with a demand shift.

So far, we know that if the apple price changes dramatically—for instance, if it leaps from $3 to $6 per dozen—we possess no information on which to act. In isolation, this price movement tells us nothing about the apple-production process and, thus, the profitability of the apple producers.

However, what if a new and authoritative study reveals that people who eat apples every day can greatly reduce their risk of catching common strains of the flu virus? Well, in this case, we would have our answer: A positive demand shock has occurred, resulting in a spike in the demand for apples. Correspondingly, we also then know that consumers will be willing to pay a higher price for apples because there is now an added value attached to eating them. Economists refer to this situation as an outward shift in demand, and there's a lot going on behind the scenes.[1]

As the price of apples goes up, producers will have an incentive to harvest more apples. They will now make an effort to collect apples in those hard-to-reach places, or even sell the smaller apples they might have skipped over in the past. In the short term, the price of apples and the quantities transacted will unambiguously increase.

How large these increases will be depends greatly on the supply elasticities of the apple growers. If the size of a country's apple crop is static, or fixed, and there is no way to import any more apples, any new demand will have to be satisfied through price increases. Here, the same quantity of apples will be transacted, but at a higher price—and, thus, at a higher profit. In stock market terms, inelastic supply in the apple industry will make for high-beta apple-industry stocks—stocks that will climb in price in the wake of positive demand shocks. (This should sound familiar: It is our regulated-airline story of the 1960s.)

But let's say, on the other hand, that there is ample supply of the fruit in the rest of the world at the market price when the shock occurs, and extra apples *are* imported. In this case, the incremental demand on the good news that apples prevent the flu will be satisfied through imports *without* any additional increase in the price of apples. There is still an outward shift in demand, yet prices hold. This is a classic example of stocks with a beta of 1, which signifies that they are in line with the market and thus will rise and fall with the market.

Of course, such perfectly elastic or inelastic situations are not the norm. The more general case is one in which there is a finite elasticity of supply, and shifts in demand are satisfied through a combination of price and quantity changes. But the extent to which each occurs will continue to depend on the supply elasticities of individual industries. And down the road, equilibrium once again will be achieved: Over time, an increase in the apple price will cause more apple trees to be planted. Soon enough, this will mean a greater supply of apples, which, in turn, will bring the unit price of the apple back to its long-run, or equilibrium, price.

Follow That Apple: Supply Shift

Swings in aggregate supply also impact prices. Let's again say that the price of apples shoots up, but this time we read in the papers of a dreadful disease that is decimating the apple-tree population. Decimated trees do not produce fruit, so we now understand that there is a shortage in the supply of apples.

Demand for apples in this case remains the same (because no event heightened demand), so we can describe the apple-tree blight as an inward shift of the supply curve, in which the price of apples has increased as a way of rationing the lower supply of apples. In addition, because the price of apples now is higher, some consumers will no longer find it desirable to consume apples and, thus, will switch to bananas or oranges or perhaps away from fruit altogether.

We also can view a supply shift in terms of a price decline.

Suppose there is a stretch of incredibly good apple-growing weather that results in a bumper crop of apples. What then? Here we have an outward shift of the supply curve, with a corresponding *reduction* in price becoming a way of inducing people to buy more of that bumper crop.

In this case, we might or might not want to invest in apples. The lower apple price will not necessarily mean lower profits because a greater quantity of apples is being transacted. Here, the determinant of profitability will be the flexibility of consumers to purchase more apples at a lower price. The more elastic that demand is, the greater will be the increase in units demanded.

Same Smoke, Different Signal

Just as the nature of companies and industries (i.e., whether they are elastic or inelastic) determines how they respond to economic shocks, the nature of shocks determines the all-important relationship between quantity and price.

Demand shifts produce a movement along the supply curve and, in equilibrium, result in a *positive* relationship between price and quantity. By "positive," I mean that the prices of apples, the quantities of apples transacted, and the profits related to apple production will all move in the same direction—they will rise together when demand increases and fall together when demand declines.

For example, if studies show apples to be the next wonder drug, the demand for apples will increase, as will the price of apples—at least, in the short term, until the quantity of apples rises to meet the new demand. In contrast, if it is broadcast that the seasonal crop of apples has been infested by worms, not necessarily destroying the apples, but making them unappetizing, demand for apples will fall off, as will the price.

Supply shifts, meanwhile, produce a movement along the demand curve and, in equilibrium, result in a *negative* relationship between quantity and price. In this situation, the price of apples and the quantity of apples transacted will move in the opposite direction. For example, a bumper crop of apples will lead to *more* apples at *lower* prices; a disease that kills a large number of apple trees will result in a *lower* amount of apples transacted at *higher* prices.

In this way, price increases or decreases can be consistent with either higher *or* lower quantities of a certain good in the production pipeline, with each situation having drastically different investment implications. Clearly, in many cases, price smoke will look the same, although the signal will be *very different*.

The Press and Prices: Approach with Caution

Of all the smoke generated by the market and the economy, price smoke ranks among the most valuable. For this reason, I so often am dismayed by the financial press: With regularity, this branch of the media skips or botches any attempt to decode a price reference in terms of supply and demand. Here are a few statements concerning price that have appeared in U.S. newspapers in recent years, followed by some quick analysis:

- "In spite of ever-increasing imports, consumers are not faced with higher prices that would curb their demand for goods." One suggestion here is that higher prices go hand in hand with higher volumes transacted. Is that true? Well, sometimes it is, and sometimes it is not.

- "Without price inflation, corporate profit margins may still not reach pre-recession levels." This implies that profits rise alongside prices. True in all cases? No again.

- "The better the economic news gets, the more negative it seems to financial markets. That's chiefly because a higher growth rate translates into higher prices." One conclusion here is that economic growth causes price inflation. It does not.

- "Lower prices mean lower corporate profits." It doesn't get more straightforward—or more misleading—than that.

The financial press gets it right when it generalizes about the correlation between profits and *share* prices: When the net earnings of companies increase, it is extremely likely that their stock prices will climb. Of course, investors want to own shares of companies that are good profit-generators today and stand to increase their profits in the future. However, contrary to much of the conventional wisdom, no perfect correlation exists between the direction of *consumer* prices and the direction of corporate profits (or the future path of GDP or the stock market).

It does seem intuitive that if a company can sell its products at higher prices, it will stand to profit more from those sales. But this won't necessarily be the case if it costs that company more to produce its products, or if the higher price of its products represents a shortage of some commodity or good used in the manufacturing process. Sometimes higher prices coincide with *lower* corporate profits; at other times, lower prices result in *higher* profits. This means that the convenient rules of thumb the financial press uses do not always hold and must be ruled out for investors interested in above-average performance.

For example, had you acted as an investor on a rule-of-thumb rationale such as "higher prices mean higher corporate profits," you would have profited in the situation in which apples prevented the flu, but you would have suffered in the case of the apple-tree blight. If you held to "lower prices mean lower corporate profits," you would have protected yourself if the apple crop was invaded by worms, but you might have missed out when a bumper crop led to an increase in the number of consumer transactions.

Shock Study: The Twenty-First-Century Bears

Generalizations can be convenient, and early in an analysis, they can be very useful. But when they substitute for thorough analysis, they can become very misleading.

When it comes to media generalizations about price, one that I find particularly deceptive is the notion that *all* price increases act like tax hikes on consumers, thus having the effect of confiscating consumer dollars. The corresponding generalization is that all price declines are the equivalent of subsidies, or free money. These relationships are correct only some of the time. Critically, the tax-hike effect is true only when there are *supply-led* increases in price, whereas a *demand-led* increase in price is not a tax hike at all.

Here I update of one of our earlier shock studies to make this point.

One of the bigger financial stories at the start of the twenty-first century was the climbing price of oil and the resulting increase in gasoline prices. On the surface, this was the same one-two punch that Americans were dealt in the 1970s, a period of high inflation and economic stagnancy (what has come to be known as "stagflation"). Three decades ago, high energy prices did indeed act as a tax on consumers—and also many businesses, which saw the costs of producing and transporting their wares climb to profit-damaging heights. But let's flash forward to the first half of the 2000s. Alongside high energy prices, the U.S. also experienced high economic growth, record corporate profits, and a climbing stock market. Not quite the 1970s.

As an investor during this period, if you subscribed to the generalization that high energy prices act like a new tax on consumers and businesses—a generalization that ran rampant through the media—you likely took a very bearish view of the direction of the economy and the stock market right when you should have been bullish.

Whether you knew it or not, this bearish view was attached to the notion that higher gas prices were a supply-led phenomenon. Here's how the supply-shift argument went: OPEC is still an effective cartel and, thus, able to tinker with supply levels like a monopolist to generate the highest possible profit; oil supply disruptions due to global economic strife (such as war in the Middle East) are great enough to severely damage world oil supply; and, for good measure, the world is running out of oil, so the price of an increasingly scarce commodity will continue to climb.

Such arguments were *de rigueur* in the newspapers, and it's hard to blame the average investor for latching on to this forecast. But when it comes to price movements as they are presented in the media, you must do your due diligence, applying scrutiny to every price assertion you encounter. Here's how I approached the gas price debate a few years back:

To begin, I asked, if OPEC is still an effective cartel, why is the inflation-adjusted price of a barrel of oil much lower today than it was in the early 1980s (just prior to when President Ronald Reagan decontrolled energy prices and, as I like to say, broke the cartel's back)?[2] I also applied this same rationale to the geopolitical argument: If world supply has been so greatly damaged by disruptions in Venezuela (due to worker strife), Iraq (due to war), and elsewhere (due to a variety of localized shocks), why hasn't the inflation-adjusted price of oil jumped to a new peak? As for the world running out of oil, if this were true, why hasn't OPEC taken great advantage of the circumstances by curtailing production and thus driving up the barrel price even more?

It turned out that not only was the supply-led forecast full of holes, but it was, in fact, a pessimist's forecast at a time of unprecedented global growth. Indeed, when you viewed high energy prices in terms of a global *demand* shift (in good part due to the rising economies in India and China), a rainy-day story turned quite sunny: Oil prices increased because the demand for oil increased, and that demand increased because the world economy was growing. It was an optimist's story, one in which greater global wealth and prosperity increased the demand for and price of a commodity.

Is Pricing Power All-Powerful?

You will often see the term *pricing power* bandied about by the financial press. By definition, pricing power is the ability of companies or industries to determine price levels in the marketplace, with strong pricing power equated with the ability to generate high profits. I say "by definition" because this rationale, like so many concerning price, can be misleading. In the converse, it is very possible for companies or industries that *do not* theoretically have strong pricing power to be very profitable.

I re-enlist another of our shock studies to make this point:

The arrival of the personal computer and the Internet has led to an impressive increase in productivity across industries, resulting in a greater supply of products and services at lower prices. This clearly has been the case with personal computers, the star of the technology revolution. High price tags, difficulty of use, and limited functionality pushed the general consumer away from computers in the 1980s. However, as the price tag lowered and functionality and ease-of-use increased during the 1990s and thereafter, the masses embraced personal computing.

But to what extent have the developers of the technology increased their profits? Because the trend has been for the price of computing to go down, haven't computer suppliers exhibited *low* pricing power and, hence, low profitability?

By definition, today's computer companies *do* exhibit low pricing power, but low profitability is another story.

Charting the computing revolution, the trend toward lower-priced computers has led to a movement along the demand curve, with the quantity demanded increasing and the price declining. On the other hand, a lower sales price means less revenue per unit sold. This is what many in the media might generalize as a "subsidy" effect, whereby consumers get a price break at supplier expense. But suppliers can and often do generate profits in this situation.

Importantly, technological innovations that bring about increased productivity also lower production costs. The consumer also matters here. If consumers are elastic enough, they will purchase enough low-priced computers to make this a profitable business.

One reliable rule of thumb is that when demand is very elastic, sales for a business will increase better than 1 percent for each 1 percent decline in price. On the other hand, when demand is very inelastic, technological innovation will result in only lower prices without any increase in unit sales, for a net loss of revenue for the producers.

Prosperity Measures and Price Movements

A qualitative aspect is involved in judging how consumers will behave in the marketplace shock to shock, but the analysis becomes much more quantitative and straightforward when you embrace a top-down worldview.

Consumers react to products in the marketplace in terms of price, their income levels, the value they perceive in different products, their ability to substitute the purchase of one product for another at a better price, their emotional attachment to particular products and services, and so on. At the microeconomic level, we can call this shopping. But from a macroeconomic perspective, one can, to a good degree, forecast consumer activity, resilience, and flexibility in terms of the level of economic growth and a variety of other prosperity measures.

Think of a scenario in which gross domestic product and personal net worth have risen, unemployment has lowered, and the stock market has rallied. At the same time, think of a corporate environment in which competition between suppliers remains strong, productivity high, and prices low. Here I have described the economic recovery that began in the early 2000s, a period marked by consistent double-digit gains in corporate profits and economic growth (gains well above the averages of the last 25 years), greater individual prosperity, *and* the absence of pricing power.

The prevailing investment insight is that when increases in *productivity* lead to lower prices, a lack of pricing power is not a hindrance to profitability. The more elastic the demand, the more responsive will be the demand and the more likely it will be that suppliers will compensate for their per-unit revenue loss through higher volume and the cost savings that productivity gains engender.

The media's rules of thumb about pricing power, just like those about price, is correct only some of the time. True enough, when production (supply) and consumption (demand) are *inflexible*, pricing power is synonymous with profitability. Yet paradoxically, when production and consumption are *flexible*, productivity gains will lead to a lack of pricing power and *higher* profits.

There's a saying in the economics profession that "a rising tide lifts all boats." In terms of pricing power, this is often true. When positive economic shocks bring about a rising tide of prosperity, even the boats with "low" pricing power stand to profit.

Price-Smoke Detectors

Let's imagine back a few centuries: Two Native Americans from peaceful tribes are conducting a smoke discussion concerning the details of an upcoming celebration. They are speaking to each other from two hilltops, with a mile of valley in between. Below them, crossing that valley, is a column of settlers on horseback. These settlers see the smoke rising to their left and right, but because they have no knowledge of the code behind the smoke, they have no idea what the Indians are talking about. Worse, they begin to come to some wrong conclusions, ones that have them arguing whether to hide in the foothills, go on the offensive, or retreat out of the valley.

Had they possessed the code, however, they would have proceeded toward their destination as planned.

In the same way, price movements must be decoded if they are to be instructive. If a demand shift generates a price change, one gets a very different outlook than if a supply shift generates an equal movement in price. In shorthand, we can say that price increases due to demand shifts and price declines due to supply shifts are all quite *bullish.* Contrastingly, we can say that price increases due to supply shifts and price declines due to demand shifts are all quite *bearish.*

Understanding price movements in terms of their unique natures will likely bring about proper action within a portfolio, as opposed to the hit-or-miss action that can come from adhering to generalizations about movements in price. The foremost rule when it comes to price smoke is to never take the conventional wisdom at face value; to do so often is the equivalent of accepting false information as true. The second rule, simply, is always to place price movements into the context of supply and demand, the code that turns price smoke into a true signal:

Bullish Price Smoke

- Price increase, demand shift

  Description: The price of a good rises in response to an increase in the demand for that good, a situation in which suppliers stand to earn much greater profits.

  Examples: Eating apples, it is discovered, can help prevent the flu, an event that raises the demand for apples. The demand for oil increases because of a dramatic increase in world economic growth.

- Price decrease, supply shift

  Description: A greater supply of a good in the marketplace causes the price of that good to drop, a situation favoring the suppliers that can operate in the most cost-efficient manner.

Examples: A bumper crop of apples leads to a lower apple price but more apples transacted. A new technology brings about greater productivity and, hence, more output at a lower price.

Bearish Price Smoke

- Price increase, supply shift

  Description: A reduction in the supply of a good results in less of that good in the marketplace at a higher price.

  Examples: An apple-tree blight leads to fewer available apples, with those apples rationed in the market at a higher price. An oil supplier preys on the inelasticity of consumer demand by reducing supply, thus bringing about higher oil prices.

- Price decline, demand shift

  Description: A good falls out of favor with consumers, thus causing a decline in the price of that good.

  Example: The recent hepatitis scare related to the sale of contaminated spinach decreased the demand for and price of spinach.

A Word on Windows of Opportunity

In describing price smoke as either "bullish" or "bearish" our discussion climbs to the most macro level. In the big picture, the tandem of lower demand and lower prices is a double negative for profits. Here, society is in trouble. Release the bears. Higher prices and higher demand on the other hand are a double positive for profits. Here, society is in good shape. Bring out the bulls.

And, in each case, price needed to partner with a supply-and-demand determination for it to be of any use.

Undeniably, when viewed in isolation, a price shift can carry just as much misinformation as information. However, when you determine the nature of the shock that brought on a shift in price, you have a window of opportunity on which to act within your portfolio. Importantly, these windows often stay open for an actionable period of time, from a few quarters to several years or more. Additionally, in many cases, you can anticipate these openings and closings.

This ushers in the concept of *timing*, our subject (and something of a controversial one) for the next chapter.

Endnotes

1. In the late nineteenth century, the economist Alfred Marshall formalized a supply-and-demand model that has since been used rigorously within the economics profession. This model has two axes: The left-vertical axis regards price, and the right-horizontal axis concerns the quantity of goods being transacted. By plotting the supply and demand "curves" across these axes, economists are able to draw many conclusions about the impact of price and/or quantity shifts on businesses, industries, and economies. In this chapter, I use some of the terminology related to this model, such as "outward" or "inward" shifts in supply or demand.

2. Canto, Bollman, and Melich (1982).

12

Making Hay While the Sun Shines: The Case for Predicting, Forecasting, and Timing

In investment circles, the word *timing*, or more the phrase "market timing," carries a lot of baggage. Generally, *market timing* is the practice of timing the purchase or sale of assets to predicted swings in the market. The idea has been defined as "buy low, sell high" and further can be described as purchasing assets that are deemed undervalued currently and are forecasted to increase in value. This latter description is closer to what concerns this book: Instead of attempting the more timing-dependent and very active strategy of buying individual stocks low to sell them later at a higher price—a practice that can occur day to day, if not minute to minute—we here are in search of the cyclical periods when asset classes can be considered undervalued and are likely to gain in value.

This is a quarterly, semiannual, or even annual regimen. Yet because many investors and investment counselors subscribe to the idea that shorter-term swings in the market are random and, hence, not predictable, they equate any timing strategy with gambling. They also counter with an investment plan that clings to the performance of asset classes over the historic long term. Here the forecast doesn't change all that much. It posits that because assets did such-and-such over the last 30 or so years, they can be expected to do about the same over the next 30 or so years. Buy them, hold them, and ride out the ups and downs. Timing isn't all that necessary to this formula, nor are the rigors of forecasting and predicting.

Investors are not wrong for embracing such a strategy. (This is the one that will deliver average performance.) But it stands to reason that if swings in asset classes *can* be forecasted, a better way of investing exists. Additionally, if asset-class swings can be predicted, we should be able to *time* our investment actions to these swings.

In this chapter, I test and support the firmness of this conviction.

To begin, I set forth just what goes into constructing a reliable investment forecast. Experience matters here, as does our ability to extract actionable information from the economic data and financial news. But the forecasting process itself is straightforward, and to describe it, I employ a knowledgeable guide: the farmer. Indeed, if in pursuit of being a good investor you were to model your behavior on a common-world activity, I would recommend farming—*above-average* farming, that is.

From here, we look for the economic prompts by which we can time our investment actions. Tax- and monetary-policy changes constitute significant shocks to the economic system, with each dictating periods when certain types of assets will outperform others. Because neither of these events is ever much of a surprise, each adds a good degree of predictability to our forecasts. Business cycles, inflation rates, and the level of interest rates similarly come into play—and once again, predictability joins the forecasting process. This is a key combination. When predictable events make for reliable forecasts, the timing of our actions becomes exceedingly certain.

The Art of Forecasting: A Farmer's Perspective

Investors who collect reliable information and time their actions to predictable shifts in asset-class return cycles on average will outperform investors who buy and hold for the long run. Simply, they will make hay while the sun shines, just as above-average farmers make the most of good weather and clear skies.

This is a nearly one-to-one parallel, as I see it: How the farmer goes about the process of gathering information, building a forecast, and acting on that forecast mirrors how cyclical asset allocation is properly performed.[1]

At the outset, one would expect the above-average farmer to be well acquainted with his crops, land, pests, insecticides, seeds, and machinery. He also knows what the quality and quantity of his product should be if he is to earn the most when it is shipped to market. All this puts him in the game, so to speak. However, if he consistently is to be an above-average performer, meaning that he will more often than not produce a high and quality yield, he arguably will time his actions in the field with admirable precision. Primarily, he will excel at coordinating his actions with the weather.

Of course, the good farmer working in the field keeps his eyes open. He watches the skies and the clouds, and he knows that storm clouds, in particular, are packed with information. When clouds gather on the horizon, he estimates how long he can continue to plow before the rain will stall his work. By checking the clouds against the wind and appraising their shade and shape, he attempts to determine whether he has hours or just minutes to get his equipment in the barn. This is a judgment that *experience* brings; the farmer's practical experience allows him to make a forecast and act on it.

But in most cases, the information he collects with his eyes and the application of that information are not enough to ensure an above-average yield year to year. He must rely on a bit more information than that.

Weather shifts predictably, although not perfectly, with the seasons, and it shifts less predictably week to week and day to day. This requires the good farmer to be a forecast collector for both the longer and shorter terms. Seasonally, and perhaps weekly, he checks in with his local agriculture forecasting service, the people who track the weather diligently and scientifically, and every morning he listens to the weather forecast on the radio or watches one on TV. Each of these forecasts helps him determine the most favorable times to plant, pick, water, fertilize, and spray.

At this point, the information carried in a forecast, the reliability of that information, and personal experience all converge to bring about a conviction to act. When that conviction level rises, timing becomes more precise.

Specifically, the farmer adjusts his actions in the field based on a sum-total rendering of the forecasts he collects—whether they are derived from advanced scientific evidence, the analysis of a local weatherperson, or his own eyes and experience. Additionally, none of these forecasts is a sure thing; at times, each will be off. In theory, if a weather forecast is always right, the farmer always will know what to do. He similarly always will know how to act if a forecast dependably is wrong. But the more real-world example is one in which a forecast is right only some of the time.

Let's say, on average, that a particular weather forecast is right only 67 percent of the time. In this case, the farmer has to make a judgment call on whether to act on this report. He also will want to know if there are additional pieces of information that will help him improve that forecast.

The timing of the forecasts themselves also matters a great deal.

Let's say a forecast is for sustained stormy weather. If received just before planting, the forecast might cause a delay in planting; if received during the harvest, it might cause an acceleration of the harvest; if received in between planting and the harvest, it might elicit no response whatsoever. Thus, the extent to which a forecast causes a change in behavior depends on both the historical accuracy of the forecast and the stage of the crop when the forecast arrives.

These are the variables the good farmer must weigh as he builds a reliable plan of action. And these are your variables, too:

- Know your strategies and asset classes.

  Just as the good farmer knows his seeds, crops, and machinery, and worries about what to plant and what seeds to use…

  …you must grasp the fundamentals of the investment process, of asset classes to use in your investment process and how the overall environment affects the rate of growth and your investment returns (such as those discussed in this book).

- Know your shocks.

  Just as the good farmer understands how the weather plays into the quality and yield of his crops…

  …you must ground your understanding of economic shocks, the companies and industries they impact, and, hence, the stocks they affect in the laws of elasticity and supply and demand.

- Keep your eyes open.

  Just as the good farmer watches the skies and checks the weather reports daily to detect near-term shifts in the weather…

…you must make it a daily habit to track the political, global, and financial news. You needn't act on this information every day, but you will be able to spot economic and policy trends in the earliest stages when you stay abreast of current events.

- Be a forecast collector.

Just as the good farmer relies not on his eyes alone…

…you must collect the quarterly and annual economic forecasts generated by major newspapers and various financial magazines. Reference these whenever possible to see if the pros corroborate your understanding of the future economic environment. (More on this shortly.)

- Apply your forecast to a proven framework.

Just as the good farmer reflects on his forecast in terms of the demands and promise of the specific crops he grows…

…you must view your economic forecast in light of an investment framework that not only promises the results you desire, but also has proven to generate such results. For the most part, economic forecasts that trigger changes in a portfolio or investment process are important only to active (or semiactive) investment frameworks because passive investment frameworks rarely adjust to the economic winds.

- Rely on experience when experience has served you well.

Just as the good farmer gains invaluable experience with the weather and his crops as he matures in years…

…you must count on your ability to become a better investor over time. You might be able to develop a strategy that enables you to deviate from the long-run allocation to take advantage of predictable fluctuations in the market. Indeed, cyclical asset allocators typically improve with each new quarter and every new year. Although their forecasts (and investment calls) are not always correct, in time they will be right more often than not. Additionally, their experience very often enables them to improve on a forecast that is not so certain.

- Act (or don't act).

  Just as the good farmer bases his actions on a sum-rendering of the forecasts he collects and his experience over the years…

  …you must make reasoned adjustments to the assets in your portfolio when you possess a high conviction level that your forecast is correct. If that conviction level is not high and/or there is no reason to adjust your allocations, leave your allocations alone.

Farmers must serve Master Weather just as good investors must serve Master Shock. Yet each of these masters can be managed. The farmer develops a weather forecast by collecting information from a range of sources, and he times his actions in the field based on his experience with that information. He must know his crops and equipment to get in the game, but he must know them in relation to the weather if he is to apply them with the best possible effect.

Similarly, good investors must know the characteristics of the separate asset classes. If they are to allocate to them with the best possible effect, they must understand them in relation to the range of powerful macroeconomic variables that include taxation, monetary policy, interest rates, and inflation.

Timing Happens All the Time

Timing, in all its investing shapes and forms, is a dirty word to those who have little faith in the various forecasting methods that attempt to predict short-term swings in asset prices. But here I ask a basic question: Why *do* asset classes swing away from their long-run trends for shorter periods of time?

The most obvious answer is that enough investors from time to time act in the same way and thereby cause pronounced swings in the price of distinct groups of assets. In other words, enough investors will have bought or sold enough of the same types of investments to cause a significant price movement in those investments.

Now I ask a follow-up question: *Why* do enough investors suddenly act in the same way? Is this randomness? Coincidence? The result of a cause that even if known today was not predictable yesterday?

I'm not so sure it's any of these. In fact, when enough people act in the same way at the same time, I am from the school that believes there is not only a tangible or identifiable reason for this collective action, but that the reason might be behavioral and predictable.

A simple marketplace example can describe this.

Surely you are familiar with retail come-ons, such as "Shop Our Blowout Memorial Day Sale: All Prices Slashed!" or "Only Ten Days Left to Shop Our Incredibly Low Prices!" Stores preannounce sales, or even price increases, all the time. But the behavioral effect of the former, the preannounced sale, is much different than that of the latter, the preannounced price increase.

For starters, few of us will shop a store the day before a preannounced sale—the only ones who might are those who are ignorant of the coming sale or for some reason *must* have an item in that store on that particular day. And who are these full-price shoppers? Well, whether they are ignorant of a pending sale or not, if they *must* purchase an item at the going price, despite the fact that it will very shortly lower in price, we can say they are inelastic consumers. Meanwhile, those who possess full knowledge of an oncoming sale and have flexible schedules will be able to take advantage of lower prices when the sale goes live.

As for the preannounced price increase, rather than a timed delay of activity, we will see a timed acceleration. If prices in a store are to increase tomorrow, consumers will have a strong incentive to purchase items in that store today. As expected, only those with inflexible plans and/or a lack of knowledge of a price hike will shop a store on the day of that hike.

Consumers—at least, the elastic ones, who have knowledge of a pending price increase—will bask in the sunshine of the current lower prices; they will purchase more before the price goes up. Similarly, consumers with knowledge of an upcoming price decrease will wait for the sun to shine; they will plan their purchases for when prices go down.

When it comes to prices—and saving a buck or making a buck—strong behavioral forces determine group action. Indeed, timing happens all the time, and it is often a predictable event.

Shock Study: Preannounced Tax Policy

This analysis easily graduates from the consumer experience to a macroeconomic shock that preys on human behavior, the direction of the economy, and the price movements of major asset classes: tax policy. Although tax increases and tax decreases are different animals, they are alike, in that they usually are preannounced. Hence, each event can be the basis of a forecast that is very accurate.

For example, when new tax legislation passes, anyone can know the exact date that the tax change goes into effect, with that date either representing the beginning of a storm or a clearing of the skies. There's a nuance to this, however. In the case of tax cuts, legislation can be phased in; in the case of tax increases, the current lower rates can be phased out. But the actions of taxpayers in all cases are predictable: As a group, they will avoid the higher-tax storms and bask in the lower-tax sunshine.

A very clean example of this occurred during the second term of Ronald Reagan's presidency. Back in 1986, on the administration's prompting, Congress lowered the top marginal income-tax rate to 28 percent from 50 percent, with this cut scheduled to be phased in over a two-year tax period. At the same time, the new legislation increased the capital gains tax rate to 28 percent from 20 percent. So we had a preannounced tax increase *and* a preannounced tax decrease, indicating two different periods when the sun presumably would shine on taxpayers.

In the case of the preannounced tax increase, investors with accumulated capital gains largely chose to realize them before the capital gains rate was lifted to 28 percent. This is an obvious case of making hay while the sun shines, although there is more to the story.

Because the prospect of higher capital gains tax rates in the future led to more people paying taxes at the current lower rate, more taxes were paid, which fattened the tax-revenue coffers at the federal and state levels. In some states, officials projected these revenue gains to continue, and in doing so, they mistook a one-time windfall for a permanent event.

In my own California, for instance, spending was increased to match the higher revenue projections. And when the higher revenue did not materialize, the state went into deficit. To make matters worse, instead of cutting back on spending, California raised taxes and pushed the state into recession, all while the federal economy was also slowing down. (Thinking back to the location effect, it's not surprising that California as a whole and its small-cap companies, in particular, suffered a worse fate than the average of the other 49 states.)

Tax changes have far-reaching and predictable implications, and we can view this again in the case of the Reagan income-tax cuts of 1986.

These cuts were phased in over two years, a period that coincided with an economic slowdown. And why did the economy slow? Our store example can help answer this.

Recall that when stores preannounce sales, consumers will delay their purchases until the sale prices take effect. This delay will cause store sales to slump. And taxpayers react to incentives or disincentives just like consumers: They will delay activity if they know they will profit by doing so. Because the Reagan income-tax cuts of 1986 were phased in, there was a negative impact on behavior from the consumer level to the corporate level in the short run. In economist terms, the postponement of economic activity at the consumer level and the juggling of the books on the corporate level had the effect of delaying income recognitions—but only until the full rate cuts went into action.

And once they did, guess what? The economy boomed, with the GDP gaining by double digits.

If consumers and taxpayers can time their behavior with precision to periods when the returns will be greater, to the periods when the sun shines, there's no reason investors can't also. The challenge then becomes to detect, or forecast, that sunshine. We begin this process by searching for patterns of relative performance between stocks and bonds.

Predicting Fixed-Income Cycles

I have stated that the stock/bond (or equity/fixed-income) decision within a portfolio is the most important one an investor can make. The reason is simple: Bonds produce lower returns with lower risk, while stocks produce higher returns with higher risk. Everyone wants higher returns, but the level of risk we can stomach varies greatly person to person. Hence, so does the level of returns.

However, if we can discover persistent patterns of relative performance between these bellwether asset classes, it stands to reason that we can mitigate much of the heartache associated with this choice while also maximizing our earnings over the long haul.

So let's take a look.

Pillaging through the quarterly returns of the S&P 500 (my stand-in for the performance of stocks) and the ten-year Treasury note (my stand-in for the performance of bonds) for the last three decades, I identified seven full cycles in which bond returns systematically out-performed stock returns (see Table 12.1).[2] These "fixed-income" cycles are about equally divided between those that lasted 6 quarters and those that lasted 12.

As an aside, perhaps the distinct duration of the cycles lends sup-port to the idea that election cycles at the congressional level (every two years) and the national level (every four) affect the direction of economic policy and, thus, cycles of relative performance in the stock and bond markets. This tidbit adds some grist to our cyclical mill. But more to the point, the fact that these relative-performance cycles per-sist *at all* means there is a possibility of developing a strategy to exploit them.

TABLE 12.1   Fixed-Income Cycles

Beginning	End	GDP	Business Cycle	Inflation	T-Bill	Real Rate
1973.1	1974.3	0.9	Mixed	7.41 Rising	7.46	0.05 Falling
1976.2	1978.1	5.91	Expansionary	6.17 Falling/ Rising	5.33	–0.84 Falling
1981.2	1982.3	–0.4	Recessionary	6.85 Falling	12.81	5.96 Falling
1983.4	1986.3	3.25	Expansionary	2.46 Falling	3.72	1.26 Falling
1991.2	1994.1	3.02	Expansionary	2.46 Falling	3.72	1.26 Falling
2000.2	2003.1	1.22	Mixed	2.02 Falling/ Rising	4.12	2.1 Falling
2003.2	2005.4	4.1	Expansionary	3 Falling/ Rising	1.96	–1.06 Falling

Let's first look to a usual suspect: recessions.

It is sensible to expect stocks to underperform bonds during recessions, when the GDP is contracting, and outperform during recoveries, when the GDP is expanding. Simply, investors will protect themselves with safer bond or cash positions—or fixed-income positions—when the economy turns sour.

Yet the recession record as it relates to fixed-income cycles is not perfect. According to the National Bureau of Economic Research, in only three of our fixed-income cases was the business cycle either all or part recessionary, while in four cases, the fixed-income cycles coincided with expansions. Thus, the data shows conclusively that economic recessions are neither a necessary nor sufficient condition for fixed-income cycles.

Is inflation our indicator? Again, the correlation is not perfect: Fixed-income cycles have occurred when inflation has trended both upward and downward.[3] However, when you subtract the inflation rate from the Treasury bill yield, essentially removing the effect of inflation, you get what is known as the *real rate*. And in our study, each time a fixed-income cycle occurred, the real rate was *falling*.[4]

From this result, we can draw a quick investment rule:

> *A rising real rate is bullish for equities and bearish for fixed income.*

The phrasing of this rule is important. Even though a falling real rate is a good indicator of fixed-income cycles, I *cannot* conclude that a falling real rate is bullish for bonds or necessarily bearish for stocks. That's because there are different degrees to which stocks and bonds, as distinct groups, perform cycle to cycle. Indeed, when the real rate is falling—a generally nice time to be invested in fixed-income instruments—stocks also have performed well enough.

This brings us to the concept of *valuation*, what we estimate the relative value of assets or asset classes to be. When forecasting how stocks and bonds will perform in the near term, we want to grade the economic conditions from least to most favorable, a process that brings economic policy and economic performance neatly together.

Putting a Value on Stock and Bond Cycles

Likely as many economic forecasters exist as weather forecasters. And they each select from a broad basket of data when developing their forecasts. For the economic forecaster, these data points might include consumer prices, interest rates, corporate profits, commodity and producer prices, currency exchange rates, unemployment rates, productivity and wage levels, and on and on. They also look at exogenous factors that are outside the control of individual investors and the collective financial markets. These might include war and peace, national strife and passivity, or the effects of unexpected disasters, both manmade and natural. However, despite the breadth of data at their disposal, many economic forecasters put the greatest weight on just two of their conclusions: the future direction of inflation and the real (or inflation-adjusted) rate of growth for GDP.

Table 12.2 describes the level of stock and bond performance in relation to the direction (increasing or decreasing) of each of these variables, inflation and GDP. The results are based on monthly data from 1948 through 2004, and they make a lot of sense.[5]

TABLE 12.2   **Average Monthly Stock and Bond Returns During Different Combinations of Rising and Falling Inflation and Rising and Falling Real GDP Growth (1948–2004)**

Stock Returns

	GDP Growth	
	Increasing	**Decreasing**
Inflation: Increasing	0.33%	0.22%
Inflation: Decreasing	1.17%	0.87%

Bond Returns

	GDP Growth	
	Increasing	**Decreasing**
Inflation: Increasing	–0.44%	0.17%
Inflation: Decreasing	0.30%	0.51%

Sources: National Bureau of Economic Research and Ibbotson Associates

Stocks performed best when inflation was on the decline and the GDP was increasing, what we might call a bullish economic environment. Turning the tables, when inflation was on the rise and the GDP was declining, stocks fared the worst, although, as a group, they did turn in a gain of 0.22 percent. Bonds did the best when inflation and the GDP were both decreasing, and the worst when both were increasing.

Fifty-six years of data is a nice sample, and from it we can draw some pretty firm conclusions about how stocks and bonds will perform in relation to a very simple rendering of the economic environment:

Stock and Bond Performance in Relation to GDP and Inflation Growth

Stock Returns

Best: Falling inflation/rising GDP

Second-Best: Falling inflation/falling GDP

Second-Worst: Rising inflation/rising GDP

Worst: Rising inflation/falling GDP

Bond Returns

Best: Falling inflation/falling GDP

Second-Best: Falling inflation/rising GDP

Second-Worst: Rising inflation/falling GDP

Worst: Rising inflation/rising GDP

It stands to reason that if you are to take advantage of these rules of thumb, you want to possess a reliable forecast of the directions of inflation and GDP. However, such forecasts can range in their accuracy from excellent to quite poor. A good explanation for this disparity is that often economic forecasts do not account for public policy.

In particular, shifts in tax rates and the procedures the Federal Reserve use are greatly related to the future direction of GDP and inflation. A forecast that does not account for these shifts stands an excellent chance of being wrong.

For instance, lower tax rates on workers will increase the incentive to work more, earn more, and put those earnings into action, while lower taxes on business and capital will bring on business expansion and higher employment. This is economy-stimulating stuff that results time and again in a rising GDP. What good is a forecast that misses the impact of such policy?

Meanwhile, a Federal Reserve that adjusts the amount of money in circulation by reacting to the direction of prices in the overall market stands the best chance of holding inflation in check. Here, the thinking is that whenever prices rise above a certain target range, too much money exists in circulation, and when prices fall below that range, there is too little money in the pipeline. However, the Fed can control this simply by tracking prices in the aggregate and acting appropriately on that information.[6] Nevertheless, a sound inflation forecast must attempt to discover the direction of Fed policy, regardless of the sensibility of that policy.

A Framework for Your Forecast

Because you can read the newspapers and watch TV, you can monitor fiscal and monetary policy on your very own. And because these policies are excellent harbingers of the GDP and inflation, respectively, you stand a good chance of formulating reliable economic forecasts. But there's nothing like a second opinion, particularly an expert second opinion.

Just as seasoned meteorologists develop forecasts that are correct more often than not, the more experienced top-down economic forecasters boast good track records when it comes to anticipating behavioral changes in the market. Even better, major newspapers regularly poll a variety of these analysts, putting together what they call "consensus" forecasts on the future direction of the stock market and economy.

How good are these forecasts?

As a financial advisor, I formulate my own forecasts, and I also sit on financial advisement boards that construct consensus opinions on the economy quarter to quarter. These forecasts have missed at times, but they have been right much more often than not. This is good news, not just for me, but for every investor who is grounded in the forces of supply and demand.

I make this last point because we can profit from an economic forecast only if we can apply it to a proven investment framework. And the most provable one I know is that which projects public policy and the range of macroeconomic variables forward to the supply-and-demand responses they will illicit. This is the framework I set forth in this book. If you subscribe to it, it is the framework to which you will apply the economic forecasts you both build and collect.

Here's an example of how the procedure might work:

At the start of 2005, the *Wall Street Journal's* consensus economic forecast called for a 1.4 percent increase in the short-term interest rate (Treasury-bill yields) and a 0.89 percent increase in the long-term rate (ten-year Treasury-bond yields). Bond prices are inversely related to yields, so the predicted increase in yields was a bearish signal for bonds. The *Journal* also called for a low 2.5 percent inflation rate and a strong 3.6 percent GDP growth rate, an environment that historically has favored stocks over bonds.

The *Journal's* consensus was bullish, to say the least, although this forecast historically has not always been correct. But if in 2005 you understood the relationship between economic policy and the relative performance of the separate asset classes, particularly the stock/bond split, you would have been just as bullish.

In the six quarters prior to the start of 2005, the GDP had been trending upward, a response to the 2003 tax-cut package that included lower rates on capital gains and investor dividends. Few, if any, signs in early 2005 indicated that this period of sunshine was about to end. Other data trends included lower unemployment, rising corporate profits, strong productivity, and record high tax revenues—all marks of sustained economic expansion. Finally, on the monetary front, fears were bubbling that higher future inflation was a threat. Yet, regardless of whether it was, all signs pointed to the Fed holding it in check: The Fed had begun the anti-inflationary procedure of raising interest rates six months earlier, and most statements from the Fed said this process would continue in a measured way.

This confluence of indicators should have had you investing properly. If you read the papers, understood the relationship between public policy and future economic realities (in other words, if your framework was correct), and backed up your opinions with a well-known consensus forecast, you might have favored stocks over bonds during 2005. And you would have been right to do so. For the year, stocks as a group gained 4.2 percent, while bonds fell 1 percent.

Reacting to Cycles Is Not an Everyday Event

We live in a world of a tax hike here and a tax cut there, of a year when the Fed and other central banks managed inflation handily and a year when they made a mess of the monetary works. As a result, we live in a world of bond moments and stock moments with many shades of stock/bond gray in between.

But in most countries, the legislative process is long and drawn out, so there is plenty of time for anyone so inclined to figure out what policies are coming down the pike. And although it is true that final legislation is never identical to initial proposals, policymaking is rarely an impromptu activity; in most cases, final policy law is related to earlier bills that have long been discussed.

In this way, "timing," as it relates to cyclical asset allocation, is not an onerous process—it is *not* day to day. This is a good reason why big investment firms make a habit of meeting quarterly to decide their major allocation moves: They understand that the markets shift in relation to significant world events. And although they make daily allocation decisions based on the minutiae of market data, for the most part, they react to the "big stuff" at quarterly intervals.

Anticipation is involved in this process, and anticipating cycles is a better strategy than reacting to cycles: When you anticipate, the window in which you stand to make above-average gains stays open that much longer. This strategy, however, is not without peril: Sometimes your forecast will be wrong and you will have to adjust. When unexpected macroeconomic shocks or unanticipated policy changes occur, ones that have you suddenly poorly allocated within your portfolio, you should cut your losses, correct your forecast, and allocate to the new cycle.

That said, more often than not, your forecast will be correct if you perform the due diligence described in this chapter. Doing so also will have you improving your performance year to year and cycle to cycle. Overall, if you behave like the above-average farmer who merges appropriate action with forecasted swings in the weather, you both will make hay while the sun shines and protect your portfolio when storm clouds threaten.

Endnotes

1. Modern meteorology certainly is more of a pure science than modern investing. Weather patterns conform to the rules of atmospheric and oceanographic physics, and the use of supercomputers has enabled meteorologists to monitor a broad range of physical factors and historical patterns and, thus, greatly increase the accuracy of their forecasts. Yet while some

claim investing can never be considered a science, I counter that empirical regularities in the data can facilitate our ability to act scientifically, to accurately forecast the collective behavior of the investment markets in a scientific way.

2. In preparing Table 12.1, I used a simple shorthand to describe quarterly returns year to year, with 1973.1 signifying the first quarter of that year, 1974.3 the third quarter of that year, etc. The inflation characteristics (rising or falling) are generalizations of the major trends within the periods.

3. Paul Volcker switched operating procedures at the Federal Reserve in the 1970s from a quantity-rule approach, which in the simplest terms watches the supply of money, to a price-rule approach, which lets real-world prices indicate the direction of inflation. When he did so, inflation began to fall. Correspondingly, if you view the inflation rate in terms of when the Fed was operating under a price-rule and when it was not, you will notice distinct and divergent results regarding the inflation rate. One lesson here is that cycles are everywhere, and understanding changes to public policy will help you identify many of them.

4. To understand why falling real rates correspond to fixed-income cycles, you have to grasp the nature of fixed-income instruments. Very simply, bonds are like stocks with fixed earnings: You know what you are going to get at the time of purchase, depending on inflation. An increase in the real rate—the interest rate adjusted for the effects of inflation—leads to a higher discount rate, which is the benchmark rate used to put a value on cash streams. When the discount rate turns higher, it produces a lower value of the coupon payment (or the specified interest rate) attached to fixed-income instruments. In the most basic terms, a rising real rate causes a decline in the value of fixed-income instruments, while a declining real rate brings on an increase in their value.

5. In formulating Table 12.2, I used a 3-month moving average to identify rising and falling interest-rate cycles and a four-quarter moving average for real GDP to determine rising and falling periods of economic growth.

6. The Federal Reserve can either increase or reduce the money supply through open-market operations. By selling government bonds in the open market, it reduces the quantity of high-powered money circulating in the economy. By purchasing back those bonds, it increases the quantity of high-powered money in the economy.

13

The Fight Is On: How to Invest Properly Relative to Regulations, Inflation, and Taxation

Imagine a prize fight in which the boxer in one corner is a 5-foot-tall, 125-pound featherweight, and the slugger in the opposite corner is a 6-foot-tall, 250-pound heavyweight. Doesn't quite seem fair, does it? Well, in business, these mismatches occur all the time, although appearances can be deceptive.

Let me first define the circumstances of these bouts, which indeed they are when viewed in terms of the performance of the different asset classes within a portfolio. *Regulations, taxes,* and *inflation* direct the behavior of all companies; they affect the economic stage, the ability of firms to turn profits, and, ultimately, the level of stock prices. Simple enough. But in an important sense, these three factors determine the ring conditions under which *all* businesses must come to blows. And this is where the mismatches come in. Sometimes the ring is slippery and favors the nimble, quicker fighter. Other times the ring is small, favoring the bigger, more powerful punchers.

Think of it. At times we can say that the burden of regulations, taxes, and inflation within a country is high. Taken together, these economic variables set a very dangerous and treacherous stage. Only the lighter and more nimble fighters will be able to negotiate the stage. The nimble fighter will take on all challengers within a country's borders. Yet not all fighters are built the same. Let's say that in Country A, Large-Cap A has sales of $100 *billion* and Small-Cap A has sales of $500 *million*. Clearly, these are fighters of a different stripe. How will each perform in the domestic economic ring? Just the same? Certainly not.

The fix is in, of course. As a group, businesses in the free market always will be victorious over the combined burden of regulations, taxation, and inflation, the specific set of shocks that concerns us in this chapter. The new equilibrium will be achieved. But the rounds of these fights are worth watching. Sometimes we'll see a company bob and weave and score points early on, only to run out of steam later in the fight. Other times we'll see a business get pummeled in the opening rounds, only to land a knock-out blow before the final bell. Fundamentally, when uncertainty emerges within national borders, you want to know which of its opponents deserve your investment dollars and in which rounds. This chapter gives you such expertise.

Getting to Know Your Investing Venues

If a boxer with national appeal had the option of fighting in the high-school gymnasium in Anywhere, U.S.A., or in Madison Square Garden in New York City, which venue do you think he'd choose? One would presume the latter because it would offer a larger audience, a greater dollar volume at the gate, and, hence, a superior purse. So it is with our public companies. Motivated by profit, companies seek the widest audiences—the largest and most visible venues—possible. For a time, the high-school gymnasium will have to do, but the persistent compulsion is toward center ring at the Garden.

Of course, the catchphrase that "size matters" is used with a little naughtiness these days, but in business and investing, it matters a great deal. Among our pair-wise portfolio choices is large-cap versus small-cap, a simple delineation based on size. Small-caps, in general, have dollar sales in the hundreds of millions; large-caps in the hundreds of billions. Small-caps and large-caps will perpetually coexist. However, within industry groups, the largest companies will at times enjoy inherent advantages over the smallest simply because they are bigger. Specifically, larger companies will have an advantage when the costs of doing business become "fixed," or predictable.

Let's say that it will take a fixed amount of paperwork to introduce a new product into a country, regardless of how many units are likely to be sold. With that paperwork comes a new fixed cost. It follows that the largest companies within sectors will be better suited than their smaller competitors to pay back these costs, a reality that will lead to increased consolidation and fewer (larger) companies eventually dominating each industry.

For a quick case study of this move toward the large and of how fixed costs play unequally on companies in relation to their size, we can look to the megaregulation known as the Clean Air Act.

In 1970, legislators in Washington passed the first full-fledged version of this act, establishing the EPA as its enforcement agency. With cleaner American air and better fuel mileage as the stated goals, the act mandated that carmakers conform to a set of strict emission rules—a full *90 percent* reduction in automotive discharge.

One solution was to outfit all new cars with catalytic converters, exhaust-system devices that turn pollutants into more acceptable atmospheric gasses. Largely, as a result of antirust regulations, GM,

Ford, and Chrysler—the Big Three automakers at the time—each set out to develop these converters, which, from my point of view, meant that Detroit would develop two catalytic converters too many. The costs for developing these converters were roughly the same for each of the firms, which, in addition to other fixed costs related to the Clean Air Act, had a clear size-related impact. Because greater capacity begets greater efficiency, which begets lower costs, the unit costs would climb the most for the smallest of the Big Three.

At the time, GM was a giant, Ford was relatively large, and Chrysler was a distant third in terms of size. Not surprisingly, Chrysler was put at a competitive disadvantage once the new regulatory rules were established and suffered the most during the period, even when you account for the energy crunch, runaway inflation, and heightened foreign-car competition that characterized the 1970s (see Table 13.1). When catalyst-endowed cars first rolled off U.S. assembly lines, some in the industry began talking of the "Big Two," *sans* Chrysler.[1]

TABLE 13.1   Big-Three Automotive Revenues and Net Income 1970–78*

	Chrysler Revenues	Net Income	Ford Revenues	Net Income	GM Revenues	Net Income
1978	13,618	**–205**	42,784	1,589	63,221	3,508
1976	15,537	**423**	28,840	983	47,181	2,903
1974	10,860	**–52**	23,621	361	31,550	950
1972	9,641	**221**	20,194	870	30,435	2,163
1970	7,000	**–8**	14,980	516	18,752	609

° U.S. dollars in millions

Source: Ward's Motor Vehicle Facts & Figures

As the smallest of the domestic Big Three, Chrysler sucked it up for much of the 1970s. But it persisted in the decades that followed, nibbling away at the market share of its U.S. competitors. Eventfully, it merged with Germany's Daimler-Benz in 1998 to create a truly global concern, and though DaimlerChrysler stumbled a bit out of the gate, Chrysler's move to the large—and toward the minimization of the impact of fixed costs—has been near textbook.[2]

A few monster prize fighters competing in one intraplanetary ring in pursuit of a mega payday? Is this the future?

To a degree. Globalization is a compelling argument for the largest of the large-caps capturing an outsized chunk of the profits within their industries in the decades and centuries to come. But I am not, by any stretch, suggesting that you put all your money in this one super-basket and call it a day.

Just as certainty in business and investing will never be 100 percent, a true single market will never completely materialize. Pockets of differentiation always will exist. Smaller venues, offering smaller purses, will attract the lighter-weight prize fighters: the small-caps. There forever will be a California or France that regulates itself toward disadvantage on both a regional and global basis. There perpetually will be a Hawaii or South Pacific that, based on the natural endowments of sand, palm, and sunshine, will draw specific tourist dollars that other locations cannot claim. There always will be a Dominican Republic, my small pond of birth, where some small-cap businesses will flourish below the large-cap radar. (In my D.R., organic farmers have done just that.)[3] There perpetually will be a Country A that lowers taxes and a Country B that raises them—and the flight of capital toward Country A that ensues.

Consequently, we can talk of two "venues," *national* and *global*.

The global venue is the future single world market—a work in progress, eternally perhaps, but nonetheless an increasingly prevailing force. This grand stage is for the super large-caps, those companies with facilities all over the world and the ability to shift production toward the most advantageous economic environments. Because these companies are so big and can mechanically shift operations in the direction of advantage, they are the most shock-resilient.

Then there's the national venue, across which the winds of uncertainty often travel. This can be described as any global location where tax, monetary, regulatory, and trade policies differ from other locales. Earlier we discussed the location effect in terms of the economic shocks that bring about pockets of market differentiation. The lesson still applies: Erase the borders on your globe as they are currently drawn and retrace them based on the levels of transaction costs that exist between regions when economic shocks occur. That said, there are, in fact, times when the transaction-cost borders as they are currently drawn will serve you just fine.

We already know that the relative size of companies will relate directly to their performance when economic shocks occur. In California, when regulatory controls on energy led to the lights going out, small-caps performed much worse than large-caps because the former, many of which have single plant facilities, were stuck in the state and the latter could shift production outside the shock zone. In this example, size became our proxy, or stand-in, for companies that had the ability or inability to shift production outside of a region. In other words, company size allowed us to determine the level of locational, or physical, elasticity. And we derived an important rule from this: When negative shocks impact specific locations, locationally inelastic small-caps likely will underperform locationally elastic large-caps.

But when focusing on elasticity with respect to the combined burden of regulation, taxation, and inflation, size becomes a proxy for the ability of companies to adjust to the changing economic environment.[4] This turns our earlier locational rule on its head:

> When shocks—in particular, those related to regulations, inflation, and taxes—affect national economies, large-caps likely will underperform small-caps.

To see this in the clearest light, we must further separate our fighters by weight class.

Classifying Stocks: From Nimble to Brawny

Taxes and regulations are typically targeted at the largest companies within national borders; when governments tax and regulate, they like to go after big game.

As for taxes, big is where the greatest potential revenue is, while the populist tendency of governments is to tax the larger, "richer" companies at a higher level than the smaller companies, which might be stifled under a tax burden that is too lofty. As for regulations, small-cap favoritism also exists: Governments frequently stick provisions into legislation that exempts smaller companies outright or protects them from stricter levels of compliance.

Inflation, meanwhile, causes what economists call "bracket creep." Simply, it pushes people and businesses into higher tax brackets, essentially increasing their tax rates.

Putting all this together, like lightweight fighters, small-caps will appear nimble and quick when adverse changes to taxes, regulations, and inflation threaten or arrive. Indeed, bobbing and weaving are the fortes of small-caps, which might "hedge" against inflation (putting assets into safe havens), "shelter" themselves against high taxes (through legal but crafty means), or "skirt" regulations (for example, by morphing the way business is done so that certain regulatory rules no longer apply). And how will our large-caps perform at this juncture? Like slow-footed behemoths.

But these are the earlier rounds of the fight. When uncertainty increases, the costs are not fixed. And when they do fix and certainty returns—meaning the tax, regulatory, and inflationary environments become knowable and predictable—the combined regulatory burden becomes something of a stationary target, one that is tailor-made for the corporate power punchers, those big, brawny (and national) large-caps.

Would You Always Bet on a Fighter Who Wins Two-Thirds of the Time?

If I were to show a chart of the relative performance of small- and large-cap stocks over the last 31 years to professionals in the investment community, I would more often than not receive a shrug. Since the dawn of asset allocation, which wasn't all that long ago, small- and large-cap stocks have exhibited periodic behavior, whereby one beats out the other for a few years before switching.

Well, in Figure 13.1, I have provided such a chart, and from where I sit, a shrug is hardly the right reaction.

The table shows the annual returns of U.S. large-caps (shaded boxes) and small-caps (white boxes) between 1975 and 2005.[5] If we overlook the one-year size shift that occurred in 1988, considering it to be an anomaly for now, five distinct size cycles come into view. From my perspective, random periodic behavior this is not.

Reflecting on this chart, an investment analyst who adheres to the sentiment that small-caps are the best bet for investors over the long run would say my data is a further endorsement of investing fact. And he'd have a point. Indeed, small-caps beat out large caps in 21 of the 31 sample years—more than two-thirds of the time.

However, I'd ask, "Would you *always* bet on a fighter who wins two-thirds of the time?"

"Yes," he'd respond. "In the long run, I'll make money if I place equal bets on all of his fights."

"But what if you had a strong sense of *when* this fighter would lose that one-third of the time? Would you still bet on this fighter to win all of the time?"

"No, I wouldn't," he'd respond, catching my drift. "But it's difficult to know such things. That's why I 'bet' the long-run trends. It's the safest way to go, and not a bad business."

	1975	1976	1977	1978	1979
1	S 52.8	S 57.4	S 25.4	S 23.5	S 43.5
2	L 37.2	L 23.8	L -7.2	L 6.6	L 18.4

	1980	1981	1982	1983	1984
1	S 39.9	S 13.9	S 28	S 39.7	L 6.3
2	L 32.4	L -4.9	L 21.4	L 22.5	S -6.7

	1985	1986	1987	1988	1989
1	L 32.2	L 18.5	L 5.2	S 22.9	L 31.5
2	S 24.7	S 6.9	S -9.3	L 16.8	S 10.2

	1990	1991	1992	1993	1994
1	L -3.2	S 44.6	S 23.4	S 21	S 3.1
2	S -21.6	L 30.6	L 7.7	L 10	L 1.3

	1995	1996	1997	1998	1999
1	L 37.4	L 23.1	L 33.4	L 28.6	S 29.8
2	S 34.5	S 17.6	S 22.8	S -7.3	L 21

	2000	2001	2002	2003	2004
1	S -3.6	S 2.5	S -15.3	S 38.8	S 22.5
2	L -9.9	L -13.1	L -23.7	L 28.7	L 10.7

	2005
1	S 7.68
2	L 4.91

FIGURE 13.1 Annual Returns: Large-Cap Versus Small-Cap

At this point, I would smile and nod, perhaps shrug, and walk away. There always will be those investors who, in the safe pursuit of profit over the long run, resign themselves to losing one-third of the time—or even more. But cyclical investors are motivated to capture the fractional historical differences that the purer long-run investors toss aside.

Indeed, if you know your recent U.S. economic history, Figure 13.1 becomes a scorecard on which to base decisive future action. For each period in the sample, when small-caps beat large-caps, the economic environment can be described as one in which inflation, taxation, and regulation were in flux—an uncertain environment. And when large-caps beat small-caps, inflation, taxes, and regulations were steady, for the most part—a proven recipe for certainty.

In what follows, I describe each of these cyclical periods in detail, an exercise that will help you describe both certain and uncertain economic environments in the future. But first I restate a warning: I have my political views and you have yours, and they might be as diametrically opposed as night and day. But who really cares? As investors, we should stand in cold allegiance, basing our actions not on political emotion, but on the hard facts. If Political Action A causes Economic Result B nearly all the time, we possess reliable information and, hence, a pretty good basis for investment action.

So on with the national fight.

Business vs. Uncertainty, Round by Round

The venue is the United States of America. The years are 1975 to 2005, a period in which the uncertainty monster climbs in and out of the economic ring. Our corporate fighters—our nimble and lightweight small-caps, our brawny and heavyweight large-caps—are gloved and ready for battle.

Place your bets.

1975–83: Small-Cap Effect

The period 1975–83 can be divided into two phases: an initial seven years of profound uncertainty and a two-year transitional period when businesses and the economy weaned themselves off the doubt and dismay that characterized most of the previous decade.

Inflation infamously swelled during the 1970s, while tax policy in this environment was hesitant and temporary—two moods that only nourish the uncertainty beast.[6] And then there were the regulations. Regulations in America historically have come in waves, and a great regulatory tidal wave hit in the 1970s in response to the environmental and safety movements of that era.[7] With each new act and agency (there were dozens) a stack of new rules and restrictions landed on the corporate desk—not to mention reams of added paperwork and legal fees. Of course, it would not have been the 1970s without energy-price controls of nearly every size and stripe.

But the scene shifted dramatically with the turn of the decade. In 1981, the fledgling Reagan administration passed a landmark tax-cut package, the centerpiece being a steep cut in individual tax rates. The cuts were phased in, helping prolong uncertainty until they were fully implemented in 1984, although uncertainty was clearly on the way out. For instance, even though small-caps outperformed large-caps in 1982 and 1983, large-caps did not perform poorly during these years.

Additionally, by 1984, it was evident that the Fed had gotten inflation right: In January of that year, inflation was down to about 4 percent from nearly 12 percent at the start of 1981. The Reagan administration also had been diligently trimming back the regulatory burden. Initially, it required agencies to outline new regulations in terms of "net benefits," the difference between the social benefit and social cost.[8] It also significantly reduced the annual flow of major new regulations (from triple to double digits) while lifting price controls on oil and gas.[9]

With taxes lowering, inflation (at long last) settling, and the regulatory burden lessening, certainty—and a sustainable large-cap cycle—finally emerged.

1984–90: Large-Cap Effect

The period 1984–90 is storied for its economic certainty. In these "seven fat years," as former *Wall Street Journal* editor Robert Bartley termed them, inflation held relatively steady between 3 and 5 percent (dipping near 1 percent in late 1986), a momentous turnaround from the previous decade.[10]

In 1986, individual tax rates were slashed again (the top rate falling to 28 percent), corporate income taxes were lowered (the top rate dropped to 34 percent), and personal exemptions were increased. During the seven fat years, businesses enjoyed the certainty that fiscal policy, for the most part, would be favorable and monetary policy stable. The regulatory story, by and large, also was consistent: The Reagan administration continued to slow the flow of red tape and strike hundreds of restrictions from the books.

A complete-certainty world? No. Every cycle has its bumps, and sometimes these bumps foretell a cycle's end.

One of the bigger bumps of the Reagan years was the savings and loan (S&L) crisis. This is an involved story featuring shady political deals, questionable regulatory oversight at the agency level, and outright crooks. Jumping to the outcome, it culminated in the elimination of more than a thousand S&Ls (roughly a third, by way of bankruptcies and mergers) and a bailout by the federal government in the hundreds of billions of dollars.[11] It also led to much stricter regulations for all banks. In 1989, the American Banking Association said regulation already had reached a "crisis stage" and that the pro-regulation fever of policymakers in the wake of the S&L disaster was only making matters worse.[12]

In the last of the fat years, the transition back to greater uncertainty also included the start of a recession and the denouement of one of the greatest political blunders in modern presidential history. After gaining office on the pledge of "Read my lips: no new taxes," President George H. W. Bush signed a bill in the Rose Garden that hiked taxes on tobacco, gas, alcohol, and other items.

1991–94: Small-Cap Effect

Inflation pushed over 6 percent in 1990 but was pulled back to the 3 percent range in 1991, the year in which a brief eight-month recession also ended.[13] But the damaging interaction of higher inflation, taxes, and regulations stuck around a little longer.

As vice president under Reagan, Bush Sr. headed that administration's regulation-reduction task force. But in his one term in the Oval Office, Bush helped fatten the regulatory burden, the primary thickeners including the Clean Air Act (1990; an expansion), the Americans with Disabilities Act (1990), the Federal Deposit Insurance Corporation Improvement Act (1991; a sweeping S&L crisis reform), and the Nutrition Labeling and Education Act (1992).

Then in 1993, the freshman Clinton team raised fuel, individual, corporate, and Social Security taxes. Correspondingly, the Clinton agenda featured sweeping health care reform, an idea that grew into a 1,342-page regulatory bill that, if passed, would have nationalized the country's health system.

But the 1991–94 cycle is notable for its lightness and shortness: Small-caps were the winners for the four-year period, but large-caps didn't perform too shabbily overall. Though new layers of uncertainty had blanketed the economy, apparently they were not too thick.

1995–98: Large-Cap Effect

A prevailing fear among businesses in 1993 and 1994 was that the Clinton health care plan would become reality. The program portended an enormous government expansion—one that would have to be funded somehow (i.e., tax increases)—as well as a potentially huge increase in the regulatory burden. Forty percent of corporate executives polled in a 1994 *Fortune* survey revealed they had reduced their employment plans based on fears of these higher costs.[14]

Apparently, similar fears gripped members of Congress, and in 1994, the Clinton health care plan was firmly defeated. Then in the midterm elections that year, Congress flipped majority parties from Democrat to Republican, an electoral nod to restraint over bigger government. This GOP "takeover" was termed a revolution by the victors, who carried to Congress a platform of tax-rate reductions, spending cuts, and deregulation. This put the executive and legislative branches in opposition, stances they would retain for most of the next six years.

In 1995, as the new Congress settled in, the president pulled out his veto pen, something he would do many times in what have come to be known as the gridlock years. And businesses didn't mind at all. *Newsweek's* Wall Street editor wrote in 1998 that "for savvy U.S. business people, political gridlock is almost as much fun as making money. If Clinton (or Gore) and Congress spend all their time fighting each other … they're more likely to leave the rest of us alone."[15]

An additional factor supporting certainty was that the only alternative to gridlock was consensus; the president and Congress would have to meet in the middle if they were to meet at all. And for businesses, the middle wasn't so bad. In the vein of compromise, the president signed a tax bill in 1997 that included a reduction in the top capital gains rate from 28 to 20 percent.

1999–2005: Small-Cap Effect

Deeds *and* words both add to certainty (or uncertainty). In late 1996, while the economy was enjoying another year of expansion and stock markets were humming along, then–Federal Reserve chair Alan Greenspan entered two words into the national lexicon that forever will be equated with uncertainty: "irrational exuberance."[16]

Greenspan had managed monetary policy with a deft touch to this point and also did so for the near term that followed. But that phrase hung heavy in the air, and for good reason: It pointed to the fear that the Federal Reserve might very well put the brakes on the economy through interest-rate hikes to calm a vibrant bull market—one that, if left unchecked, would collapse of its own weight and bring the economy down with it (or so the theory went). Y2K concerns—the fear that computers would not be able to distinguish 1900 from 2000 at the turn of the century, a "bug" that would shut down businesses globally—were also ripe in the air. The tone of the Federal Reserve increasingly became one of restraint and caution.

And in 1999, the deeds followed. In an attempt to cool off the economy and, hence, the stock markets, Greenspan began to increase the regulatory burden through a series of interest-rate hikes that he continued through May 2000—six hikes in all that lifted the overnight interest rate from 4.75 to 6.5 percent.[17] In March 2001, the economy began what would be an eight-month contraction. The Fed's cooling effort had a chilling effect.

At the start of 2001, the Fed began a reverse policy of interest-rate cuts in an attempt to re-energize the economy. But on September 11, 2001, at the tail end of the recession, terrorists steered airplanes into the World Trade Center and the Pentagon, and everything, as they say, changed for good.

At this point, the Fed began adding a large amount of liquidity (or cash readiness) to the economy, partly as a response to the shock of 9/11 and partly to cure what had become a deflationary recession. By

June 2003, it had reduced the federal funds interest rate to a historically low 1 percent, where it held for a year. Additionally, in 2003,
Congress passed and President George W. Bush signed an investment tax cut that immediately lowered the capital gains and dividend
tax rates each to 15 percent. The economy surged almost instantly
and climbed in a sustained way in the coming years. But the small-cap
cycle persisted, for a number of reasons.

Geopolitical uncertainty locked itself in place on 9/11. Suddenly,
the U.S. was at war, war being yet another synonym for uncertainty.
Then there's regulation. In 2002, after a string of corporate accounting scandals rattled investor confidence, Congress passed the Sarbanes-Oxley Act. This enormous regulation, an attempt to elevate the
quality and transparency of financial reporting, greatly increased
paperwork, SEC compliance costs, and legal fees for American businesses, costs that would not "fix" right away because certain provisions of the act were rolled out. Compliance "established" itself as an
ongoing, developing, and sometimes head-scratching matter.
Bizarrely, but not surprisingly, this legislation earned its very own "for
dummies" book, *Sarbanes-Oxley for Dummies*.[18]

Uncertainty—the interaction among taxes, inflation, regulations,
and sometimes more—has a way of piling up.

Investing across Inflation, Tax, and Regulatory Cycles: The Payoff

A dollar invested in our basket of large-cap stocks in January 1975
would have grown to $50.04 by the end of 2005. That is a 13.45 per-
cent compounded annual rate of return and, historically, not a bad
return at all. (For comparison's sake, Jeremy Siegel, in his *Stocks for
the Long Run*, shows that large-caps returned about 11 percent
between 1926 and 2000 on a compounded annual basis.)[19] Meanwhile,
a dollar invested in small-caps in 1975 would have grown to $198.54, a

phenomenal gain that translates to an 18.61 percent annual return. If you invested your entire nest egg in small-caps during this period, you would have generated returns that exceeded the large-cap benchmark by 5.16 percentage points annually. As a pure long-run strategy, you would have to be considered among the smart investors if you held to a small-cap program for the full 31-year period.

However...

If you employed a cyclical switching strategy between 1975 and 2005, whereby you acted on the size performance of asset classes in relation to the prevailing levels of economic certainty and uncertainty, you would have proven *much* smarter.

One dollar invested in small-caps in January 1975 and appropriately switched thereafter based on the small- and large-cap cycles through December 2005 would have grown to a whopping $424.46. This strategy would have produced a breakneck 22.38 percent compounded annual rate of return, outperforming the all-small-cap strategy by 3.77 percentage points per year and the all-large-cap strategy by 8.93 percentage points annually.

As a result of the interaction among inflation, taxes, and regulation, economies switch between uncertainty and certainty without asking your permission. But as an investor, you have every opportunity to switch between the appropriate "fighters" during each of these environments. It's really only a question of whether you want to win some of the time or most of the time.

An Investor's Certain Advantage

How about winning all the time? Well, one must be realistic. Capturing the full breadth of every size cycle within national borders is difficult because the effects of tax rates, regulations, and inflation on asset values don't always respond on cue. Responding "near cue," though, is another story. During each of the five size cycles discussed in this chapter, once the environment emerged, it stuck around for a good while—for several years and more.

The job, then, is to track changes to inflation, tax rates, and regulation as they develop and to act once they establish.

Let's say it is 1982 all over again and your U.S. indicators are beginning to blink "certainty." Taxes have been lowered. The regulatory flow has been lessened. And inflation is trending down. Still, small-caps are outperforming large-caps. Same for 1983, although you notice that both small-caps (+39.7 percent for the year) and large-caps (+22.5 percent) are doing well. Then it's 1984, and large-caps finally beat out small-caps (with small-cap returns actually turning negative). Well, it might be early 1985 by now, but because you took these actions, you made the appropriate switch to large-caps in the U.S. portion of your portfolio:

1. You watched economic certainty—produced by lower tax rates, regulations, and inflation—gather and then establish.

2. You understood that tax, regulatory, and inflation cycles tend to last several years or more.

3. You knew that large-caps tend to be inelastic with respect to changes in tax rates, the inflation rate, and the regulatory burden, and thus will outperform small-caps when these variables are low or declining.

4. You recognized that small-caps are elastic with respect to taxes, inflation, and regulation, and thus will outperform large-caps when these variables are high or increasing.

Despite a one-year blip in 1988, when small-caps beat out large-caps (although both did well), you would have been correctly allocated for most of the next *six* years.

But what if you caught only five years of this cycle? Or four or three? In truth, the differential in performance between large- and small-caps is great enough to suggest that capturing even a fraction of these cycles will enhance your portfolio returns in a significant way.

When you think of it, you have a *certain* competitive advantage over the stocks you invest in. One year you can be large-cap, and the next year small. No company can do that, and you need only develop the confidence to act on this advantage. Here, your ability to spot distinct economic environments and your understanding of how asset classes behave in these environments are inseparable: The more you know about the cyclical nature of asset classes, the more certain will be your investment actions and the better will be your performance.

Of this, I am certain.

Endnotes

1. Allan J. Mayer and James C. Jones, "Chrysler's Shake-Out," *Newsweek*, 14 July 1975, 61.

2. Describing the natural move "to the large" in terms of the auto industry has its difficulties. At the start of the new century, Ford and GM were still giants in their field, although they probably received more press about their predicted bankruptcies than anything else. Over the years, Detroit has always struggled to meet one cost variable: its unions. Worker pay, health benefits, and retirement benefits have all been bid up in the union negotiation process, to the detriment of the cost-effectiveness of Detroit. Product matters, too, and Detroit's output has not always matched up with the burgeoning foreign competition. One can look at Toyota: Once an innovative, fleet-of-foot start-up, it is now a "Big Four" member, along with DaimlerChrysler, Ford, and GM. But there it is again, that move to the large. Union woes, poor management, bad breaks, and ill-conceived products aside, the moral of the story still holds: It is in the DNA of public companies to grow.

3. When the doors to free trade opened in the Dominican Republic, farmers there were in a bit of a pickle. How could they compete with the U.S. agricultural business? What would they
   grow? It turns out that the answer was right in front of them. In
   the coveted U.S. produce market, organically grown fruits and
   vegetables were (and still are) in high demand, an offshoot of a
   cultural movement toward health and wholesomeness. But
   D.R. farmers had been growing organically for years mostly
   because chemical fertilizers are so expensive. So right from the
   start, they had a competitive advantage: When it came to growing organically, they knew what they were doing, and soon
   enough these small-cap farmers were competing for retail
   space in the U.S. and Europe.

4. The investing strategy for the mega large-caps, or what we
   might call the super heavyweights, must be separated from any
   strategy concerned with investing specifically within national
   borders. Because these big hitters are not bound by the rules of
   any one country, investing in them should become a matter of
   estimating which industries will perform the best in relation to
   the global economic environment.

5. In computing the results reported in Figure 13.1, I used the
   S&P 500 as the proxy for domestic large-cap stocks, and the
   Russell 2000 and S&P 600 as the proxies for domestic small-
   cap stocks.

6. Inflation data in this section is based on the consumer price
   index as compiled by the Bureau of Labor Statistics. Historical
   federal tax-policy data is available from a range of sources,
   including the U.S. Treasury Department.

7. Information on major U.S. regulatory programs is made available by the Office of Management and Budget (OMB). Following is a list of several of regulatory acts and agencies to emerge
   during the 1970s: the National Highway Traffic Safety Admin-

istration (1970), the Clean Air Act (1970), the Environmental Protection Agency (1970), the Occupational Safety and Health Administration (1970), the Clean Water Act (1972), the Consumer Product Safety Commission (1972), the Noise Pollution and Abatement Act (1972), the Safe Drinking Water Act (1974), the Materials Transportation Board (1975), the Toxic Substances Control Act (1976), the Resource Conservation and Recovery Act (1976), the Community Reinvestment Act (1977), and the Office of Surface Mining Reclamation and Enforcement (1977).

8. "Report to Congress on the Costs and Benefits of Federal Regulations," OMB, 30 September 1997.

9. Philip Shabecoff, "Reagan Order on Cost-Benefit Analysis Stirs Economic and Political Debate," *New York Times*, 7 November 1981.

10. Robert L. Bartley, *The Seven Fat Years* (New York: Free Press, 1992).

11. "An Examination of the Banking Crises of the 1980s and Early 1990s," Federal Deposit Insurance Corporation (December 1997).

12. "ABA Report Attacks Red Tape," International Banking Report, Informa Plc., 1 November 1989.

13. Business-cycle expansions and contractions are monitored by the National Bureau of Economic Research.

14. "Fortune Forecast," *Fortune*, 6 September 1993, 17.

15. Allan Sloan, "The Real Bottom Line," *Newsweek*, 28 December 1998, 56.

16. Alan Greenspan, "The Challenge of Central Banking in a Democratic Society," remarks at the Annual Dinner and Francis Boyer Lecture of the American Enterprise Institute for Public Policy Research, Washington, D.C., 5 December 1996.

17. Historical data on the intended federal funds rate is maintained by the Federal Reserve Board.

18. Jill Gilbert Welytok, *Sarbanes-Oxley for Dummies* (Indianapolis: Wiley, February 2006).

19. Jeremy J. Siegel, "Long-Term Returns of NYSE/AMEX/Nasdaq Stocks Ranked by Size, 1926–2000," *Stocks for the Long Run* (New York: McGraw-Hill, 2002).

14

Ending the Never-Ending Debate: Active vs. Passive Investing and Why You Can Take Both Sides

Did a lone gunman assassinate JFK, or was there a second shooter on the Grassy Knoll? Is Hamlet really insane, or does he just feign madness? Did Shoeless Joe Jackson help throw the 1919 World Series, or is he vindicated by his .375 batting average across those games? Who makes those crop circles? Farmers on tractors or little green aliens?

Coke or Pepsi?

Attempt to publicly answer any of these questions, and you are sure to receive a truckload of rebuttal for your efforts. This is the personality of the never-ending debate, which is characterized by the absolute conclusions drawn by the opposing sides. Lee Harvey Oswald killed JFK, period. Shoeless Joe took the money, so he threw the series.[1] Contestants in a never-ending debate might cede ground on a point or two, but their conclusions rarely waver. "Despite the findings of my opponent, some of which may be worthy, I still hold to my original opinion that…"

Debate can be good sport. But what about debates that have *a lot* to do with how well you will perform over your investing life? What about, in particular, the great debate over whether to go active or passive with your investments? This is *your* money we're talking about, and sport this debate is not. Yet despite temporary gains in argumentative momentum on either the passive or active side, I do not foresee an end to the dispute—which is a shame, for in reality, this does not need to be a dispute at all.

At this point of the book, it should be clear that I hold to the formula that sometimes you want to "go" active in your portfolio, and at other times you want to act passively. This is because I believe your investment decisions should be founded in the cyclical nature of economies and markets. If you can acknowledge the existence of cycles—if you understand that there are predictable economic environments in which small-caps will beat out large-caps, when stocks will eclipse bonds, or when any pair-wise investment choice will outperform—then you also must grasp the idea that sometimes passive investing makes the most sense, and at other times active is the way to go.

In this chapter and the following chapter, I hope to bring this argument to a conclusion, at least within the framework of this book: One absolute passive or active formula is not a perfect fit for any investor interested in above-average performance over the long run. Practically speaking, this must be true if you are to invest across cycles: To do so, you have to actively switch between the major asset classes from time to time. But there's an additional practicality at work here: Just as there are asset-class cycles, there also are *passive and active cycles*.

At this point of the above-average-investing story, we make a decided turn toward the practical. Understanding the foundational rules of market cycles, industry and corporate elasticity, and price shifts in the context of supply and demand will have you prepared intellectually to invest in an above-average way, but at some point you have to, well, actually invest. In this chapter, I incorporate the investment vehicles most often accessed by modern investors, among these index funds, exchange-traded funds, and mutual funds. In Chapter 15, "A Rational Walk Down Wall Street: Darting Between Passive and Active When the Odds Are in Your Favor," we turn to the managers who oversee active investment funds, developing rules for how and when to choose between them. In Chapter 16, "Alpha Bets: The Case for Hedge Funds and a Greek Letter You'll Want in Your Portfolio," we investigate our final portfolio choice, the hedge fund, which might be out of your reach today but at some point could supercharge your portfolio. Finally, in Chapter 17, "Tilting Toward Success: A Step-by-Step Guide to Above-Average Asset Allocation," we put it all together, reviewing the complete strategy for above-average cyclical asset allocation and how you can practically apply it to your starting world portfolio.

For now, I take my initial stab at ending the active versus passive debate once and for all.

Meeting or Beating the Market?

Let's review what's at stake here. *Passive investing* is based on the idea that the stock market is efficient, that all available information is priced into the market at any given time, so no other "smaller" set of information can consistently beat the market. It's as if the market were one giant brain made up of the millions of brains that invest in stocks and bonds and thus determine the prices of those investments. How can one active brain consistently beat that?

Advocates of pure-passive investing yield points here: They admit that, from time to time, some investors and active fund managers will indeed be able to outperform the market, and they might attribute this performance to luck or excellent investment timing. However, because only a relative few can sustain such performance, the passive proponent offers the formula of indexing your investments.

When one "indexes," one buys and holds a good representation of the market; one purchases the big market brain, or a facsimile of it, such as an index fund that mirrors the performance of actual stock or bond indexes. In this way, investors gain access to the true performance of the market. And because markets have proven they *will* climb upward over the long haul, this is smart, safe, market-average investing.

Active investing, on the other hand, is founded on the belief that there are opportunities to perform better than the stock and bond markets. Stock pickers, who base their actions on seemingly uncountable methods, from charting stocks to evaluating company fundamentals to seeking undervalued, as-yet undiscovered opportunities, are the most active investors. But mutual funds can be considered active vehicles, and this is exactly where active investing thrives. When you own shares of a mutual fund, as more than 54 million U.S. households and 91 million investors do, you own part of a managed vehicle, with the managers regularly adjusting fund allocations in an attempt to bolster fund performance.[2] It stands to reason that the better your manager is, the better your performance will be.

Any investor wants to "beat" the market. The only question is, is it possible to do so with regularity? Of course. The probability of doing so, however, changes from market cycle to market cycle. And this, from my perspective, is where the active versus passive debate ceases to be a debate at all.

The Allure of the Average Argument

When I speak of the "long haul," I mean the total length of time you will be invested in the stock and bond markets. For latecomers, this can be 10 or 20 years; for those who start out young, 30 or 40 years. Over such periods, passive investing indeed appears to beat out active investing.

John Bogle, founder and former chairman of the Vanguard Group and a passionate advocate of passive investing, reports that the average S&P 500 index fund returned 12.8 percent annually in the 20-year period between 1983 and 2003, while the S&P 500 index, the benchmark for the fund, returned a nearly equivalent 13 percent.[3] This is a clear indication of passive investing doing exactly what it should: delivering market-average results.

But Bogle also reports that the average stock mutual fund (or active fund) returned only 10 percent in this period, a full 2.8 percentage points below the average index fund. Many similar studies show that stock indexes and the passive funds that mirror them beat active funds, on average, over long periods of time. Add in the fees attached to owning these funds—transaction costs and tax penalties that do not apply to passive investments (at least, not to the level of active funds)—and the pure-passive case strengthens that much more.

Active managers, however, defend their fees. If you expect an active fund to outperform the market, why shouldn't it cost you more than an index fund that only mirrors the market? Indeed, the knowledge of the active manager and the caretaking he or she provides must come with a price. Active managers point to periods of excellent performance, times when their funds ran circles around slow-footed passive investments. They do so because 1) they have indeed at times generated market-beating performance, and 2) they very much want your business.

Over the long haul, some fund managers will be more deserving of your business than others; they will beat the market more often than not. However, because it might be difficult to select such managers (never is there a year when all active funds "beat the market"), the passive argument gels into a homogenous whole: Stay safe, stay steady, believe in the efficiency of markets and that you are not smarter than the markets, invest in index funds, avoid transaction costs that don't always justify themselves, realize sound gains, and enter retirement with average results.

Average, in the passive lexicon, is *not* a dirty word. It's the law. Says Bogle,

> We [in the investment profession] continue to focus nearly all of our attention on the search for the Holy Grail of achieving superior performance for our own clients, seemingly ignoring the fact that all market participants as a group earn average returns. Put another way, in terms of the returns we earn for our clients, we in the investment community are, and must be, average.[4]

Must we?

The Same People Shop at Costco and Nordstrom

The investment community is pretty much divided into the active and passive camps. Though few in either camp will tell you this, you are free to roam between the two. Costs are involved in this practice. For one, there are the added taxes and fees that are a part of active investing. The fee, again, is the price of accessing the knowledge of the fund manager, while the added taxes come about when fund managers switch between investments, with each switch becoming a moment when capital gains taxes are realized.

Fund to fund, the added cost of taxes and fees varies. Taxes are attributable to the *turnover rate* of the funds, with low turnover (say, around 25 percent) representing a much more tax-advantaged situation than high turnover (say, 80 percent or more). Fees, including management and administrative costs, can run anywhere from 0.5 percent to 2 percent (or more) annually. Taking taxes and fees together, this *is* a hurdle. But it *can* be worth it.

True enough, even switching from an active to passive mode, or vice versa, has its costs: Often taxes are due when one leaves one investment for another. But because we have seen not only the existence of cycles, but the *persistence* of cycles over many years, I firmly believe that switching between the active and passive investment modes at the appropriate times will deliver gains that can easily hurdle these transaction costs.

This is really the crux of the active versus passive problem, as I see it. In terms of the debate, both parties are too absolute in their beliefs for any one investor's good. Simply, I don't think it is in the nature or best interest of any investor to be so rigid as to go all-passive or all-active all the time.

When you think about it, an investor is little more than a shopper, someone who compares and contrasts the range of investment products and purchases the ones that fit. As a consumer, do you shop in just one type of store? Or does it take of range of stores, from the lower to higher end, to meet all your shopping needs?

I would wager that you, like most readers, fall in with the latter group.

Let's think of two diametrically opposed stores: Costco and Nordstrom. Costco, among the largest of the nationwide warehouse clubs, sells low-priced (and often quality) goods in bulk. You can buy name-brand clothes here, which you can select from giant bins. You also can purchase a whole rib-eye section of a cow, which, priced for bulk, is a lot cheaper per pound than beef at the supermarket. This shopping is very do-it-yourself: You grab a cart, cruise the wide and towering aisles, and select from an array of reasonably priced products that, though plentiful to the eye, are strictly limited to what Costco management could stock that day or week.

You compromise when you shop at Costco. If the bins fill with fleece jackets and you want one in blue, you might have to settle for one in black. If you need a box of Cheerios, you might have to buy three (or a king-size box because Costco sells in bulk). If you want to barbecue ribs tonight, you might have to switch to pork chops if that's all the pig Costco has in stock. (It's hard to tell Costco what you're having for dinner; Costco usually tells you.)

Now let's drive over to Nordstrom, where the scene changes dramatically. Instead of bins, industrial pallets, and 40-foot-high metal storage shelves, there are trendy departments, creative merchandising displays, name brands galore, and a good many service personnel at your disposal. Here you are not necessarily a shopper, but a client. If you buy a pair of pants in Costco that need alternations, you're on your own. At Nordstrom, they adjust them on the premises. Need a personal shopping assistant? Nordstrom will oblige. And if Nordstrom doesn't have an item you're looking for, the notoriously uber-accommodating clerks will go out of their way to order it for you or find an alternative. Yes, this is a high-priced store, but in terms of selection, quality, and service, one can argue that you get what you pay for.

Even if you never have shopped at Costco or Nordstrom, my message here should be evident: No one store can provide all consumers with all the products they need to meet the requirements of their diverse and modern lives at the appropriate levels of price and value. Higher price, higher value? This is often *not* the case. But often it is. Sometimes you need a tailored suit, not a Costco specialty. Sometimes you need a few pairs of generic white socks, items that do not require a trip to Nordstrom.

Likewise, when you purchase active or passive investment products, you receive different things. Passive products are not necessarily "Costco-grade," nor are all active products Nordstrom's-equivalent. But as you slide from passive to active, you move from bulk items to more customized fare:

In the passive, lower-cost, standardized aisle, you have index funds that mirror the stocks or bonds in specific indexes, with some of the big brand-name providers including Vanguard and Fidelity. Then there are exchange-traded funds (ETFs), funds that mirror individual indexes (or asset classes, as they are reflected in indexes) and can be traded like individual stocks. Some of the more prominent ETF brand names are PowerShares, iShares, SPDRs (or "Spiders"), and ProShares. Over in the active, higher-cost, and customized aisle, the selection shifts to mutual funds (and on the higher shelves, hedge funds, which we investigate in greater depth in Chapter 17. Mutual funds are managed portfolios of stocks and bonds that are offered by a broad range of companies—JP Morgan, American Express, Goldman Sachs, Vanguard, Fidelity, Scudder, T. Rowe Price, and Dreyfus, to name a few. Mutual funds can be very thematic in how they are composed, falling into categories such as large-cap, small-cap, growth, value, international, and fixed income—and the full range of combinations of each. There are also sector funds that track various industries (health care, retail, technology, utilities, etc.), global funds that invest both domestically and abroad, and lifecycled funds that will rebalance the equity/fixed-income split as you age.

Transaction costs, again, also increase as we move from passive to active, as does risk, in many cases. Yet so does the possibility (and, at times, the probability) of increased return, even after transaction costs are counted.

A Chink in the Passive-Only Armor

In 1970, Eugene Fama, working off his dissertation from the University of Chicago, constructed the ammunition store from which scores of passive advocates flocked to load their guns.[5] Fama is the father of the *efficient market theory*, which boils down to the postulate that markets are smarter than you and that all relative market information is reflected in the *current* price of stocks. Thus, according to the theory, the future path of stocks cannot be predicted because no one person can possess such information (at least, not legally). The resulting prudent investment action *must*, then, be to index.

Without proof, such conclusions are rhetorical, but the passive crowd comes well armed with data. I already have reported John Bogle's numbers, which show that the average active stock fund underperformed the average S&P 500 index fund by 2.8 percent between 1983 and 2003. Does this say that all active funds underperformed across the period or that all will underperform across any period deemed statistically long enough? Not at all, and here we can begin to discover a chink in the passive-only armor.

Rex Sinquefield, a co-founder of Dimensional Fund Advisors, a firm that helped pioneer index-fund investing, is a well-versed passive-investing advocate. In various speeches and articles, he has pointed to a range of studies that show how passive investing has a strong edge over active investing. In a speech in 1995, Sinquefield reported, "In the most recent and comprehensive study done to date, a dissertation at the University of Chicago, Mark Carhart studies a total of 1,892 funds that existed any time between 1961 and 1993. After adjusting for the common factors in returns, an equal-weighted portfolio of the funds underperformed by 1.8 percent per year."[6]

The Carhart study remains important; to this day, it is frequently referenced in the passive literature. But for our purposes, it is somewhat suspect. The sample size of 1,892 funds is statistically sound, as is the sample period, which covers a total of 16,109 fund years.[7] In arranging his data, Carhart formed "ten equal-weighted portfolios of mutual funds" and tracked performance using a range of involved technical measures. Results aside for the moment, I'm very interested in one variable that both Carhart and Sinquefield mention: that of an *equal-weighted* portfolio. Bogle also uses an equal-weighted measure in ranking certain aspects of mutual-fund performance, leading us to wonder, what is an equal weight and why do proponents of passive-only investing regularly use it?[8]

In the simplest terms, an equal-weighted index puts an equal value on each of the stocks it tracks. A capitalization-weighted index, on the other hand, gives a greater value to some stocks over others (see the sidebar "How Benchmark Indexes Are Constructed"). Because each stock in an equal-weighted index has an equal impact on the direction of that index, up or down, this same rule *must* apply to any equal-weighted ranking of mutual fund performance.

How Benchmark Indexes Are Constructed

Most benchmark indexes today are *capitalization-weighted,* or cap-weighted. Every publicly traded company has a market capitalization, which can be computed by multiplying the number of a company's outstanding shares by the current share price. Let's take the case of two different companies with different market capitalizations and see how a cap-weighted index of these firms would be constructed. If Company A has 1 million shares outstanding and each is worth $3, its market cap is $3 million. If Company B has 500,000 shares outstanding and each is worth $14, its market cap is $7 million. If we were to build a cap-weighted index of just these two companies, the index would assign a 30 percent weight to Company A (market cap $3 million) and a 70 percent weight to Company B (market cap $7 million). Very simply, a greater value will fall to Company B because it has the higher market cap.

We can draw an important conclusion from this: The largest stocks in a cap-weighted index hold more sway over the direction of that index. If the big stocks in a cap-weighted index have a very good day, the index will climb significantly more than if the small stocks had a good day. Using our sample cap-weighted index, if Company A's stock rises 10 percent, from $3 to $3.30 a share, the entire index will climb only 3 percent, or 30 percent of that 10 percent share-price increase. On the other hand, if Company B's stock rises 10 percent, the index will climb 7 percent, or 70 percent of that 10 percent share-price increase.

This scheme is put into place for the theoretical reason that the sum total of an index's market capitalization reflects the current value of the capital stocks in an economy. Stated alternatively, the price movements of larger stocks in a cap-weighted index will best reflect or best capture overall market conditions. As an extreme example of this, if sales at Wal-Mart are slumping and a small-cap surf apparel chain is doing a bang-up business, which result will tell you more about the state of the overall retail environment and the economy? The Wal-Mart result, of course.

An *equal-weighted* index paints a much different picture. If we construct a hypothetical equal-weighted index of 10 stocks, each stock accounts for 10 percent of the index's weight. This is a more "democratic" way of building an index, and it is intended to capture the *market breadth* of the economy. We can say that a broad market exists when more than 50 percent of the stocks in an index are outperforming that index, and that a narrow market exists when less than 50 percent are outperforming. Put another way, the greater the market breadth, the greater the number of winning stocks are in the market. An upside to the equal-weighted scheme is that it gives strong emphasis to emerging companies, those that start small and grow bigger and bigger, the global progression toward the large. The downside is that it also gives great emphasis to dying companies, those that are losing market share (and, thus, weight in the cap-weighted indexes).

Table 14.1 offers a visual comparison of cap-weight and equal-weight index construction. The fictional cap-weighted index of ten stocks is considered "top-heavy" because only three of the stock names (or 30 percent) make up 50 percent of the index's weight.

TABLE 14.1   How Cap-Weighted and Equal-Weighted Indexes Are Constructed

Stocks in an Index	Market Capitalization in Descending Order	Cap-Weighted Index Weights	Equal-Weighted Index Weights
1	25	25%	10%
1	15	15%	10%
1	10	10%	10%
1	9	9%	10%
1	9	9%	10%
1	8	8%	10%
1	7	7%	10%
1	7	7%	10%
1	5	5%	10%
1	5	5%	10%
10	100	100%	100%

The S&P 500 index, an extremely popular benchmark for passive index funds, comes in two forms: cap-weighted and (more recently) equal-weighted. In the equal-weighted index, all the S&P 500 stocks are assigned a fixed weight of 0.2 percent and are rebalanced quarterly based on the price movements of the stocks. For the most part, therefore, the individual performance of each stock in the index will have an equal bearing on the direction of the index. For investors looking to capture the performance of the total market, this scheme has its advantages: If one large stock in the index has a bad day, it won't disproportionately sway the index; if a *group* of stocks in the index have a good day, the index will reflect this performance in an orderly way.

Indeed, if we apply an equal weight to the performance of a set of active mutual funds over a period of time, we will see an averaged performance of all these funds, where both the smallest and largest funds will have had an equal influence on the result. This gives us the Carhart/Sinquefield 1.8 percent underperformance of active funds over 32 years. Is this a fair result?

Well, if we apply a cap weight to the performance of these funds, we will identify a 50/50 weighted split of over- and underperformance. Sometimes one or a few funds will generate this outperformance (our cap-weighted stock index equivalent would be Wal-Mart on a good day), and at other times multiple funds will drive outperformance (say, a surf apparel chain, plus quite a few other small-caps, on a good day).

Critically, in this scheme, there always will be losers *and* winners, a division that, on average, will run 50/50 on a weighted basis, even though the *number* of fund names providing that performance can and will differ greatly.

And if there always will be winners, it is my belief that an opportunity exists to locate them.

Size Cycles and the Active Opportunity

We've come full circle to the idea that at any time in your investing life, you will want to have your portfolio correctly allocated to capture the overperformance of the economic times and avoid the underperformance. Because we now *know* that 50 percent of active funds must outperform at any time on a cap-weighted basis, we also know that the opportunity to capture these results at least perpetually exists. Undoubtedly, the passive-only recommendation that the only prudent way to invest *must* be to index *must* be wrong.

Importantly, however, and on a cap-weighted basis, the window of opportunity for active investing shifts from wide open to barely open and back again across your investing life. But of equal importance is the existence of a foolproof indicator of this shift: *the size cycle.*

In the following chapter, a rational walk down Wall Street and a few games of darts help bear out the fact that size cycles and the active versus passive choice are inextricably linked. Know your size cycles, and the active/passive decision becomes a process of turning a switch rather than making a one-time investment-life decision.

Endnotes

1. Known as the "Black Socks Scandal," eight players on the Chicago White Sox were accused of throwing the 1919 World Series for monetary gain. Shoeless Joe Jackson, one of the accused, hit .375 for the series and committed no errors—proof, some say, of his innocence, even though he might have "naïvely" accepted the money.

2. "U.S. Household Ownership of Mutual Funds in 2005," Investment Company Institute (ICI), October 2005. The ICI reports in its *2005 Investment Company Fact Book* that in the ten years between 1995 and 2004, the number of U.S. mutual funds grew from 2,811 to 8,107 (excluding mutual funds that invest in other mutual funds).

3. John C. Bogle, "The Relentless Rules of Humble Arithmetic," *Financial Analysts Journal* VOL 61,NO.6 (November/December 2005): 22–35.

4. Ibid.

5. Eugene F. Fama, "Efficient Capital Markets: A Review of Theory and Empirical Work," *The Journal of Finance* 25, no. 2, (1970): 383–417.

6. Rex A. Sinquefield, "Active vs. Passive Management," Schwab Institutional Conference in San Francisco, 12 October 1995.

7. Mark M. Carhart, "On Persistence in Mutual Fund Performance," *The Journal of Finance* 52, no. 1 (1997): 57–82.

8. Bogle, Ibid. Bogle, for instance, uses an equal-weighted measure to show how firms operating relatively few mutual funds outperform firms operating a relatively large number of funds.

15

A Rational Walk Down Wall Street: Darting Between Passive and Active When the Odds Are in Your Favor

In 1973, Burton Malkiel delivered what would become a seminal tome on the virtues of passive investing. Entitled *A Random Walk Down Wall Street*, Malkiel's book, now in its eighth edition, takes on all forms of active investing, from rigorous fundamental analysis to the outlandish idea of basing stock movements on the results of the latest Super Bowl. Malkiel's conclusion, consistent with the passive-only mantra, is that when the added costs of active investing are factored in, passive investing will regularly beat active investing over the long run.

Again, *average* is not a dirty word to the purveyors of passive investing. But these advocates also understand that the term "random walk" rings foul in the ears of active investors. This is why Malkiel used it in his title, a jab at the active managers who believe there are predictable (nonrandom) patterns in the market data that regularly can be exploited for profit. Writes Malkiel, "On Wall Street, the term 'random walk' is an obscenity. It is an epithet coined by the academic world and hurled insultingly at the professional soothsayers. Taken to its logical extreme, it means that a blindfolded monkey throwing darts at a newspaper's financial pages could select a portfolio that would do just as well as one carefully selected by the experts."[1]

In a strict sense, this analogy will hold up: Blind dart-hurling monkeys could well beat out the sum total performance of all active managers over a long-enough period of time. But this result is only an average result over the long term, one that masks the fact that there are winning active managers (and funds) at any given time.

Think of this: Using Malkiel's imagery, let's say a number of blind-folded monkeys are throwing darts at a blackboard that contains the names of all the stocks in the S&P 500. On a cap-weighted basis—which, we determined in Chapter 14, "Ending the Never-Ending Debate: Active vs. Passive Investing and Why You Can Take Both Sides," means that some stocks in an index, based on their market capitalizations, will be given a greater value over others—the chance that any one monkey will hit a winner always must be equal to the number of stocks that are outperforming the index at any one time. If only 40 percent of the stock names are outperforming, a monkey has only a 40 percent chance of hitting a winner and a 60 percent chance of nailing a loser.

The *number* of stock names within the cap-weighted scheme is of critical importance here. A cap-weighted index can (and often will) show a disproportionate number of stocks in the bottom half of the index because it takes fewer stock names with heavier weights to fill out the upper half. (For instance, if 50 companies in an index have a weight of 1 percent and 10 companies have a weight of 5 percent, those 50 companies will sit in the bottom half of the index, while those

10 companies will fill out the top. Such top-bottom disproportion is a common feature of cap-weighted indexes.) Similarly, 50 percent of the weight of an index will always outperform and 50 percent will always underperform, with the number of stock names represented by each 50 percent also being inconstant.

In Table 14.1 in the previous chapter, I showed a fictional index of ten stocks that, after dividing by weight, had three stock names in the top half and seven in the bottom. If the stock names were jumbled and placed on a wall, a dart-throwing monkey would enjoy a 30 percent chance of hitting a name from the top half of the index and a 70 percent chance of hitting one from the bottom. Now, what if we are in a small-cap cycle, meaning that the smaller stocks in the bottom half of the index would, on average, outperform? Well, this would mean that our monkey would stand an excellent chance (more or less 70 percent) of hitting a winner.

The concept of market breadth is at play here. As described in the last chapter, we can say that a broad market exists when more than 50 percent of the stock names in an index are outperforming that index. Hence, the greater the market breadth, the greater the chance that an active fund will outperform its benchmark—or *the greater the chance that active investing will beat out passive investing.*

One easily can apply this dart-throwing test to the world of active funds, and I do so in a most revealing way in this chapter. But first a word on *actively managed funds.* Just as there are large-caps and small-caps, there are large-cap and small-cap funds that are managed by professionals who actively switch between stocks in search of the best-performing mix. As I pointed out in Chapter 8, "Pipelines to Our Investment Returns: How We Get What We Want, in the Amount We Want, and When We Want It," mutual funds tend to have mandates whereby they purchase "like" assets, such as mostly value, growth, small-cap, large-cap, or international stocks. Fund managers, in other words, are often constrained by size and style, and here we can put this insight to good use. If we believe in the existence of size cycles, we also must believe that there will be periods when actively managed large- and small-cap funds will move in and out of favor.

The Broader the Market, the Greater the Active Opportunity

We discussed in Chapter 13, "The Fight Is On: How to Invest Properly Relative to Regulations, Inflation, and Taxation," how small- and large-cap cycles are predictable, in that the former emerges during periods of economic uncertainty and that the latter manifests in the converse, more certain, environment. For the most part, the level of economic certainty can be described in terms of the burden of inflation, taxation, and regulation at any given time. Because small-caps exhibit more nimbleness than large-caps within national borders (they can morph and adjust to skirt regulations, hedge against inflation, and avoid certain taxes), they will outperform during periods of uncertainty, when tax, inflationary, and regulatory conditions are in flux. Large-caps, on the flip side, will beat small-caps when these burdens fix and times are certain.

By applying this knowledge to the stocks in your portfolio, you will know when to favor large-caps over small-caps. But in terms of active versus passive, the switch is not as clear-cut as leaning toward active large-cap funds during large-cap cycles and active small-cap funds during small-cap cycles. To see this, we need to add weighting schemes to the concept of market breadth.

The market caps of the stocks in a cap-weighted index will, by definition, vary. If we take any cap-weighted index and rank the stocks in descending order by market cap, we will see a disparity in the number of stock names in the top and bottom halves. Typically, there will be fewer, heavier-weight stocks in the top half and more lighter-weight stocks in the bottom half. Hence, in a small-cap cycle, more than 50 percent of the names in a broad index (the bottom, lighter half) will outperform the index. This makes small-cap cycles and active management (in general) perfect partners.

From here we can narrow the discussion based on the mandates placed on fund managers. In general, small-cap fund managers will select from a basket of small-cap stocks and attempt to beat a small-cap benchmark, such as the S&P 600. At one point in recent years, the largest company in this cap-weighted index had a weight of about 0.7 percent, while the top ten holdings represented less than 6 percent of the weighted index. Contrast this with the large-cap S&P 500 at the same time, when the largest company in the index had a weight of more than 3 percent and the top ten holdings accounted for more than 19 percent of the index's total weight. Clearly, the small-cap index appears much less top-heavy than its large-cap cousin, which is usually the case when comparing small- and large-cap indexes.

In a way, the scheme of a cap-weighted small-cap index is closer to that of an equal weight, meaning that the number of names outperforming the index will be nearer to 50 percent at most times. This indicates that the odds of a small-cap fund beating a small-cap benchmark at any time will hover near 50 percent and that a small-cap fund manager needs only a small edge to regularly come out on top.

And what about large-caps? What are the odds that a large-cap fund will beat a large-cap benchmark? Two snapshots of the large-cap S&P 500 reveal some drastically different conditions for active large-cap managers. At one point in the later, large-cap 1990s, the ten largest companies in the S&P 500 accounted for a full 50 percent of the index's weight. Because these were large-cap days, this meant that a full 490 companies would, on average, underperform the index. With such a narrow window for picking the outperforming stocks, a passive indexing approach at this time would have made very good sense. Put another way, large-cap active funds and large-cap cycles are *not* perfect partners.

More recently, in an index snapshot taken during the small-cap cycle of the early twenty-first century, it took the largest 50 companies in the S&P 500 to account for 50 percent of the index's weight. In a world of 500 stock names, this result is not *that* much different from the one in which ten companies made up half the index's weight. But here the conditions drastically change for the large-cap manager, who would have a much greater chance of picking an outperformer among the 450 stocks in the lower half of the index (because, presumably, the smaller stocks in the lower half would outperform during the small-cap cycle).

This discussion boils down to the fact that there indeed are times when active funds will beat their passive benchmarks and that the existence of size cycles makes these opportunities predictable. Next I present some size-based stock data to help us form some decision rules on when to switch between an active and passive mode.

A Rational Game of Darts

Mutual fund managers (most of them) are not monkeys. They are smart human beings who, in the pursuit of outperformance, work very hard to select the right mix of investments for their funds. Their jobs and reputations are always on the line, so they have a very good incentive to beat the market. Sadly for them, the odds are not always stacked in their favor—or equally in their favor, based on the constraints of large- and small-cap fund management.

Table 15.1 reports the percentage of stock names in two S&P indexes—the large-cap 500 and small-cap 600—that beat their respective indexes during the 1998–99 large-cap cycle and the 2000–05 small-cap cycle. (*Note:* In Chapter 13 and in Figure 13.1, I indicated that 1999 was a small-cap year, which, in terms of overall stock returns and per the conversation of certainty, it was. For the record, both small-caps and large-caps were strong performers that year, up 29.8 percent and 21 percent, respectively. But in contrasting the S&P 500 and 600 indexes, I am forced to consider it a transition year from large-cap to small-cap, favoring the large-cap result. Simply, when comparing size results between different indexes, you will sometimes get different results.) Returning to our dart throwers, elevated here from monkeys to humans, we can come to some general conclusions about the promise of active large- and small-cap strategies during different size cycles.

TABLE 15.1   Percent of Stocks Outperforming Their Benchmark Indexes

Cycles	Large-Cap		Small-Cap					
	1998	1999	2000	2001	2002	2003	2004	2005
S&P 500	33%	31%	63%	69%	64%	55%	62%	51%
S&P 600	48%	36%	47%	54%	54%	47%	48%	43%

Source: Research Insight

- A dart thrower has a better chance of outperforming any index during a small-cap cycle.

  Simply, when a size cycle switches from large-cap to small-cap, the number of stock names outperforming each benchmark index will increase. For the large-cap S&P 500, this is a function of the bottom half of the index (or the smaller-weight names) providing the outperformance during the small-cap cycle.

  The odds of a dart thrower outperforming an index change systematically over the course of a cycle, and the odds of a larger-cap dart thrower change the most.

  Averaging out the results, 32 percent of the large-cap stocks outperformed the S&P 500 benchmark during the large-cap cycle, while 61 percent outperformed during the small-cap cycle. That's a *big* difference: a full 29 percentage point swing. In comparison, 42 percent of small-caps outperformed the S&P 600 during the large-cap cycle, while 49 percent beat the

same index across the small-cap cycle. This is a smaller systematic change, yet 7 percentage points is important nonetheless.
Note, again, that the smaller-cap S&P 600 will perform more
like an equal-weight index at most times. As a result, the index
will reveal a smaller shift in the level of out-performance
between cycles.

- During a small-cap cycle, a large-cap dart thrower has a better
  chance of beating a large-cap benchmark than a small-cap dart
  thrower has of beating a small-cap benchmark.

  The only place we see greater than 60 percent outperformance
  is within the large-cap universe of the S&P 500 during the
  small-cap cycle, while there is only a 49% chance of outperforming the small cap S&P 600 universe during the small-cap
  cycle. Again, these is a direct result of the capitalization
  weights. In percentage terms, the stock names outperforming
  the large-cap index is much larger than the percentage of the
  number of stocks outperforming the smaller capitalization
  index S&P 600. Therefore, the odds tend to favor the larger-
  cap manager. Averaging out both indexes across the small-cap
  period, relative-to-benchmark outperformance favors large-
  caps by 12 percentage points (61 percent minus 49 percent).

- During a large-cap cycle, a small-cap dart thrower has a better
  chance of outperforming a small-cap benchmark than a large-
  cap dart thrower has of beating a large-cap benchmark.

  It does sound ironic that a large-cap fund manager will be at a
  stock-picking disadvantage during a large-cap cycle. But there
  is no escaping the realities of the weighting scheme as it relates
  to market breadth. During large-cap cycles, the largest of the
  large will get only that much larger, pushing more names into
  the bottom half of an index, which is out of favor during a large-
  cap cycle. In the 1998–99 large-cap period, only 32 percent of
  large-cap stocks outperformed the large-cap index, meaning

that 68 percent underperformed on average—poor odds for a dart thrower. Over at the S&P 600, the outperformance odds, at 42 percent, were more in favor of the small-cap dart thrower. Still, the odds of underperformance were 58 percent.

- A dart thrower is better throwing during small-cap cycles in general.

Fund and index constraints aside, the odds that an active stock-picking strategy will prevail always will be higher during a small-cap cycle. At these times, there simply are more winning names floating around.

An Active/Passive Litmus Test

If we momentarily shift away from the size-cycle mindset, we can perform a litmus test on the viability of an active/passive switching strategy within a portfolio.

Not so long ago, Standard & Poor's began publishing an equal-weighted version of the S&P 500 index. In this scheme, because there are 500 stocks, each stock is assigned a weight of 1/500, or 0.2 percent, meaning that each stock in the index enjoys the same level of importance. In blind-monkey terms, each stock return in the index becomes a stand-in for the average return that can be achieved by tossing darts at the S&P 500 board of stocks. And if we take the analogy to its extreme, turning our active fund managers into blindfolded monkeys, we can equate the performance of the equal-weighted S&P 500 with that of the universe of actively managed funds. As goes the equal-weighted index, so goes active management. Meanwhile, we can use the cap-weighted S&P 500 as a stand-in, or benchmark, for passive performance because this historically has been the case.

Table 15.2 pits the performance of the cap-weighted S&P 500 against the equal-weighted version from 1989 to 2005, with the bolded results showing the triumphant index year to year. Not only is the cyclical nature of the results obvious, but so is the fact that, on average, the index in favor switches in unison with our size cycles: Passive (per the cap-weighted proxy) outperformed active (per the equal-weighted proxy) during what were, for the most part, large-cap years, whereas active beat passive during most of the small-cap years. Even though the results were a little more erratic for the 2000–05 small-cap period (the cap-weight index beat the equal-weight index two out of six times), the overall result for the period favored the equal-weight index and, hence, active management.

TABLE 15.2   Annual Returns of the Equal-Weighted and Cap-Weighted S&P 500

Cycle		Cap-Weighted	Equal-Weighted	Best
Large	1989	6.7%	**7.4%**	6.7%
Large	1990	**3.9%**	–4.9%	3.9%
Small	1991	30.5%	**35.5%**	35.5%
Small	1992	7.6%	**15.6%**	15.6%
Small	1993	10.1%	**12.5%**	12.5%
Small	1994	1.3%	**1.6%**	1.6%
Large	1995	**37.6%**	32.2%	37.6%
Large	1996	**23.0%**	**23.1%**	23.1%
Large	1997	**33.4%**	24.6%	33.4%
Large	1998	**28.6%**	11.0%	28.6%
Large	1999	**21.0%**	10.2%	21.0%
Small	2000	–9.1%	**8.2%**	8.2%
Small	2001	–11.9%	**2.3%**	2.3%
Small	2002	–22.1%	**–10.2%**	–10.2%
Small	2003	**28.7%**	26.0%	28.7%
Small	2004	10.9%	**23.0%**	23.0%
Small	2005	**8.1%**	4.91%	8.1%
Average		11.0%	12.4%	15.7%

Source: Standards & Poor's

The most important result in this investigation, however, is how well an active/passive switching strategy would have done across our

17-year sample period. The passive-only (S&P 500 cap-weight proxy) strategy would have returned a respectable 11 percent, and the active-only (S&P 500 equal-weight proxy) would have generated an even better 12.4 percent return. But the switching strategy would have delivered an outsized 15.7 percent return.

The results shown in Table 15.2 don't quite jibe with the multiple findings that passive beats active investing over the long run. But they also don't suggest the dominance of an active-only strategy. Adjusted for fees, the passive-only advocate could here make the case that active-only investing would not necessarily have outperformed passive-only across the period. But the more difficult case to make is that a switching strategy is not somehow superior.

One could, of course, hold to the efficient-market principle that the future path of stocks is unpredictable, so no such switching strategy can be implemented reliably. Yet because this active/passive switch is based firmly on the existence and proven predictability of size cycles, it becomes a fully functional and reliable strategy.

The Efficiency of a Switching Strategy

I believe in the efficiency of markets over the long run. I also believe in entering retirement having performed in an above-average way over your investment life. If you go all passive, I do predict that the long-run performance of the stock and bond markets will deliver you firm, average results. *Average,* here, again becomes a welcome and comforting word. If you go all active, on the other hand, you might or might not achieve market-beating results. Of course, with active investing comes greater risk because you and/or your manager(s) will be pitted against the collective knowledge of the market. But it is a fundamental reality of investing that the potential for greater-than-average returns exists alongside greater risk.

Thus, my proposal is nuanced on the passive versus active front: The long-run data might tend to show that passive investing is superior to active investing. But it also clearly reveals periods when active investing beats passive. The challenge, then, is to catch those periods, to be active at times and passive at others, and thus gain the best that both worlds have to offer. The challenge here is far from difficult, in that the large versus small decision will guide the active/passive switch:

- Invest actively during small-cap cycles. The odds of beating an index turn decidedly in your (or your active fund manager's) favor during small-cap cycles. At this time, you should choose actively managed funds to fill the allocation buckets in your portfolio.

- Invest passively during large-cap cycles. The odds of beating the market systematically decline during large-cap cycles. And although they decline more for large-cap fund managers than small-cap managers, you will be best served by choosing index funds and/or exchange-traded funds (ETFs) at this juncture.

In proposing this, I am not suggesting that you become some sort of bizarre cross-breed investor, although you might be accused of this. To be sure, the active versus passive debate shows no signs of abating. And if you make a habit of reading the financial literature, there will be no escaping the onslaught of argument attempting to lure you to either side.

Not surprisingly, active managers always have the better argument during small-cap cycles, while passive-only purveyors crow a little more loudly when large-caps are in favor. Maybe you can use this as your switching indicator, although I suggest that you follow a more reliable strategy of tracking size cycles (in relation to the level of certainty that exists or threatens to develop in the economy) and simply go passive when the cycle turns large-cap and active when it shifts small-cap.

Critically, these cycles persist. And there's nothing wrong with being a little late in making a switch, if the switch you end up making delivers higher returns.

Endnotes

1. Burton G. Malkiel, *A Random Walk Down Wall Street, 8th Ed.* (New York: W.W. Norton, 2003). Although Malkiel's book leans heavily toward a passive-only recommendation, it provides an excellent tour of how Wall Street works and offers very sound advice on how to invest over the long term. Malkiel also admits to taking a "middle of the road" position on active versus passive, stating, "Although it is abundantly clear that the pros do not consistently beat the averages, I must admit that exceptions to the rule of the efficient market exist."

16

Alpha Bets: The Case for Hedge Funds and a Greek Letter You'll Want in Your Portfolio

There are fees, and then there are *fees.* As one ascends the active ladder, the promise of expected return can rise precipitously, but so can the cost of entry.

Let's look ahead several years, imagining that you diligently followed the rules of a cyclical-based asset-allocation strategy and could boast a portfolio net worth of $1 million or more. Or let's say that today you have seven figures or so to put in the stock market and are interested in achieving the biggest bang for your investment buck. In either case, you would have access to the upper rungs of the investment ladder, several steps above the index fund and the almost equally accessible mutual fund. At this level, you will be asked to verify your annual income and/or net worth and, if you are deemed eligible, to pony up an initial investment anywhere from $1 million to several million dollars. And that's not all. Once you have opened your wallet wide, you will have to endure annual fees of 1 to 2 percent and relinquish in the neighborhood of 20 percent of profits if a predetermined performance standard is met.

What I describe here are the high-watermark parameters of the *hedge fund*. Estimates put this industry above $1 trillion worldwide, and it is to be considered a playground for the rich—the yacht club of investing, if you will.[1]

A rational guess is that most readers of this book are not in this net worth category. And although I believe many of you can be if you periodically and strategically adjust your investments with a broad based top-down mindset, some of you forever will think of hedge funds as forbidden territory. And who can blame you?

Partnering with tales of breakneck hedge-fund gain are just as many stories of hedge-fund woe. Perhaps you heard of Julian Robertson, a one-time "wizard" of Wall Street. Through the 1980s and most of the 1990s, his hedge-fund firm, Tiger Management, turned millions of dollars into billions, returning to investors in the neighborhood of 25 percent on an annualized basis, well above market-return averages. But in the short period between 1998 and 2000, more than $20 billion in assets sank to around $6.5 billion, and the firm shuttered.[2] Or maybe you read about Long-Term Capital Management, the former hedge-fund darling that transformed $1 billion in assets into $5 billion over four short years in the 1990s (this amount was highly leveraged, to the tune of well more than $100 billion), only to lose most of it in a few short months. This "rags" to riches to "rags" story prompted a bailout by the Federal Reserve, which feared the LTCM collapse would harm the broader financial markets.[3]

It would seem, in other words, that the high entry fees attached to hedge funds are there for a reason; only the richest among us might be able to afford the risky business of hedge-fund investing.

But the chronicles of Julian Robertson and LTCM have only added to the mythology and negativity that surround this investment category.

Outside stock picking on your own, hedge-fund investing is about as active as you can get. But "active" here does not necessarily mean taking on more risk; in many ways, it's about skirting the risks that are inherent in passive, or index, investing. When the overall market turns down, the passive investor suffers with the market. In theory, the hedge-fund investor, in a traditional sense, would be protected in such a situation because the traditional hedge fund is built to be uncorrelated with the movements of the market. By virtue of their lack of correlation with the markets, the hedge fund returns have a zero beta. In other words, a hedge fund should behave independently of the market, with performance based on the unique strategies employed by the fund managers.

A lot is at play here. We are back, in a way, to the passive versus active debate, whereby the former says you can't beat the market with regularity and the latter says you can. If you believe in the existence of cycles and agree with the arguments in previous chapters that these cycles are exploitable, you understand that sometimes passive investing makes more sense than active investing, and vice versa. But in this chapter, we take a more technical look at the differences between the two.

What does each strategy chase, when we come right down to it? Well, passive investing seeks the performance of the market, which, technically speaking, is *beta*. The overall market has a beta of 1. This *is* the market. Over the long run, a passive portfolio indexed to the market will own that 1, and for better rather than worse because markets have always risen across the historical timeline.

At this point in our conversation, you should know that you can do better than 1. Those stocks with higher betas and, thus, higher sensitivities to the market will surge to a greater extent than stocks with lower betas when the overall market is rising. For example, when the market goes up 10 percent a stock with a beta of 1.2 will go up 12 percent, whereas a stock with a 0.5 beta will increase only 5 percent. The higher beta stocks also will tumble quicker than their lower-beta neighbors when the market turns down. So when the market goes down 5 percent, the stock with the 1.2 beta will decline 6 percent, whereas the stock with the 0.5 beta will decline only 2.5 percent. For much of this book, this is where we have been. By identifying the elasticities of companies and industries shock to shock, we have been separating the high-beta stocks from the low-beta ones (something passive-only investing does not do at regular intervals). In the good times, when the overall market is rising, we want to own those high-beta stocks that are hypersensitive to the market swings, while avoiding them when economic and market conditions turn adverse. This is a simple, profitable rule for cyclical-minded investors.

In turning to the active side of investing, however, we shift into the realm of another Greek letter: alpha. Alpha is a measure of the risk-adjusted excess performance of an asset, or an asset manager, in relation to a benchmark. For our purposes, we can consider alpha to be the extra return related to investing, over and above the market return. It is what active managers and investors seek every day when they sit down at their computer screens. A simple example suffices here. A manager who delivers a positive alpha will always outperform its market by the alpha amount. So if the market goes up by 10 percent, a manager with a 2 percent alpha will deliver a 12 percent return. If the market declines by 5 percent, the manager will deliver a –3 percent return. In contrast, as stated in the previous paragraph, the 1.2 beta stock will produce a 12 percent return on the upside and a 6 percent return on the downside. Alpha is the opportunity to profit more than the beta-only crowd.

Mutual-fund investors and managers both like their alpha. They love it, in fact. It is the lure of active investing. Its mere existence— and it does exist—says that there are opportunities to beat the market during the good times when the market is going up and the bad times when the market is declining. We now dissect this Greek letter, pinpointing how and when alpha opportunities arise in the market. This brings us deep into the realm of the hedge fund, where alpha is sought in the most resourceful of ways. But importantly, we do not stray into foreign territory. In the pursuit of alpha, the laws of supply and demand still apply. Elasticity matters, as do the economic shocks that alter the elasticities of different companies and industries.

Peeking Through the Hedges

A gambler will talk of "hedging" his bets, which means he won't place all his money on 23 Black before spinning the roulette wheel. He'll place portions of his money on various numbers and combinations of black and red, or he'll move from roulette to blackjack to slots, never risking all of his money on any one game. When you hedge a bet, you diversify.

Comparatively, a *hedge* in financial terms is an investment in one or more securities that will, in theory, remove the risk of an investment in another security. And it's not gambling when performed correctly. When put into good practice, hedging, like diversification, is a risk-reducing technique.

Short-selling is perhaps the most understandable hedging practice employed today. When you sell a stock short, you make a bet that the stock price will go down. In practice, you would borrow shares of a certain stock and immediately sell them at the current price. If and when the stock price lowers, you would physically purchase the stock back at the lower price, keeping the difference from your original bet. On its own, short-selling is risky. If the stock price goes up, you would still have to purchase the stock back; at a higher price, the whole process would deliver you a loss. But as a hedging technique, short-selling can be a risk-reducing measure. For instance, a long-short investment fund holds two baskets of securities, a long basket that is expected to rise in price and a short basket that is projected to fall. In this way, the short position offsets the long position in the event that the returns of the long position do not develop as planned.

As it happens, hedging is a technique that a hedge fund might or might not employ. For instance, some hedge funds are purely speculative, stock-picking funds. Still, most hedge funds aggressively seek the alpha-extra that can exist in diverse areas of the market at any given time. Some hedge funds seek distressed securities at deep discounts—say, the equity or debt of companies facing bankruptcy. Some hunt for investment opportunities related to special events, such as mergers or corporate takeovers. Some are pure hedges, taking offsetting long and short positions. Some take a macro focus, seeking to strategically gain from shifts in the economy, inflation, and interest rates. And some are arbitrage specialists, making hay based on the difference in prices between locations.

Meanwhile, many are highly leveraged, which is to say they have borrowed heavily to magnify their return. And all are alpha hunters, seeking to exploit profitable investment opportunities before they disappear.

Finally, as a group, hedge funds are vilified more often than they are lauded. However, if most were rooted in the laws of supply and demand, we'd probably hear fewer claims that hedge funds are "accidents waiting to happen."[4]

Graduating from Beta to Alpha

When I say the supply of an industry is inelastic, I mean that it has a very limited ability to alter its production plans and, as a result, can satisfy fluctuations in demand only by raising or lowering prices. When demand increases for the products or services supplied by an inelastic industry, a higher price is the only mechanism that will clear the market. On the flip side, a decline in demand will result in lower prices. For this reason, inelastic industries experience above-average profit increases during the good times (when there is an increase in demand) and above-average profit declines when the climate turns sour (when demand falls). For the most part, the prices of inelastic stocks exhibit corresponding fluctuations: above-average gains during the good times and above-average declines during the bad. Such exaggerated swings meet the definition of high-beta stocks.

I have argued that if you can correctly identify an industry's ability to adjust to economic shocks (i.e., you can judge the elasticity of an industry) as well as anticipate the arrival of positive and negative shocks, you have the makings of a very simple and profitable investment strategy: Buy inelastic stocks experiencing positive shocks and avoid inelastic stocks experiencing negative shocks. I also have argued that economic policies have a long-lasting impact on the economy and that changes in policy will lead to predictable economic cycles. If you track the economy and economic policy, you should be able to anticipate and take advantage of the asset-class cycles they produce.

So far, and elastically speaking, this is a very beta-driven (or *high-beta-driven*) strategy. But important alpha strategies partner with these very same insights. In particular, I have in mind a strategy that focuses on muting or completely eliminating the impact of market fluctuations. Taken to its extreme, this strategy would be insulated from any market fluctuation whatsoever. Call it a *pure-alpha* strategy.

In the course of this book, we have visited several economic shocks, and here I bring a couple back, but this time with an alpha mindset.

Let's assume there is an increase of, say, 10 percent in the price of oil. All else the same, the higher oil price will lead to a decline in the demand for the activities that are dependent on oil (or the fuel derived from oil), such as air travel. Because the oil-price increase will bring about a spike in the cost of air travel, a decline in air-travel demand will result. With the onset of fewer air travelers, if the airlines industry has a 1.2 beta, overall profits in the airline industry will decrease by 12 percent.

Now consider the case of an oil substitute. The increase in the price of oil will produce a substitution effect away from oil and into oil alternatives such as natural gas. This shifted demand will result in a higher quantity of natural gas produced as well as higher profits for natural-gas producers. Assuming a 1.3 beta, we can predict a 13 percent increase in the profits of the oil substitutes.

Here, one economic shock, an oil-price spike, had two opposing results: a decline in the demand for air travel and an increase in the demand for oil substitutes. Using standard supply-and-demand models and given the proper mix of the two, it can be shown that the profit declines in the airline business will be less than the profit gains in the natural gas sector, giving us all the information we need to develop a pure-alpha strategy.[5]

So if one were to combine the profits of investing in both the airlines and natural gas industries, what would be the result? Well, during an oil-price spike, the up-shift in natural gas demand would be offset by the downward shift in the demand for air travel. But because the gains in natural gas profits will be larger than the losses in the airlines industry, jointly, the two positions will produce a net gain when the price of oil increases.

A profitable investment opportunity also exists when the scenario reverses. When the price of oil declines, air miles flown will increase, as will airline profits. The lower oil price also will produce a decline in the demand for natural gas and a resulting decrease in natural-gas profits. Jointly, the proper mix of these investment positions *will still produce a gain* when the price of oil drops.

Combining the two positions, we have developed a strategy that goes up regardless of the market fluctuations. It produces positive returns during up markets as well as during down markets.

In hedge-fund lingo, what we have constructed here is a positive-alpha, or absolute-return, strategy that is completely uncorrelated with market fluctuations. All we needed to do was identify two industries that will respond differently to the same economic disturbance—in this case, an oil shock. That's the hedge. Critically, however, these industries needed to be inelastic in nature because such industries will experience the largest fluctuations in profitability when economic shocks occur.

Elasticity is a key element of alpha strategies, as is the relationship between industries. A negative relationship, what we have just constructed, means that two industries experiencing the same economic shock will move in opposite directions in terms of demand and profitability.

Therein lies the investment opportunity. But practical questions remain: How frequent are these opportunities? And how reliable are the hedge funds that attempt to exploit them?

In Search of an All-Weather Strategy

One of Newton's laws states that everything that goes up must come down, and this is true everywhere gravity exists. Well, Wall Street has its own version of Newton's hypothesis. It is the law applied by many hedge-fund operators, and it states that a profitable opportunity can exist when the price of a commodity either rises *or* falls.

The allure of such a pure-alpha strategy is quite strong; it is the promise of a return that is independent of the direction of the economy and the stock markets. It is an all-weather strategy, so to speak— or, at least, it *can* be.

Again, a critical aspect of an alpha strategy is that it is indeed uncorrelated; in this way, the strategy will perform as expected whether the overall market rises or falls. But can any strategy truly be uncorrelated to the market (as well as the economy, which steers the direction of the market)? We can investigate this by further developing our oil/airlines example.

Alpha Pitfalls, Part I

In outlining an alpha strategy with respect to oil shocks, it would be a big mistake to proclaim that we have found a pure-alpha strategy for all seasons. Certain economic shocks might not lead to the perfect hedge and, therefore, produce a desirable alpha return.

Let's say policymakers in Washington pass a broad tax-rate cut, and the president signs it into law. As has been the case several times in modern American history, this tax-rate cut invigorates the economy and produces above-average growth of real GDP for a sustained amount of time.[6] It seems reasonable to assume that, all else the same, this higher growth rate will lead to an increase in the demand for both air travel *and* oil (as well as for oil substitutes). Well, in this case, we just lost the negative correlation that was necessary to develop our oil-shock alpha strategy. Because profits in both the airline and energy industries will presumably rise as the economy surges, the oil hedge dissipates.

Alpha Pitfalls, Part II

When it comes to implementing a pure-alpha strategy, there are sins of commission and omission.

First to omission: Is an alpha-generating hedge fund worth your money if it does not account for the range of macroeconomic forces that can at times erase the hedge on which the strategy is based? Decidedly, no. As shown, an alpha strategy aimed at exploiting one type of relationship (e.g., oil shocks) can fail miserably when a different type of shock occurs (e.g., tax-rate cuts, deregulation, or a general improvement in the macroeconomic fundamentals). This is more than a theoretical possibility.

Take the recent implosion of Amaranth Advisors. This energy trader made bets on which way the spreads (or differences in price) among various fuels were going to move. For a time, this strategy had been quite successful, generating better than $1 billion in profits in 2005 and padding manager pockets with bonuses well in excess of $100 million. In 2006, however, those fortunes changed when energy prices overall began to fall at a time the hedge fund bet certain fuel sectors (in particular, natural gas) would climb. According to some reports, $9 billion in assets plummeted to $3 billion in a matter of weeks, and Amaranth had to be liquidated. Talk about a bad bet. (As a testament to the robustness of the financial markets, however, this liquidation occurred in an orderly fashion.)

Or take Tiger Management, one of the infamous hedge funds mentioned at the start of this chapter. In the late 1990s, Tiger's funds were shorting the Japanese yen. In other words, they were betting against the Japanese economy and the strength of its currency—a flawed strategy because it failed to account for major trends in monetary policy around the world in conjunction with the economic impact of fiscal policy in Japan. At the time, central banks in the U.S., Japan, and Europe were all moving toward a price rule, which means the banks would target domestic prices to the market (and not inflation) to manage the strength of their respective currencies. This meant that exchange rates would reflect differences in real returns within the economy, not inflation-rate differentials, the latter being a key component of the Tiger plan. Correspondingly, Japan lowered its tax rate from 65 percent to 50 percent. This meant that a profitable Japanese business with positive cash flow kept 50¢ per dollar instead of 35¢, a 43 percent increase in after-tax income—and the precise amount of yen appreciation across the period. Technically, the Tiger strategy failed to incorporate the impact of the tax-rate cut on the foreign exchange rate and, more generally, implemented a bearish strategy in respect to Japan at a time when it should have been bullish. The losses, in the billions of dollars, quickly mounted, leading Julian Robertson to return most of what was left of the funds to investors and close Tiger.

We can form a rule here: Certain hedges will not be true hedges if they protect against only certain types of shocks. In addition, the lack of correlation assumed in an alpha strategy will be true only as long as the shocks that are being hedged are the prevalent shocks. When other types of shocks occur, all hell breaks loose, and the assumed lack of correlation fails to hold.

Now to commission: a 2 percent fee plus 20 percent of profits if the fund manager's performance goals are met. Is it worth it? Yes, but with certain provisions: First, the alpha fund must be truly uncorrelated to the market *and* other hedge funds within a portfolio. Second, its hedge must hold up rain or shine.

A potential error of commission occurs when an investor includes several alpha strategies in a portfolio that might not be truly uncorrelated. For starters, why buy four of a thing when one will do you just fine? In addition, diversification—or the gambler's idea of hedging his bets—also decreases when you insert several correlated alpha strategies in your portfolio. Over time, a set of correlated pure-alpha strategies will deliver superior returns (if, indeed, the pure-alpha hedges hold up) but will do so with greater volatility along the way. Why the extra volatility? Simply, when you invest in more of the same thing, you lose diversification, with high diversification being an investment synonym for lower risk.

On the other hand, the commissions related to a set of uncorrelated pure-alpha strategies might be well worth it. Indeed, assuming that one can identify pure-alpha strategies that do not overlap, the ideal would be to lump several together within a portfolio. The reason for this is straightforward. Let's say you discover a pure-alpha strategy that is truly viable *and* solid across shocks. And now let's say you identify additional alpha-generating hedges that are *unique* (relative to your portfolio), viable, and solid. Well, for each strategy you add, you increase the diversification of your portfolio and thus reduce portfolio volatility. In other words, given alpha, additional uncorrelated strategies increase the risk-reward ratio of an overall portfolio.[8]

The old phrase is that you can never get too much of a good thing, and here this applies as long as the good "pure-alpha" things are uncorrelated and fully functional (that is, the hedges hold up across shocks).

Every Portfolio Can Have Its Alpha

From the point of view of cyclical asset allocation, your portfolio has several levels. In Chapter 10, "Your Benchmark Portfolio...and Beyond," we developed a standard portfolio allocation based on the world allocation to the various asset classes. This is your beginning, benchmark, allocation, and it is based on four distinct choices: stock/bond, location (domestic/international), size (large-, mid-, and small-cap), and style (value/growth). The world portfolio is an optimal and diversified starting point and easily attainable by purchasing targeted exchange-traded funds (ETFs) and index funds. If you buy and hold this allocation, you will own valuable, though average, beta through your investing life.

Taking this allocation to the next level, by strategically switching among these asset classes *based on the strategies provided in this book*, you will capture both those high-beta opportunities when certain asset classes will outperform the market and those alpha moments that active management can deliver. Prior to this chapter, we discussed active management in terms of the mutual fund. This is a wide universe that enables you to fill any or all of the asset-class buckets in your world allocation, thereby meeting your beta requirements while adding the alpha-extra that active mutual-fund managers can provide.

But note here that you have to take your alpha with your beta. This *can be* an excellent mix, and it *will be* when you arrange and periodically adjust your portfolio based on the top-down, elasticity-minded strategy I have set forth.

Importantly, however, there is one more level to go: the pure-alpha level. At this point, we can briefly discuss it in terms of *portable alpha.*

This is a newer expression in the investment community, and it is quite in vogue. Simply, it means that you can separate your alpha from your beta (or from the market effect) to realize that full, pure-alpha return. But more than that, the term means that you can transport or port the alpha to any other investment of portfolio. To generalize, you "port" your alpha by physically extracting it from the beta portion of a portfolio and letting it do its magic on its own. Put into practice, however, this is a little more involved and ushers in techniques used by highly skilled active managers.

I illustrate portable alpha in a very hypothetical and bare-bones way. Let's say you identify a superior large-cap manager with a 3 percent alpha. This means that, on average, the manager beats the S&P 500 by 3 percentage points. Let's say that you have $1,000 to invest and that you want to have a return that is independent of the market movements. In short, you want to isolate the manager's alpha. How would you go about doing it? Well, one way to do it is as follows: You go to your broker (for an institutional investor or hedge fund, this would be your prime broker) and sell short the S&P 500 in the market. The broker then puts that money to work earning interest in his prime brokerage account. He then invests his original $1,000 with the superior manager. If the market goes up 10 percent, the manager delivers the market plus alpha, or 13 percent. He loses the market return in selling short, or 10 percent and net 4 percent worth of interest. In this simple strategy the hedge fund is netting a 7 percent return, regardless of the market conditions. Not too shabby. One way to further increase the returns is to increase the leverage of the investments. The point we need to stress here is that the return is totally uncorrelated with the market and, as such, has no beta.

The alpha the previous investments generated can now be ported to another style or strategy. By "porting," we mean that the alpha or excess return over the benchmark can be extracted and transported or grafted on to any other investment or portfolio. All you have to do is add the desired beta to these returns. Let's say that you get hired to beat the small cap index. How would you go about doing that? Well, all you do now is borrow $1,000 from your prime broker and pay him the 4 percent for the money. The proceeds are invested in the small-cap index. Say the small-cap increases by 16 percent. What is your total return now? You get the 3 percent alpha of the large-cap manager, plus 4 percent net from shorting the large-cap index, minus the 4 percent for borrowing money from your prime broker to invest in the small-cap index, plus the 16 percent generated by the small cap index. The net return is 19 percent, for a 3 percent alpha on your "small-cap" strategy. You have been ported.

Again, this is all very bare bones, but it does diagram how skilled investors, fund managers, and pension-fund administrators attempt to squeeze the most alpha out of a portfolio as they can. Notwithstanding your ability to develop a high level of investment skill on your own, you might be best served by farming out the pure-alpha or ported-alpha segment of your portfolio to a professional.

But at the very least, now you know the alpha rules:

A Checklist for Seeking Alpha

- When you purchase shares of an alpha-generating fund, be sure that it is uncorrelated with the market to the greatest degree possible. If not, you can port the alpha return of any superior manager. In this way, you remove beta exposure from your alpha investments and thus purify (or maximize) your alpha returns.

- Be sure that your alpha-generating investments are shock resilient—either that they will hold up when economic and market conditions shift or that your alpha-fund managers will make the proper adjustments when these conditions shift.

- Size up your pure-alpha investments against one another, being sure that each employs a unique strategy. By adding uncorrelated pure-alpha investments in your portfolio, you add diversification and thus decrease risk.

You might never have access to hedge funds and the pure-alpha they can produce. Or you might want to avoid this investment category altogether. But either way, you always will have access to alpha—the investment return over and above the market average. (Once more, active mutual-fund managers can provide this, although it will be bundled with their beta.) And if you can make the acquisition of alpha predictable—by paying attention to the direction of public policy, the economic environment, and the asset cycles each of these produce—there is no reason why you cannot or should not possess it.

Endnotes

1. The Hedge Fund Association estimates that there are approximately 9,000 active hedge funds today, representing $1.1 trillion under management.

2. For play-by-play and ballpark figures relating to the downfall of this hedge fund, see "The End of the Game: Tiger Management, Old-Economy Advocate, Is Closing," *New York Times*, 31 March 2000; or "Tiger Is Licking Its Wounds," *Business Week*, 13 March 2000, 126–128.

3. See Kevin Dowd, "Too Big to Fail? Long-Term Capital Management and the Federal Reserve," Cato Institute, for background on the demise of LTCM and its subsequent bailout by the Federal Reserve.

4. As quoted in "So Many Hedge Funds, So Few Strategies," *New York Times*, 1 August 2004.

5. By using traditional supply-and-demand models, it can be shown that the gains in natural gas are larger than the losses in the airlines industry when the price of oil increases, and that the gains in the airline industry are larger than the losses in the natural-gas sector when the oil price declines. In terms of the oil-shock hedge, each of these joint positions produces a net gain.

6. In modern American history, broad-based tax-rate cuts were initiated by the JFK/LBJ, Ronald Reagan, and George W. Bush administrations. In each case, the tax cuts reinvigorated the economy and produced sustainable above-average real GDP growth.

7. LTCM was founded by John Meriwether, formerly of Salomon Brothers, with inaugural board members including Nobel laureate economists Myron Scholes and Robert Merton.

8. Technically, the standard deviation of the average return of a collection of pure-alpha strategies declines in direct proportion to the inverse of the square root of the number of strategies. This is a lofty, though important detail: A decline in the standard deviation means that the range and volatility of the average returns of the combined strategies decline. Thus, as one adds alpha strategies, the information ratio—the ratio of the alpha returns to the standard deviations of the alpha returns—increases in direct proportion to the square root of the number of strategies. You can use this formula at your own discretion, or you can take my simple advice: Add as many (truly) pure-alpha strategies to your portfolio as you like, but be sure that no one strategy is correlated to another.

17

Tilting Toward Success: A Step-by-Step Guide to Above-Average Asset Allocation

In *The Millionaire Next Door*, a bestseller from a few years back, authors Thomas Stanley and William Danko attempt to uncover just what makes the modern millionaire tick.[1] Drawing from an exhaustive survey of more than 1,000 millionaires, the authors conclude that most in the seven-figure crowd work hard, are frugal, plan their every move, and are unpretentious in their consumption. On this last point, it seems that a good many millionaires don't drive fancy cars, or dine very often at five-star restaurants, or live in mansions. They're rich, it turns out, *because* they don't spend their money conspicuously. They are savers—and, importantly, they are investors. What kind of investors? Here's how the authors describe it:

Nearly all (95 percent) of the millionaires we surveyed own stocks; most have 20 percent or more of their wealth in publicly traded stocks. Yet you would be wrong to assume that these millionaires actively trade their stocks. Most don't follow the ups and downs of the market day by day. Most don't call their stock brokers each morning to ask how the London market did. Most don't trade stocks in response to the daily headlines in the financial media.

These millionaires sound like my kind of investors. But to conclude that they are not "active" investors is a semantic discrepancy. For some people, active investing means stock picking and aggressive trading day to day. For me, active investing is all about making reasoned adjustments to a portfolio from time to time that are too obvious and profitable not to make. And it appears that a good many millionaires would agree. According to the authors' survey sample, about 2 percent of millionaires trade their stocks on a daily or weekly basis, less than 7 percent switch their investments monthly, 9 percent hold their investments for less than a year, 20 percent hold between one and two years, 25 percent hold between two and four years, 13 percent hold between four and six years, and 32 percent hold for more than six years.

I have no precise idea of what these millionaires invest in or what particulars prompt their investment switches. But overall, I like the pace of their adjustments. By and large, it appears to be a cyclical pace. When it makes sense to switch out of losing investments and into winners, the rich apparently make their moves. I call this adjustment process *tilting toward success,* and it's the exact prescription I have set forth in this book.

Tilting, or adjusting your allocations in a reasoned way from time to time based on the shifts of the prevailing macroeconomic forces, is where the rubber hits the road in a cyclical investment strategy. In this final chapter, I summarize this process, reviewing the finer points of a strategy that

1. Is founded in the laws of supply and demand and the elasticities of businesses, industries, and consumers at any given time.

2. Is both practical and promising, based on the fact that economic and asset-class cycles not only exist, but are predictable and long lasting.

3. Has you generating above-average returns across your investment career.

In the preface to this book, I asked you to think in terms of cocktail economics, to view the world with a top-down mentality and to draw conclusions about the news of the day based on time-tested economic truths. This is exactly how you should proceed in applying a cyclical asset-allocation strategy. A skilled practitioner of cocktail economics must be well versed in political, economic, and geopolitical current events and must equally grasp how these shocks can have a dramatic impact on the direction of the economy. Like my students of years ago, such knowledge might make you a star at happy hour, but I also hold that it will make you a successful investor if you strategically and periodically apply it within your portfolio. Here are the basics of why cocktail economics and its application to a cyclical asset-allocation strategy will put you at a competitive advantage to a great many investors:

First is the fact that *market cycles both exist and are predictable.* The economy, the direction of the stock and bond markets, and the emergence and disappearance of positive and negative shocks are interrelated forces, and as they play on each other, market cycles emerge, whereby one asset class outperforms another. Because economic shocks, particularly those related to public policy, are foreseeable, and because we can judge how these shocks will act on asset classes and the economy based on like situations in the past, predicting cycles becomes a strong possibility. And because market cycles tend to last a while, often for a few years or more, there is ample opportunity to act on them. Indeed, rather than dive into a new market cycle, you can wade in, taking action once a cycle has established and likely to stick around.

Second is the fact that not everyone, by a long shot, is going to invest and adjust their investments in relation to the predictable fluctuations in the broad asset classes. Lower-risk, long-term, passive-only investing will be around forever; the great herd of average investors will forever roam. And where there is average investing, there is an opening for above-average investing.

Third is the fact that, within what we might call the active community, *not all investors will make the correct allocation calls all the time.* There will be winners and losers cycle to cycle. My firm prognosis, however, is that if you take the information in this book to heart, you will rank among the winners *much more often* than you will reside among the losers.

These three facts present the opportunity for any investor to perform better than most. And it's comforting to know that the rigors of the cyclical asset-allocation approach are on par with the even-paced investment regimen many modern millionaires employ. This is a daily strategy *only* in that you are encouraged to stay up-to-date with the financial, economic, and political news. In its application, it becomes a very manageable quarterly, semiannual, or annual strategy, junctures at which you will either tilt toward success or sit tight with your existing allocation.

The Above-Average Regimen

Above-average cyclical asset allocation has its demands. But they are the similar to the rigors that correspond to any successful venture: Study up. Keep your eyes open. Separate fact from fiction. Seek out historical relationships that can guide your understanding of the future. Trust your experience if your experience has served you well. Be a cool customer (i.e., don't act rashly), etc. In other words, act like a winner.

Taking a cue from our above-average farmer from Chapter 12, "Making Hay While the Sun Shines: The Case for Predicting, Forecasting, and Timing," I suggest that you

- Grasp the fundamentals of the core macroeconomic investment strategies (such as those discussed in this book) and the asset classes they track.

- Ground your understanding of economic shocks, the companies and industries they impact, and (hence) the stocks they affect in the laws of elasticity and supply and demand.

- Make it a daily habit to track the political, global, and financial news. Although you needn't act on this information every day, you will be able to spot economic and policy trends in the earliest stages when you stay abreast of current events.

- Collect the quarterly and annual economic forecasts generated by major newspapers and various financial magazines. You should reference these whenever possible to see if the pros corroborate your understanding of the future economic environment.

- View your economic forecast in light of an investment framework that not only promises the results you desire, but has proven to generate such results.

- Count on your ability to become a better investor over time. Indeed, cyclical asset allocators typically improve with each new quarter and every new year. Their forecasts (and investment calls) are not always correct, but in time they will be right more often than not. Additionally, their experience often enables them to improve on a forecast that is not so certain.

- Make reasoned adjustments to the assets in your portfolio when you possess a high conviction level that your forecast is correct. If that conviction level is not high and/or there is no reason to adjust your allocations, leave your allocations alone.

The final guiding premise is to either act or not act within your portfolio—to tilt or not to tilt—based on the reliability of the information you possess and the framework to which you apply it. Next I review what I consider to be the most reliable framework for above-average investing.

Framework Fundamentals: Supply and Demand

A successful cyclical asset-allocation strategy should be based on the information an investor can extract from both economic shocks and the response to those shocks. Market signals, in particular prices, are entry points through which we can search out the supply-and-demand realities that underpin all economic shocks, while the elasticities of companies, industries, and consumers enable us to determine the magnitude of response to these shocks.

Understanding price movements in terms of their unique natures—in terms of supply and demand—leads to proper action within a portfolio. In practice, you want to determine whether a price increase or decrease is either bullish or bearish, the former representing an investment opportunity and the latter indicating that you should sell or avoid an investment.

You can use two rules of thumb for when price changes can be considered bullish:

- **Price increase, demand shift**—The price of a good rises in response to an increase in the demand for that good, a situation in which suppliers stand to earn much greater profits.

- **Price decrease, supply shift**—A greater supply of a good in the marketplace causes the price of that good to drop, a situation favoring the suppliers that can operate in the most cost-efficient manner.

Alternatively, two rules of thumb exist for when price changes can be considered bearish:

- **Price increase, supply shift**—A reduction in the supply of a good results in less of that good in the marketplace at a higher price.
- **Price decrease, demand shift**—A good falls out of favor with consumers, thus causing a decline in the price of that good.

Due to media realities, I recommend that you never take the conventional wisdom about price movements at face value because to do so can be the equivalent of accepting false information as true. Anyone can talk price "smoke." But only those who can trace price movements back to supply and demand can discuss and act on price signals.

Framework Fundamentals: Elasticity

Supply and demand describe the nature of a shock. To put your understanding of these forces to proper use, you need to discover the response to a shock. Is that response elastic or inelastic?

Elasticity is all-pervading within an economy, and you can begin to identify it in the simplest of ways: Elastic companies can move either toward or away from shocks; inelastic companies are stuck. Elastic consumers can adjust their plans to get what they want at the price they want; inelastic consumers have few shopping alternatives. Elastic stocks exhibit a degree of independence from the average fluctuations of the market; inelastic stocks are slaves to market swings, often slingshoting well beyond the market's average movements. All this is directly related to corporate profit. Because profits show up in share prices, you want to understand the elasticities that bring profit swings about.

Elasticity is directly related to the concept of beta. As a quick review, the most inelastic stocks have the highest betas and exhibit the greatest "sensitivity" to markets, rocketing skyward during bull markets and falling precipitously during bear markets. Conversely, the most elastic stocks have the lowest betas and exhibit less volatility during market swings. As for stocks with a beta of 1, they fall right in the middle, riding average market performance either up or down.

Two investment rules flow from these beta basics, the idea being that high-beta, inelastic stocks will swing the most with the market and low-beta, elastic stocks will swing the least:

- During negative-return periods—when the economy, stock market, and/or consumer demand are falling—switch to elastic low-beta stocks (if you must hold stocks in your portfolio).

- During positive-return periods—when the economy, stock market, and/or consumer demand are rising—increase your exposure to inelastic (and, hence, high-beta) stocks.

Thematically, inelastic companies, industries, and stocks all tend to love the good times. True enough, what companies, industries, and stocks do not? However, when the economic forces of supply and demand favor inelastic stocks, these stocks will climb in a pronounced way.

Here's how to properly act on inelasticity:

- Hold or buy stocks in inelastic industries that are facing rising demand (or during bull markets). Prices will increase to satisfy higher demand, with those higher prices reflecting in increased profitability.

- Sell or avoid stocks in inelastic industries that are facing decreasing demand (or during bear markets). Prices will decrease to satisfy lower demand, a perfect combination for decreased profitability.

Investing in elastic companies, meanwhile, requires a nuanced approach:

- If you must hold stocks in your portfolio when economic conditions are unfavorable (or during bear markets), hold or buy stocks in elastic industries. When the economy is doing poorly, the most elastic companies will be the best able to outperform the market.

- Reduce your exposure to elastic industries when economic conditions are favorable (or during bull markets). When the economy and the stock market are doing well, elastic companies will generally underperform the least elastic (or most inelastic) companies because the latter will rise high with their high betas.

The concept of elasticity extends all the way to the products and services that consumers purchase. If enough companies are making a certain product, we can call that product a commodity—a standard, elastic, bulk good. There's nothing wrong with such products (or services), although the companies providing them won't do much to invigorate your portfolio during the good times (when those inelastic companies should be padding your returns). Therefore...

> During rising markets, delete industries or companies from a portfolio that can be classified as commodities.

All this is powerful stuff. Investors who understand and seek out the elastic/inelastic responses of industries, companies, and consumers to economic shocks will have a decided edge over the great many investors who do not.

Looking Backward to Invest Forward

From time to time, you will find it beneficial to perform a historical analysis to connect specific shocks with their most sensitive (high-beta, inelastic) investment counterparts. In doing so, you will know just which companies, industries, and, hence, stocks deserve your investment dollars and which you should avoid.

In Chapter 5, "Putting High-Beta to Work: Industry-Based Portfolio Strategies," I diagramed the historical industry-selection process in this manner:

Step 1.   Determine a shock—whether one that is in process or one that is likely to occur.

Step 2.   Measure the stock performance, good and bad, of industries when the shock occurred in the past.

Step 2 (Alternate).   Measure the performance of industries when the mirror-image shock occurred, and reverse the results.

Step 3.   Favor the stocks in industries that have historically benefited from the shock, and avoid those that have not.

This is how one properly looks backward to invest forward, a method that can be applied to companies (individual stocks), industries/sectors, and asset classes. Note that even though "elasticity" and "beta" were not specifically named in my historical approach, this method nonetheless extracts the industries (or stocks or asset classes) that exhibited the highest betas (or inelasticity) in relation to a specific shock. Because high-beta stocks rise with positive shocks and fall with negative ones, this again is very powerful, and profitable, stuff.

Where can you look back? This answer is a lot simpler today than it was a decade or so ago. The Internet, in particular, has become a vast store of data on virtually everything known to mankind, and a variety of firms list historical stock and industry data online. Many offer these services for free; others might charge a subscription fee. Morningstar, for instance, offers both free and paid services to online financial-data seekers. Much of this information is mutual fund specific, but the site (Morningstar.com) also offers historical data on a wide range of industries and sectors.

The Global Allocation Revisited

Any investor will be well served by constructing a benchmark portfolio at the outset of his or her investment career. Indeed, if you attempted to employ a cyclical asset-allocation strategy *without* an organizational starting point, you would find it very difficult to adjust your assets to the multiple shocks that often occur at the same time.

I recommend that you begin the benchmarking process by diagramming the world allocation to the stock and bond markets, just as we did in Chapter 10, "Your Benchmark Profile...and Beyond." I say "diagram" instead of "buy" at this point because you might want to incorporate some tilts to your portfolio at the outset. So get out a piece of paper and draw up a starter world allocation as follows:

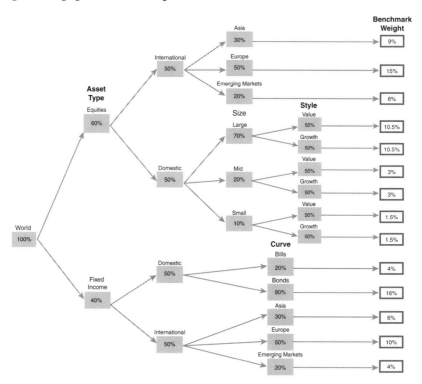

FIGURE 17.1   Starter World Allocation

This is your allocation to average performance. The percentages assigned to each of the major asset classes—or asset-class "buckets"—reflect the world market shares of these assets at this writing. Because this is a close approximation of an allocation that will maximize the long-run returns of all investors, it becomes a good place for any investor to start.

To fill these buckets passively you would use low-cost exchange-traded funds (ETFs) and/or index funds. To fill them actively, you would select mutual funds. (We review the active/passive switch later in this chapter.) Where to shop? I make no specific recommendations here because you have so many fund sources at your disposal. (Again, we are all on the Internet these days, where researching investment funds can be a painless procedure.) In earlier chapters, I mentioned Fidelity, Vanguard, Schwab, Janus, and Wilshire, all of which are reliable firms with sound investment products. A *great many more* exist, and as you shop the asset-class aisles, I only suggest that you act like a prudent shopper in a supermarket, department store, or any store: Think price/value.

On the price end, you want to make sure the fees and costs related to any desired investment are low relative to similar investments. On the value end, you want to make sure you are getting just what you want. If your asset-class tilt is for an active large-cap/growth mutual fund, you want to check the characteristics of funds so named to ensure that the stocks they carry meet these criteria. Fund characteristics might include historical performance, top-ten holdings, risk and volatility measures, pre- and post-tax return data, dividend yields, and sector weightings, among many other details. This information is important, although the strategy at hand simplifies the selection process: If your economic forecast suggests (and strongly so) that the current and future economic environment will favor large-cap/growth stocks over, say, small-cap/value stocks, and if you purchase a reputable fund at a competitive price with large-cap/growth characteristics, you will be well positioned to outperform the market (that is, if your macro forecast was correct).

From Passive to Intermediate to Active

By purchasing the global allocation, you indirectly link to the range of return-generating "fuels" that will provide your portfolio with both diversification and long-run cost efficiency. But this allocation can generate performance only on par with the world. By purchasing it and passively holding it, you guarantee yourself average performance, nothing more.

The ideal for investors wedded to the passive long-run approach is to adjust their allocations when there are major thematic changes in the business and economic environment. By adjusting to such changes, passive investors become intermediate investors, and elasticity can be their guide: From time to time, as the thematic winds change, intermediate investors should

- Add stocks to their portfolios that become inelastic as a result of economic or policy shocks
- Delete stocks from their portfolios that become more elastic as a result of economic or policy shocks

From here, the level of transaction costs (specifically, the costs associated with switching between investments) becomes the central arbiter of when to pursue an active investment strategy:

- When the transaction costs are relatively high and/or the differential of returns is low, and you have little or no reliable information, choose a passive strategy—and be an average investor.
- When the transaction costs are relatively low and/or the differential of returns is high, and you believe that you possess superior information, pursue various degrees of active strategies (and the prospect of above-average performance).

A Cocktail Construction

Your benchmark portfolio is a management tool for organizing and tracking the changes you will make to your asset-class buckets from time to time—that is, if you choose to employ a cyclical asset-allocation approach. This portfolio also helps you monitor your performance: If you indeed are adding value to your portfolio by strategically and periodically switching between the major investment classes, your return performance should be higher than those periods when you held your starting global allocation.

Adding value, or bolstering returns, is how one graduates from average to above-average performance. Is this a graduation from passive to active investing? Strictly speaking, no. Functionally, I'm talking about adding value to a portfolio by acquiring the best investment strategies at the appropriate times, and quite often these strategies can be put into action by allocating to the appropriate passive vehicles, such as broad-based ETFs. (Popular ETF brand names are PowerShares, iShares, SPDRs, and ProShares.)

In the second part of this chapter, I review the thematic adjustments you can make to your benchmark allocation across economic cycles. Here your prowess at cocktail economics—your ability to describe the world in terms of the nature of shocks and the predictable responses to those shocks—will have you constructing something of an investment "cocktail." This cocktail, or asset-class mix, will be unique to your own investment aspirations and capacity for risk. And from time to time, it will change—and likely improve in character—as you adjust with a jigger of this strategy and a jigger of that.

Icing Your Glass: The Stock/Bond Split

The most important decision you can make in a portfolio regards the stock/bond split. Basically, the greater the proportion of stocks to bonds in your portfolio, the greater will be your projected return and, technically speaking, the greater will be your risk. An 80/20 stock/bond split over a short horizon, such as a few years, carries with it high short-term risk: Stock markets can rise or dip sharply year to year. Hence, if you have a short horizon—for instance, if you are nearing retirement and expect to cash out of your portfolio in a few years—you do not want to be overexposed to stocks. Alternatively, if you have a longer horizon, such as 20 or 30 years, you want to own more stocks than bonds because stocks historically return more than bonds, while stock risk dissipates over time.

You should make the stock/bond decision on your own, but I offer a few suggestions. If you are just starting out investing and/or have a long horizon across which you will invest, heavily favor stocks: An 80/20 split might make sense. If you have an intermediate horizon, such as less than 20 years, pare that split to 70/30, 60/40, or even 50/50. If you have a short horizon of less than ten years, favor bonds (or the wide variety of safe fixed-income instruments) over stocks, switching into the least-risky investments the closer you get to cashing out.

I have described here the process of "lifecycling" your investments. As you age, reduce your exposure to market risk. This is simple, prudent stuff, although there is a sophisticated way to accomplish this risk adjustment without sacrificing all the higher returns associated with stocks over bonds: A lifecycle strategy can adjust over time in relation to beta:

> Instead of simply lessening your stock exposure and broadening your bond exposure over time, reduce your beta exposure (and the potential downsides of that exposure) as your horizon shortens.

To make the stock/bond split itself an above-average performer, you want to tilt either toward bonds or toward stocks, based on the macroeconomic fundamentals at any given time. As far as cyclical asset allocation goes, this is a relatively uncomplicated exercise, and it can serve as your initial passageway into the realm of above-average performance.

Basically, by employing the strategy of keeping your eyes open and confirming what you see with the consensus opinions of the economic pros, you will build a simple economic forecast based on the direction of the gross domestic product (GDP), the stock market, inflation, *and* public policy (you cannot skip this last variable because it could well deliver accuracy to your forecast).

Following are a few ways such an exercise might play out:

- The GDP has risen at 3 percent or more for several quarters, a trend that seasoned economic analysts expect to continue for the foreseeable future. The stock market has risen at a solid pace during this timeframe. Inflation is low and expected to decline further. No negative policy shocks (such as tax hikes) are on the horizon. *Forecast:* Bullish. *Possible action:* Increase your exposure to stocks.

- GDP growth is descending and might turn negative. Inflation is falling. A good probability exists that negative policy shocks will occur over the next year. *Forecast:* Bearish. *Possible action:* Increase your exposure to bonds.

The degree of this stock/bond tilt, as well as *all* the tilts outlined in this chapter, should be based on the level of your conviction. If you feel strongly about the future direction of the economy (either domestic or international), if your forecast is supported by reliable consensus forecasts, and if you feel your portfolio as it is currently allocated will not take the best advantage of the predicted economic environment, act decisively within your portfolio.

A Jigger of This: The Location Choice

The nature of a shock and the economic makeup of a specific geographic location combine to determine the different behaviors of the assets within that region. And because of the elasticities of each company in relation to a geographic area, the winners will separate from the losers. This location effect initially can be described in terms of mobility, the physical ability of a company to escape a regional shock:

- Mobile, multiple-plant companies can shift production toward positive shocks and away from negative ones, thus arbitraging differences between prices and regions to their advantage.

- Immobile, single-plant companies must ride out any shock in a location, good or bad, for as long as they decide to operate in that location. Unlike mobile companies, they will realize all the downside of a negative location shock, although they will enjoy all the upside of a positive one.

Because you can use a stock's size designation (e.g., large-cap, small-cap, etc.) as a stand-in for whether that stock represents an immobile, single-plant operation or a mobile, multiplant business, you can implement a location-based strategy very easily within your portfolio:

- When a negative shock hits a specific location, most likely all public companies in that location will suffer. However, small-caps likely will underperform large-caps because they are relatively immobile and will capture the full downside of the shock.

- When a positive shock lands on a specific location, most likely all public companies in that location will benefit. However, small-caps likely will outperform large-caps because they will capture the full upside of the shock.

Internationally, the location and size effects will forever partner based on the economic shocks specific to countries and political regions around the globe. Because capital is mobile and tends to flow to areas where it will see the highest return, if a positive shock makes the return for capital higher in a location, capital will stream toward that location. Eventually, as capital flows change to bring about economic equilibrium, higher rates of return will be eliminated and purchasing power parity (or PPP, a measure of the relative purchasing power of global currencies) will be restored. These capital-flow windows of opportunity open and close all the time, and capturing them can invigorate your portfolio.

For international small-cap stocks, proceed in this manner:

- When positive shocks impact global locations, buy small-cap stocks in those locations. This will put you in the best position to gain all the upside a positive location shock has to offer.

- When PPP does not hold—meaning that a disparity exists between the exchange rates of currencies and markets are not correlated—favor small-cap stocks in the regions where the local currency has strengthened.

For international large-caps, the investing rules take on a nuance. Because large-caps typically are mobile, they can move toward positive shocks (although never enjoying the full upside of that shock) while avoiding negative shocks. Hence

- Investing in international large-cap stocks should be predicated on an analysis of industries that are abundant across nations. Choose international large-cap stocks based on an understanding of the elasticities and betas of industries in relation to the economic environment.

- Do not go out of your way to buy international large-cap stocks when owning domestic large-cap stocks will offer you just as much diversification. This will be the case when PPP holds (or, in other words, when markets are highly correlated).

A Jigger of That: The Size and Style Choices

Inflation, taxes, and regulations combine to determine the level of economic certainty that exists within national borders. Certainty is an extremely important macroeconomic indicator, in that it helps direct your allocations to small- and large-cap stocks (as well as value and growth stocks) across major economic cycles.

The concept of a "national" economy is central to this analysis. We can consider a national economy to be a closed economy, where all the public companies within established borders (small and large) are subject to the policy machinations of a central governing authority. This distinction forces us to turn a location rule on its head:

- When shocks—particularly those related to regulations, inflation, and taxes—deliver or threaten to deliver uncertainty to national economies, small-caps likely will outperform large-caps.

- When certainty—as it relates to regulations, inflation, and taxes—returns to national economies, large-caps likely will outperform small-caps.

The style decision between value and growth stocks plays out in a similar manner. Basically, value stocks are considered relatively cheap, whereas growth stocks are companies with higher-than-average sales and earnings. Within the academic and financial literature, studies often show how value stocks have outperformed growth stocks over the last 30 or so years. However, value stocks tended to outperform growth stocks during more uncertain economic periods, such as the bulk of the 1970s and portions of the 1980s. Basically, growth stocks do not like uncertainty, and the uncertainty variable of higher taxation can help explain why: Corporate income taxes are directly related to the amount of cash a company can reinvest. As a result, higher corporate tax rates hurt growth stocks more than value stocks because growth companies want to reinvest the bulk of their cash to continue growing.

In practice, when tracking uncertainty to correctly allocate to the size choice, consider this style rule:

When shocks deliver or threaten to deliver uncertainty to national economies, value stocks likely will outperform growth stocks.

As with most cycles, certainty/uncertainty cycles tend to last several years or more. This enables you to watch certainty or uncertainty gather and then establish before taking action within your portfolio. If you do so, certainty of action will be on your side.

Shaken or Stirred: The Active/Passive Switch

If you are to take part in a cyclical asset-allocation strategy, you technically will be an active rather than passive investor. However, at differing times, you will want to invest in either active (mutual fund) or passive (ETF/index fund) mode.

To review, the long-run data supports the notion that passive investing is superior to active investing. But the data also shows periods when active investing beats passive. Correspondingly, if you believe in the existence of size cycles, you also must believe that there will be periods when actively managed large- and small-cap funds will move in and out of favor. The constraints of active fund management—whereby managers must invest all large-cap, all small-cap, etc.—make this so, as do benchmark weighting schemes in relation to market breadth.

For instance, during large-cap cycles, the largest of the large companies will only get that much larger and, in doing so, will push more stock names in a benchmark index into the bottom half of an index. Because this bottom half will fall out of favor during a large-cap cycle, and because it will hold more names during this cycle, it follows that there will be more large-cap losers than winners during this cycle. Hence, the odds of picking a large-cap winner decline during a large-cap cycle.

Using this same rationale, we can come to some general conclusions about the promise of active large- and small-cap fund management during different size cycles:

- The odds of a manager outperforming an index change systematically over the course of a cycle.

- The odds of a larger-cap manager change the most across a cycle.

- During a small-cap cycle, a large-cap manager has a better chance of beating a large-cap benchmark than a small-cap manager has of beating a small-cap benchmark.

- During a large-cap cycle, a small-cap manager has a better chance of outperforming a small-cap benchmark than a large-cap manager has of beating a large-cap benchmark.

- Active managers have a better chance of outperforming any index during a small-cap cycle.

These rules add depth to the discussion of a cyclical active/passive switch within a portfolio. Practically, however, this switch can be described (and applied) much more simply:

- **Invest actively during small-cap cycles.** The odds of beating an index turn decidedly in your (or your active fund manager's) favor during small-cap cycles. At this time, you should choose actively managed funds (such as mutual funds) to fill the allocation buckets in your portfolio.

- **Invest passively during large-cap cycles.** The odds of beating the market systematically decline during large-cap cycles. And although they decline more for large-cap fund managers than small-cap managers, you will be well served by choosing index funds and/or ETFs at this juncture.

Alpha Chasers

The final element of this investment strategy is the hedge fund. Love 'em, hate 'em, or don't care much about 'em, hedge funds can add plenty of firepower to a portfolio. And the reason is that they produce alpha (or, at least, they're supposed to), which can be considered the extra return related to investing, over and above the market return. Mutual funds do, in fact, generate alpha, although here you must take your alpha with your beta. For pure-alpha, if you can afford the price of entry, I recommend that you add a hedge-fund element to your portfolio. But I make this recommendation with a few stipulations:

- When you purchase shares of an alpha-generating fund, be sure that it is uncorrelated with the market to the greatest degree possible. *If not, you can port the alpha return of any superior manager.* In this way, you remove beta exposure from your alpha investments and thus purify (or maximize) your alpha returns.

- Be sure that your alpha-generating investments are shock resilient, that they will either hold up when economic and market conditions shift or that your alpha-fund managers will make the proper adjustments when these conditions shift.

- Size up your pure-alpha investments against one another, being sure that each employs a unique strategy. By adding uncorrelated pure-alpha investments in your portfolio, you add diversification and thus decrease risk.

Cocktail-Economics Hours

You are an information gatherer. You stay close to the news out of Washington, D.C.; the European Union; the Pacific Rim; the Middle East; and every other global hotspot. You understand tax policy as a good investor should—in relation to economic growth, corporate profit, and asset-class performance. Ditto for inflation, regulations, interest rates, war, strife, natural disasters, bull markets, bear markets, and on and on. You grasp elasticity, the authority on how companies, industries, and consumers will respond to economic shocks. Specifically, you understand how this response will reflect in corporate profits, which, in turn, will echo in share prices. Everything in your big-picture world is interrelated. Cycles exist. Cycles are *predictable*. Forecasts can be drawn. And success is within your grasp.

So now what?

I mentioned those millionaires next door for good reason: Their pace of investing, on average, corresponds with my pace of investing. Twenty percent switch their investments every one or two years. Twenty-five percent switch every four or six years. This is clear evidence that investing in a winning way need not be an everyday thing. In best practice, I see it as a quarterly regimen, points at which you might tweak your portfolio or maintain your existing allocations.

My business as a financial advisor regularly takes me across the United States. I often visit with clients in various cities to discuss the current economic environment, the forecasted economic environment, and the fate of the separate asset classes. Quarterly, I fly into New York City, where I meet with some top-notch investors for just these purposes. We sit in a boardroom with nice views of Manhattan and talk about the world from the top on down. We discuss financial, economic, and political news. We recall economic circumstances in the past and describe ways in which history might repeat itself—or be different this time around. Basically, we build forecasts based on what we see and our experience over the years. We then apply these forecasts to a framework for success. And then we allocate, or stick with our allocations just as they are if we have no strong feelings about our ability to add value to an existing asset mix.

You can do this, too. Four times a year, or twice a year, or even once a year, pull out the folder that carries a diagram of your current allocation mix and perhaps the characteristics of the funds filling your asset-class buckets. Then pull out the economic forecasts you have collected and contrast them with your very own rendering of the financial and political news. Then pull out this book, turn to this chapter, and start your review. Compare Macroeconomic Development A with Strategy A, B, or C. Make connections. If the macroeconomic environment has changed or you have good reason to believe it will change, test your conviction level about this development. Do this by applying what you know to what the best thinkers of the day know. (For me, these best thinkers tend to be the ones who view the world from the top down, basing their analyses on historical truths and provable correlations.) Then act—switch your investments—or don't act, repeating this process at regular intervals and adding in experience based on the times you indeed added value to your portfolio and the profit occasions you might have missed.

You can call this your cocktail economics hour because, in a symbolic sense, this is what it will be. You, something of a trained mixologist, will be pouring a very specialized concoction, made up of a dash of this asset class and a jigger of that investment strategy. At each cocktail economics hour, you will proceed in the same way, matching your knowledge of the macroeconomic environment with a proven framework for success. The cocktail mix you produce each time out might be a bit different than the one you formulated a quarter ago. Or it might be the one that has served you well for the last two or so years. It could be location-based, style-based, size-based, industry-based, active/passive-based, or stock/bond-based. It might also draw from the full range of these strategies. This cocktail will conform to your own tastes and preferences, and it will exhibit your own risk-adjusted kick. And it will improve over time, well into the range of above-average performance, if you adhere to the guidelines I have set forth in this book.

Endnotes

1. Thomas J. Stanley and William D. Danko, *The Millionaire Next Door* (New York: Simon & Shuster, 1996).

INDEX

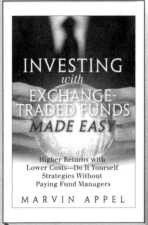

OPPORTUNITY INVESTING
How To Profit When Stocks Advance, Stocks Decline, Inflation Runs Rampant, Prices Fall, Oil Prices Hit the Roof, ... and Every Time in Between

Gerald Appel

Opportunity Investing provides tools to identify periods when stocks and/or other investment options are likely to advance, periods when market outlooks are more cloudy, and strategies that suggest changes in portfolio allocation that may be made accordingly. Other areas discussed include real estate, precious metals and other commodities, and investments that bring in high and steady levels of income. Readers will learn which forms of investment produce the best returns depending upon the general market climate. And finally, Appel identifies specific areas of investment with strategies for retirement investment. Areas covered include foreign stocks and bonds as well as domestic securities, real estate, commodities, government issues, open and closed end mutual funds, exchange traded funds (ETFs) and more.

ISBN 9780131721296 ■ © 2007 ■ 384 pp. ■ $24.99 USA ■ $29.99 CAN

INVESTING WITH EXCHANGE-TRADED FUNDS MADE EASY
Higher Returns with Lower Costs—Do It Yourself Strategies Without Paying Fund Managers

Marvin Appel

Exchange-traded funds are one of fastest growing investment vehicles because of their low cost and top performance. This book provides step-by-step instructions so that readers can use the book as a complete, self-contained investment program. Strategies included have been backtested and their history is presented for the reader to verify. Shows how to manage investments independently with just a discount brokerage account and a few minutes of internet access to gather data every month.

ISBN 9780131869738 ■ © 2007 ■ 272 pp. ■ $24.99 USA ■ $29.99 CAN